Reason and Justice

D1258320

SUNY Series in Systematic Philosophy
Robert Cummings Neville, Editor

Whether systematic philosophies are intended as true pictures of the world, as hypotheses, as the dialectic of history, or as heuristic devices for relating rationally to a multitude of things, they each constitute articulated ways by which experience can be ordered, and as such they are contributions to culture. One does not have to choose between Plato and Aristotle to appreciate that Western civilization is enriched by the Platonic as well as Aristotelian ways of seeing things.

The term "systematic philosophy" can be applied to any philosophical enterprise that functions with a perspective from which everything can be addressed. Sometimes this takes the form of an attempt to spell out the basic features of things in a system. Other times it means the examination of a limited subject from the many angles of a context formed by a systematic perspective. In either case systematic philosophy takes explicit or implicit responsibility for the assessment of its unifying perspective and for what is seen from it. The styles of philosophy according to which systematic philosophy can be practiced are as diverse as the achievements of the great philosophers in history, and doubtless new styles are needed for our time.

Yet systematic philosophy has not been a popular approach during this century of philosophical professionalism. It is the purpose of this series to stimulate and publish new systematic works employing the techniques and advances in philosophical reflection made during this century. The series is committed to no philosophical school or doctrine, nor to any limited style of systematic thinking. Whether the systematic achievements of previous centuries can be equalled in the 20th depends on the emergence of forms of systematic philosophy appropriate to our times. The current resurgence of interest in the project deserves the cultivation it may receive from the SUNY Series in Systematic Philosophy.

Reason
and
Justice

Richard Dien Winfield

State University of New York Press

Published by
State University of New York Press, Albany

© 1988   State University of New York

For information, address State University of New York
Press, State University Plaza, Albany, N.Y. 12246

Library of Congress Cataloging-in-Publication Data

Winfield, Richard Dien, 1950–
    Reason and justice.

    (SUNY series in systematic philosophy)
    Includes index.
    1. Justice (Philosophy) I. Title. II. Series.
B105.J87W56 1988   172   87-17952
ISBN 0-88706-710-7
ISBN 0-88706-711-5 (pbk.)

10 9 8 7 6 5 4 3 2 1

For my parents,
Lillian Yudien Winfield and Sidney Lincoln Winfield

Contents

Introduction

However theory and practice may differ, the quest for justice cannot be divorced from the quest for truth. The moment given authority is called into question by the demand for legitimation of actions and institutions, a problem of justification arises that is virtually identical to that entailed in the attempt to transform opinion into knowledge of truth.

In one respect the parallel is direct. Although the search for justice may have practice as its ultimate concern, that search remains blind unless it addresses the theoretical problem of conceiving what justice is. Since this requires thinking ideas about justice that are justified truths rather than unjustified opinions, the problem of knowledge is part and parcel of the problem of justice. Without resolving the difficulties of justifying truth claims in general, there can be no hope of establishing the valid concept of justice by which practice should be ordered.

Further, whether what is at stake be realizing or merely conceiving justice, there is no avoiding a problem of justification, which, though not convergent with knowing's quest for truth, still runs parallel to it. Insofar as realizing justice consists in performing those actions and erecting those institutions that are valid, reasons are called for to certify them as just rather than merely operative practice, just as reasons are required to certify the truth of knowledge claims.

In both cases not only are reasons needed to secure justification, but the qualities making something count as a validating reason are the same. To establish what is right and what is true, reasons must be supplied that are objective rather than subjective and unconditionally universal rather than conditioned by particular circumstance. If conduct and institutions have their support in nothing but subjective factors and the particularities of a given situation, their authority is as questionable as the contingent grounds they rest upon, just as if truth claims are buttressed by mere opinions and given conventions of argument, they are no more valid than the suppositions and customs with which they cohere. Might cannot make right anymore than truth

1

can lie in consensus, for in each case, what provides supposed validity are particular conditions of practical and theoretical prevalence that have no prescriptive authority, let alone necessary existence.

Traditionally philosophers have sought the reasons capable of providing justification for knowledge and action in nothing other than reason itself. Unlike the positions of the stars, the entrails of animals, the pattern of dreams or any testimony of the senses, reason has been ascribed the objectivity and unconditioned universality that would allow it to qualify as the validating factor in distinguishing right from wrong and truth from error. If reasoning has so been adopted as the privileged justifier in legitimating both actions and knowledge claims, this has not left truth and justice in the same predicament.

In reason's quest for truth, the privileged justificatory role of reason has left reason relying upon nothing other than itself. To the extent that rational argument lays claim to the objective, unconditioned universality necessary to transform opinion into knowledge, reason is autonomous in providing reasons justifying truth claims. In achieving theoretical validity, reason accepts the authority of no standard, criterion or belief that has not been certified by its own activity of reasoning. To do otherwise would mean accepting unjustified opinion as the basis of justification, with the result that no conclusions would possess an established truth.

By contrast, the quest for justice seems to entail dependence rather than autonomy. Insofar as rational argument provides the reasons justifying conduct and institutions, justice appears to depend upon reason to supply it with its measure and standard. Whereas reason must itself ordain what it must conform to in order to know the truth, action seems to be valid only if it conforms to what reason independently prescribes.

Although this unequal predicament would seem to bind the quest for justice to the quest for knowledge, it equally suggests a sharp divide between truth and justice and between reason and willing. Theory may be radically self-justifying to the extent that it moves from opinion to knowledge by relying on reason alone. Yet, whereas action depends upon reason for its norms, being just only if it conforms to rational principle, action still depends upon will for its reality. Willing, however, is a very different matter from thinking, just as knowledge of justice is hardly equivalent to the performance of just deeds and the existence of just institutions. Although justice can only be done through acts of will, the will, being voluntary, can do right as well as wrong no matter what reason may prescribe. Indeed, it is only because the will has the power to act contrary to what an individual knows to be right that criminal actions are possible. Conversely, only because the will can determine action independently of reason, do just actions require only right opinion rather than justified certainty to guide them. Accordingly, the realization of justice may require sophistry rather than rational argument if individuals can be better persuaded to do what is right by appealing to factors, such as passion, interest and prejudice, that are not themselves rationally justified.[1]

Be this as it may, if just conduct is action in accord with reason, then justice must consist in the activity of the rational will. Such a will shall be consonant with reason and thereby justified by reason even though the actions it performs need not be accompanied by knowledge of justice.

Clearly, the rational will cannot be identified with the free will, if reason be viewed as a faculty of objective universal unconditioned principles whose truth is no matter of choice. On these terms, justice demands restricting the free will, for if it is left to its own designs, there can be no guarantee that it will choose those actions in accord with reason. Yet if the will is endowed with liberty of choice, which is what calls for restriction in the first place, then nothing can limit the freedom of the will and compel it to be rational except the will itself. Reason may have compelling force in argument, just as feeling may feed inclination, but when it comes to action, only the will can command.

As a consequence, the realization of justice would appear to fall prey to the very arbitrariness that must be curtailed for rational willing to occur. Although justice may depend upon reason for its validation, the dependence of justice upon will for its realization suggests that the conformity of reason and willing, truth and justice, or theory and practice is in principle problematic.

1 The Two Traditional Approaches To Justification

In attempting to bridge the gap in reason's relation to willing, theorists of justice have ordinarily advanced the one at the expense of the other.[2] One school of thought, established by Plato and Aristotle, has sought to secure the justice of rational willing by supplanting the license of freedom with the rule of reason over the will. Another tradition has taken the opposite extreme and conceived justice to consist in the free sway of liberty beholden to no principle but itself. In pursuing their corollary approaches, these traditions have equally provided what have become the classic strategies for achieving a positive fulfillment of the quests for truth and justice. These strategies involve distinguishing the candidates for knowledge and justice from mere opinion and operative practice by appealing to either some privileged given or some privileged determiner. Insofar as both approaches root validity in a prior foundation, consisting in one case in a given determinacy and in the other case in a given determiner, they have aptly come to be grouped together under the banner of foundationalism.

1.1 The Appeal To Privileged Givens

The first of these strategies, which appeals to privileged givens in establishing the validity of theory and practice, has followed from a pair of common considerations. Motivated by the genuine need to free knowledge claims of any dependence upon opinion, numerous thinkers have agreed that justification cannot be achieved without some non-deducible self-evident reason to provide firm ground for what is to be justified. Otherwise, they have reasoned, argument is left resting upon hypothetical statements, whose own conditions are in want of an account, or upon bald assertions, as arbitrary as any counter claims. As a result, every conclusion would be equally hypothetical and arbitrary, leaving it indistinguishable from unjustified opinion.

In the same vein, many have argued that since the holding of opinions and the maintenance of institutions and ethical norms testifies only to their being and not to their validity, truth and justice cannot be found as they are conventionally determined by the subjective artifice of some conditioned, particular vantage point. Instead, truth and justice must be sought as they are by nature, according to the given determinacy that comprises their objective, justified content. Guided by these reflections, searchers for truth and justice have little choice but to begin their quest by raising the parallel questions, "What is?" and "What is the Good?". The former question asks, "What is the given determinacy or nature of reason and reality?", whereas the latter asks, "What is the given determinacy or antecedently prescribed structure to which conduct and institutions must conform to be just?". With validity taken to lie in the privileged givens of what is and should be by nature, the sought-after answers are to be had through the appropriately passive activity of contemplation. In contemplation's intellectual receptivity, reason immediately apprehends, rather than mediately constructs, the first principles of reason, reality, and justice providing the privileged givens on which all else is grounded and demonstrably knowable and right.

As history has shown, this whole approach to theoretical and practical justification is plagued by the sceptical objection that every candidate for first principle, be it of reason, reality, or justice, is equally unjustifiable due to its own privileged status. If an attempt be made to support its privileged givenness by introducing some further reason, the mediation of that support undermines the candidate's putative immediacy as first principle. Far from obtaining backing for the primacy ascribed to it, the candidate for first principle thereby gets reduced to a secondary, derivative term, predicated upon the reason on whose support it rests.

In answer to this objection, one is tempted to suggest that a proposed first principle might still be justified by showing that everything else does follow from it, rather than from any other term. Such a demonstration could not be carried through, however, unless one had prior knowledge of both what is the totality of reason, reality, or justice that must be deduced from the first principle and what constitutes valid deduction. If that knowledge depended, like everything else, upon the first principle, the demonstration would fall into a vicious circularity where its own proof rests upon what is to be proved. If, on the contrary, such knowledge could be obtained without appeal to the first principle, it would sabotage the latter's attested primacy as the exclusive source of justification.

These difficulties imply that whenever validity is based in some given, the latter has its privileged status not due to its nature, but by being determined as such by whomever has granted it its foundational role. This outcome may cast in doubt the claims of classical metaphysics and its corollary teleological theories of justice, but it does not deliver theory and practice into the hands of scepticism and nihilism. What beckons instead is the other traditional approach to truth and justice, the approach that roots justification not in a privileged given but in a privileged determiner. After all, if no given content can provide justification, it is only natural to presume that what makes something true or just must lie in its being determined by a warranted determiner.

1.2. *The Appeal To A Privileged Determiner*

Logically enough, the strategy of conceiving truth and justice by appealing to privileged givens has been historically superseded by the approach that ties validity to what is determined by a privileged determiner. Applied to the quest for truth, this approach gives rise to transcendental philosophy. It repudiates the immediate apprehension of the nature of things characterizing metaphysical contemplation, recognizing that no claim about what is can be justified simply by appealing to what is taken to be given. Instead of addressing objectivity directly, transcendental inquiry conceives it indirectly as something constituted by some condition making possible knowledge, reference, or meaningful speech. Whether this transcendental condition be described as the structure of consciousness, intentionality, *Dasein*, ordinary language, or the hermeneutic situation, it always figures as the privileged determiner that determines what can be known to be objectively valid.

Applied to the quest for justice, the appeal to a privileged determiner gives rise to the theory of right developed by the liberal tradition. Rejecting the authority of given teleological ends, such as those affirmed in the classical vision of a good life involving prescribed virtues, given means of conduct and rule by experts, liberalism instead extends legitimacy only to what the will determines in its exercise of liberty. On this basis, justice no longer consists in the dutiful embodiment of predetermined form. With all specific virtues set aside, acts of any content whatsoever count as ethical provided they are determined by the free choice of individuals without infringing on the free choice of others. As for the institutions of justice, they have their validity not by corresponding to what is good by nature, but by issuing from social contract or some other procedure of construction allowing them to be willed into being by all. On both accounts, the will figures as a privileged determiner giving action the same stamp of validity that transcendental conditions give to objective knowledge.

Although the turn to conceiving truth and justice by appeal to a privileged determiner follows from a critique of the foundational legitimacy of privileged givens, it falls victim to the very same sceptical challenge that gives it its defining motivation. All its claims are undercut by the simple fact that a privileged determiner has a content of its own that is given prior to and independently of its legitimating act of determination. That this renders all appeal to a privileged determiner ultimately equivalent to an appeal to a privileged given is well exhibited by how a transcendental condition is not constituted by its determination of objectivity any more than the will of liberal theory owes its character to its own act of choosing. Transcendental conditions may be introduced to avoid direct reference to reality, but they themselves can only be characterized in the same dogmatically direct way that reality is contemplated by metaphysics. So too, liberal theory may seek to free justice from the hold of given form, but the privileged determiner to which it appeals is still a natural will whose form is just as given as any teleological end.

Since every privileged determiner logically contains an element of given determinacy in the prior character by which it is defined, there is no way any can be made a source of validity without resurrecting the dilemmas of first principles. Judged on its own terms, everything based on a privileged determiner is unjustified precisely because that determining ground lacks the quality of being determined by a legitimating determiner, which alone could give it legitimacy.

In the eyes of many, there is an unequivocal lesson in transcendental and liberal philosophers' vulnerability to the same critique they properly direct against metaphysics and teleological theories of justice. What it supposedly reveals is the final triumph of scepticism and nihilism, leaving us nothing but the edifying occupation of deconstructing theories and systems of justice so as to uncover the given assumptions on which they rest.

2 The Challenges of Scepticism and Nihilism

Anyone concerned with truth and justice must confront the challenges of scepticism and nihilism arising from the problems of traditional theories. Their challenges, however, are of very unequal weight, for like truth and justice themselves, scepticism and nihilism have significantly different characters, despite their parallel features.

In its absolute, must radical form, scepticism denies that opinion can be transformed into knowledge, that reason can be autonomous and self-justifying, that knowlege claims can command unconditioned universal validity, that thought can transcend subjective bias and achieve objectivity. Analogously, nihilism denies that action can ever transcend its conditions and attain universal validity, that conduct and institutions can ever be rationally justified, that norms of justice can ever rest on more than belief. Even though they similarly challenge the justifications allowing knowledge and right to be distinguished from opinion and convention, scepticism and nihilism have completely different theoretical force. Although the dependence of the quest for justice upon the quest for knowledge might suggest that the challenge of scepticism is more formidable than that of nihilism, the exact opposite is the case. In a word, whereas scepticism is senseless when taken to its extreme, nihilism is perfectly coherent.

The nullity of radical scepticism is legion. As much as *particular* theories can have their truth challenged by showing how their claims issue from premises having no validity of their own, absolute scepticism's rejection of all truth is patently absurd. By blanketly denying the ability of theory to justify knowledge claims, absolute scepticism casts itself in the self-destructive predicament of advancing a putatively universally valid claim of its own whose critical force depends upon the very objectivity it repudiates. If, in recognition of this problem, the sceptic were to admit that the sceptical denial of truth cannot consistently be a justified knowledge claim, then scepticism becomes a mere opinion with no more argumentative weight than the counterposition that theory can arrive at truth. Either way, scepticism collapses of its own weight, inadvertently indicating how no argument can ever be given to disqualify the quest for truth undertaken by philosophy. It may be current fashion to treat philosophizing as an activity whose only purpose lies in curing men of the malady of seeking truth through reason, but the hopelessness of philosophy cannot be validly argued without engaging in the same philosophical activity whose abandonment is being championed.

If this leaves scepticism unable to provide any justified reason for forsaking philosophy's quest for truth, nihilism's challenge to the quest for justice cannot be so easily dismissed. Nihilism must be taken seriously for the simple reason that it need not rely upon scepticism to challenge the quest for justice. Instead, nihilism can question the possibility of justifying conduct and institutions without having to deny the possibility of justifying knowledge claims. Whereas scepticism self-destructs by denying truth while asserting the truth of its denial, nihilism can quite consistently claim truth for the proposition that there is no objectively determinable right and wrong since that in no way contradicts the proposition that there is truth that can be known.

This logical coherence of nihilism does not, of course, disqualify the quest for justice. What it does serve to do is focus the alternatives left before us.

3 The Current Impasse In Normative Theory

3.1. The Rehabilitation of The Foundational Approaches to Justice

One alternative consists in holding at bay the amorality of nihilism by stubbornly rehabilitating the classical appeals to privileged givens and privileged determiners as foundations of justice. This alternative continues to be pursued on two broad fronts, paralleling the two basic forms of foundationalism.

On the one hand, many contemporary thinkers remain advocates of teleological theories of justice, where normative validity is grounded in ends given antecendently to action. Observant Marxist-Leninists, for instance, portray the just society as a fulfillment of the fallen essence of human species being, awaiting revolutionary retrieval as the telos of historical necessity. In a similar vein, neo-Aristotelians, such as Hannah Arendt,[3] Leo Strauss[4] and Alasdair MacIntyre,[5] draw inspiration from the polis, whose realization of certain privileged human functions provides a context of sanctioned practices, in pursuit of whose ends a life of prescribed virtues remains possible. These practices may no longer involve slavery or the exclusion from citizenship of women, laborers, and members of different ethnic groups, but they still comprise a given institutional framework mandating which goals must be fufilled to render conduct valid.

On the other hand, the alternate foundationalist approach of liberal theory stands in the midst of its own contemporary revival. Thinkers such as Robert Nozick[6] reaffirm the Lockean strategy of founding justice on the given rights of individuals, deriving just political institutions as instruments for realizing private entitlements. Alternately, John Rawls[7] and his followers have resurrected the Kantian version of the appeal to privileged determiners with a procedural justice that recasts the social contract in terms of a privileged choice procedure replicating the deliberations of practical reason. On its basis, what makes principles of justice valid is not their given content, but whether they would be chosen as the outcome of this procedure. Similarly, Karl-Otto Apel[8] and Jürgen Habermas[9] have outlined a communicative ethics that grounds the determination of ethical norms in an ideal speech situation where all participants are able to engage in unconstrained discourse. Unlike Rawls' choice procedure, this framework does not deprive its participants of knowledge of their own endowments and social position, nor of the particulars of their society. Still, none of these factors independently dictate standards for justice. Rather, what makes actions and institutions just is that they conform to whatever principles are agreed upon under the conditions of free reciprocity governing the situation of unconstrained discourse. Hence, Apel's and Habermas' ideal speech situation serves just as much as a privileged determiner of justice as the individual will of Nozick and the choice procedure of Rawls. These three theories may differ in how they describe the source for the determination of justice, but they all accord in supplanting the teleological appeal to given ends with recourse to a privileged determiner as the foundation of the principles of right.

To the extent that all these undertakings embrace the foundational strategies of their classical forerunners, they cannot overcome the challenge of nihilism. However teleological ethics be resurrected, it still faces the dilemma of justifying the given ends to which it makes appeal. Rooting the norms of conduct in set functions and human potentials leaves unanswered why these givens deserve any prescriptive role. Even if only in reference to such functions could conduct have any ends not rooted in personal arbitrariness, this would still not establish why the ends of one or any such function should be ethically binding. So long as their justification is sought in either their own content or that of any other privileged given, the problems afflicting the justification of first principles cannot fail to reenter.

Similarly, contemporary rehabilitations of the liberal appeal to a privileged determiner cannot coherently legitimate the exclusive role ascribed to whatever structure of willing or discourse is made the source of ethical norms. In every case, the recourse to a privileged determiner rests on two ethical assumptions — first, that justice is not determined by appeal to any teleological ends, and secondly, that liberty has primacy, such that ethical problems revolve around adjudicating the equal claims of the competing interests of individuals. Only if the teleological appeal to prescribed ends is illegitimate does it make sense to invest validity in a determining source of ethical norms, rather than in the embodiment of given ends through the exercise of correspondingly given virtues. Insofar as the teleological strategy cannot be justified on its own terms, its repudiation by the liberal approach might be taken as a mark in the latter's favor. However, abandoning the appeal to teleological ends is not enough to justify ascribing exclusive validity to what individuals choose, be it in exercise of their natural liberty or as participants in a Rawlsian social contract situation or a Habermasian communicative community. In each case, the move from realizing prescribed ends to granting sway to the deliberations of choosing individuals is compelling only if the repudiation of teleological ends is accompanied by an establishment of the exclusive validity of personal choice. For unless the exercise of liberty has an affirmative value of its own, the embrace of liberty is just as arbitrary as obedience to any set of given ends. Only when liberty is already endowed with normative primacy is it appropriate to supplant rule by experts with a system of justice issuing as the outcome of some privileged structure of choice where the interests of individuals have equal weight.

Needless to say, the authority of the choosing will and the equal worth of personal interests cannot be established as the outcome of any such choice procedure without begging the question. Hence, the exclusive authority of the chosen privileged determiner cannot be justified in conformity with its own principle of legitimation. The primacy of individual rights cannot be legitimated as a product of personal choice both because that would take for granted what is in need of legitimation and because the structure of personal choice is not the outcome, but rather the presupposition of any exercise of liberty. Consequently, if justice consists in what is chosen with liberty, the normative primacy of liberty cannot satisfy its own standard of right. Either it is based upon choice, which would be circular, or it is rooted upon a different standard of normative validity, depriving the procedure of choice of its privileged status as the sole source of ethical norms.

3.2 The Resigned Embrace of Descriptive Theories of Justice

In light of these difficulties, a more meaningful alternative for contemporary ethics would seem to lie in the transformation that the theory of justice must undergo if nihilism can be sustained. In the case that nihilism prevails, the theory of justice will have to cease being a prescriptive philosophical science concerned with conceiving the valid norms of conduct and institutions and instead become a non-philosophical, positive, descriptive science limited to observing the workings of given systems of justice and deconstructing the ways in which their norms are conditioned by whatever particular, historical, subjective factors are responsible for their promotion as well as for their lack of universal validity.

This reduction of ethical theory from a prescriptive to a descriptive science is accepted today to such an extent that it even informs many of the current "rehabilitations" of the traditional foundational strategies in ethics. In fact, it is this resignation to descriptive analysis that distinguishes these "rehabilitations" from the original theories that provide their inspiration. Examples abound in both camps.

The triumph of nihilism is well reflected in Marxist as well as neo-Aristotelian rehabilitations of the teleological approach. Embracing historicist notions that norms are relative to each age, much Marxist theory accordingly limits its normative analyses to descriptions of how "bourgeois" and "proletarian" justice are conditioned by class interests rooted in a historical economic system. The proletarian interest may well be ascribed a uniquely universal character, making the working class the harbinger of an allegedly preeminent system of justice. Nonetheless, the failure of Marxist analysis to provide an ethical theory legitimating the norms of communist society independently of historical givens, such as the inconsistently realized values of bourgeois society, leaves proletarian justice just as relative as its bourgeois counterpart.

Similarly, when MacIntyre advances the Aristotelian ideal of an institutionally embedded ethic, where given functions and practices define the parameters of virtue, he detaches these functions and practices from any anthropological or metaphysical mooring and makes them products of historical convention.[10] As a consequence, although the practices constitutive of virtue may still involve ends internal to them, the general structure of such practices neither prescribes any particular institutions, any particular ends, nor any particular corresponding virtues. Instead, the concept of ethical practices remains a formal notion, expressing the contextual grounding of virtue without restricting normative validity to any specific institutional order. MacIntyre's analysis thereby renders ethics relative to conventional practices, in conformity with the nihilist verdict that no particular institutional framework nor any particular set of virtues can command exclusive validity.

The embrace of nihilism is equally pronounced among current advocates of the appeal to privileged determiners of justice. Instead of offering *the* theory of justice, which establishes the exclusively valid relations of right, Rawls expressly constructs merely *a* theory of justice designed to demonstrate how accepted norms of political and social organization can be made consistent with the accepted moral values of a given society. Although he offers an elaborate social contract argument, grounding detailed prescriptions for social and political justice, Rawls remains obedient to a method of "reflective equilibrium," according to which the aim of normative theory can be no more than to clarify our considered ethical judgments and bring them into coherence with our ethical intuitions. On these terms, the social contract argument becomes a pragmatically useful tool, which may be of special interest for our particular political culture, but not for determining a universally definitive concept of justice.

Analogously, Jürgen Habermas restricts his communicative ethics to prescribing the formal situation of unconstrained discourse from which just decisions are to be made. In contrast to Rawls, Habermas refrains from determining any particular ethical principles, institutional structures, or policy decisions from his privileged determiner of justice, suggesting that none of these can be conceived antecedently to the actual deliberations of the participants in the ideal speech situation. These participants are themselves bound by just one rule of rational deliberation, allegedly endemic to their unconstrained argumentative position: that what they acknowledge as normatively valid be only those rules and practices whose universal implementation entails consequences that all can agree to insofar as these consequences satisfy the interests of each.[11] What saves communicative ethics from an altogether empty formality, Habermas maintains, is that its interlocutors, unlike the participants in Rawls' social contract, have full cognizance of their society and of their own goals, endowments and social position. Hence, although the theory of communicative ethics provides nothing but an outline of the situation of unconstrained discourse,[12] the practice of communicative ethics results in particular agreements predicated upon the concrete historical situation in which the deliberating individuals find themselves. In this respect, the conventional claims of the existing institutional context assert themselves in conjunction with the purely procedural demands inherent in the pragmatic situation of practical discourse.

However, insofar as the situation of unconstrained discourse mandates no further universal principles of conduct and institutional organization, there can be nothing of ethical significance in the general structure of given convention. Furthermore, what satisfies the interests of each and every participant must equally defy a priori prescription, since otherwise a rational account of interest satisfaction would preempt the exclusive determining role of the ideal speech situation. Hence, whatever measures are there decided upon remain opaque to reason, depending as they do not only upon historical contingencies but upon collective decisions whose outcome cannot be anticipated even with knowledge of the given institutional background. Thus, Habermas' communicative ethics brings the appeal to a privileged determiner of justice to a *reductio ad absurdum* in that it renders ethical theory incapable of specifying any measure as just, while reducing normativity to a purely positive, arbitrary outcome.

Of late, it has become common to justify these endeavors by arguing, as Gadamer and MacIntyre have done,[13] that all theories of justice and ethics inevitably rest upon given frameworks of practice and discourse that cannot be justified without presupposing their own terms and values. To support this nihilist view and its consequent elimination of prescriptive ethics, two reasons are advanced, neither of which is satisfactory.

One is the attested collapse of the two common traditions of natural right theory, the teleological praxis theory classically formulated by Aristotle and liberal social contract theory. From their presumed failures it is concluded that no theory of justice is possible in a prescriptive sense. However, unless it can be shown that these

theories exhaust the possibilities of conceiving justice, their breakdown only testifies to their own inadequacy.

The other reason advanced is the conventionalist holist claim that
all discourse, including all attempts at justification, is contextually
determined within conceptual and linguistic frameworks whose
authority rests on nothing more than tradition and pragmatic agreement. The proponents of this popular position, most notably
Gadamer and Rorty, may deny its self-referential inconsistency.[14] Yet
they still fall into the familiar absurdity of scepticism insofar as they
relativize all discourse by characterizing it as contextually determined
while asserting that very claim in an unconditioned way.

Unfortunately, those, such as Leo Strauss,[15] who have opposed
the current nihilist reduction of prescriptive to descriptive ethics have
done so by maintaining allegiance to the foundationalist notion that
the only alternative to conventionalism in ethics is natural right theory, which seeks validity in given contents instead of in products of
convention, whose posited character supposedly makes them relative.

4 The Alternative of A Systematic Philosophy Without Foundations

In order to meet the challenge of nihilism and to pursue the quest
for justice in theory, it is necessary to surmount the opposition of
these positions, understand their limitations, and demonstrate that
the quests for truth and justice are not exhausted by the problematic
efforts of foundationalists on the one hand and conventionalists on
the other. As much as privileged givens and privileged determiners
may fail as sources of validity, the prevalent failure of thinkers to
consider any positive alternative to them does not prevent the logical
possibilities of determinacy from allowing a third option. This option
attempts to free the quests for truth and justice of all privileged givens
by seeking justification in self-determined determinacy or freedom. In
regard to the quest for knowledge, this involves developing an
autonomous reason that, instead of resting on foundations, generates
its own method and content in the course of its self-determination. In
regard to the quest for justice, this entails conceiving valid practice to
lie in the reality of freedom, understood not as the liberty of the
natural will, but as the self-ordererd system of the institutions of self-
determination, whose various modes of non-natural, conventional
autonomy are exclusively determined by the very institutional
framework that their own exercise comprises.

Of course, it might appear that any such attempt to invest validity in self-determination only resurrects the foundationalist strategy of advancing some privileged given as the ground of truth and justice. However, when self-determination is more closely analyzed, it becomes apparent that far from comprising a privileged given or privileged determiner, it represents something that has no given content at all. Since what it is is what it determines itself to be, self-determination must be, at the outset, utterly indeterminate. Hence, investing validity in self-determination is tantamount to taking no content or juridical standard for granted. In this respect, the logic of self-determination is a presuppositionless logic, which succeeds in grounding itself by giving itself its own character as a result of a development resting on no antecedently given terms. As such, self-determination is as much presuppositionless as it is self-grounding and unconditioned. Thereby, it realizes what all prior attempts at justification have sought, be they theoretical or practical. In the domain of theory, a logic of self-determination realizes the radical self-responsibility and independence that reason has traditionally claimed in attempting to obtain wisdom. In the field of practice, the reality of self-determination establishes a self-ordered system of institutions beholden to no standards that are not self-imposed. Insofar as autonomous reason and autonomous action derive their character not from any antecedent givens, but through their own self-determination, they are both foundation-free, and accordingly surmount the dilemmas of foundationalism.

Nevertheless, this freedom from foundations might seem to be an invitation to theoretical and practical anarchy, resulting in the same conventionalism embraced by the current avatars of holism and edifying philosophy. However, self-determination is anything but arbitrary. Theoretical and practical anarchy both issue from a given determiner, namely an independent thinker and independent agent, whose intelligence and choosing will are given preconditions for the theories and institutions they determine. Hence, when the theoretical or practical anarchist directs the course of theory and action, the resulting conceptions and activities are not self-determined but determined by the prior agency from which they issue. Similarly, the theoretical and practical anarchists do not determine their own agencies in the course of their constructions, since they already possess their determining character as the antecedent condition of their determining act.

This should indicate that a self-determined theory would no more depend for its ordering upon the agency of a given investigator, than self-determined action would derive its character from the arbitrary choices of a natural will. On the contrary, the method of a truly autonomous theory must be internal to its content, just as the form of agency of self-determined individuals must reside in conventional modes of autonomy that are products of their own activity. Although a foundation-free theory is still conceived and written by a given thinker, no contribution made by that thinker plays any juridical role in establishing what order and content it should have. On the contrary, to the extent that its subject matter is self-determined, the form of its development is just as internally generated as the content it involves. Similarly, self-determined actions and institutions may be the work of individuals with choosing wills whose natural liberty underlies, rather than results from, their activities. Nevertheless, this does not prevent them from engaging in conventional modes of freedom, such as are entailed in property, family, social, and political rights, whose agencies owe their character to the very institutional framework realized in the exercise of their artificial autonomy.

Further, if the demands of normativity are uniquely met by self-determination, then the institutions of justice must be none other than the reality of freedom. Hence, freedom proper cannot consist in a natural liberty, inherent in the given structure of the individual agent, but must rather involve an institutionally determined activity, whose artificial modes of agency entail the interactions of right and duty in which justice lies. Moreover, if these institutions are not to be held together by an agency violating the terms of justice, an institution of freedom must unite them all into a self-determined whole, and thereby seal the foundation-free, self-grounding reality of justice. In other words, justice must be crowned by a self-determined political order, which realizes all the other institutions of self-determination in conformity with its own exercise of political freedom. Therefore, the reality of freedom that coincides with the reality of justice will comprise a self-ordered system of institutional modes of autonomy, wherein individuals exercise non-natural freedoms irreducible to the natural liberty with which they are endowed.

Although the approach following from these considerations remains largely ignored, it has not gone unexplored. On the contrary, the foundation-free systematic philosophy inaugurated by Hegel has attempted to conceive truth and justice in terms of self-determination in order to escape the dilemmas of foundationalism and the attendant opposition of natural right and conventionalism. Despite the debatability of Hegel's success in working out this option, it does provide a strategy that meets the challenge of nihilism and allows for a prescriptive conception of right comprising the theory of justice.

The viability of the resulting systematic philosophy of justice can best be understood by first comprehending the logic and illogic of the traditional alternatives of teleological conceptions of justice and social contract theory, and the metaphysical and transcendental philosophies to which they correspond. Once their appeal and internal collapse is grasped, the alternative of systematic philosophy and its conception of justice can be taken seriously.

The following work attempts to legitimate the systematic philosophy of justice and to develop its basic features.

Parts I and II analyze the internal logic and internal dilemmas of the two traditional approaches to the quests for truth and justice. In the course of these analyses various thinkers will be discussed and the labels, "metaphysical" and "transcendental" will be applied to the foundationalist strategies exemplified in certain features of their thought. It should be understood that no attempt is made to provide a comprehensive interpretation of these thinkers. Reference is made to them only insofar as it serves to illustrate the implications of the strategy under investigation. Similarly, the use of the terms "metaphysical" and "transcendental" to name the two foundationalist approaches should not be taken to imply that when these terms have been employed elsewhere, they merely designate these strategies. Nor should it be presumed that philosophers who have placed themselves or been placed by others under one or the other banner have followed these strategies either exclusively or at all. The analyses of the "metaphysical" and trancendental" approaches are intended solely to uncover the logic of two fundamental strategies for theoretical and practical philosophy, and to lay bare their internal collapse.

In face of that collapse, Part III seeks to demonstrate how foundation-free systematic philosophy offers a strategy avoiding the difficulties of traditional theories and meeting the challenge of nihilism.

Part IV considers the basic relations of justice as the resulting systematic philosophy allows them to be conceived. In the course of this investigation, each of the institutions of freedom will be examined, so as to provide an outline of the entire system of justice.

Part I

Dilemmas of the Metaphysical Approach to Truth and Justice

Chapter 1

Given Determinacy and Justification

1.1 Positive Science and the Problem of the Given

In an age when philosophers trumpet their inability to conceive truth and justice, nothing seems more appropriate than turning to what is given and examining it as offered, duly refraining from all further pretension. With philosophical thought abandoning the real and the good, and resigning itself to exercises in logical consistency and edification, the study of truth and justice seems to have been handed over to positive science for its limited comprehension.

If nothing else, this might signal relief from the unparalleled contestation afflicting philosophy, whose history of ever opposing systems of thought offers no achievement whose worth is not disputed. In other disciplines some initial consensus always reigns as to what defines the subject matter and the standards by which to examine it, making possible cumulative progress. Even if given paradigms are overthrown, they always make way for some new framework whose specification of topic and procedure provides the common terms for some shared sense of theoretical advance. In philosophy, however, object and method are perennial matters of controversy precisely because they themselves are philosophical issues that must be addressed within philosophy if philosophers are not to rely on unjustified opinion to guide their quest for truth.

Such problems never arise so long as one remains in the arena of positive science. Unlike philosophy, positive science takes up a given subject matter and investigates it as such, recognizing that the accessibility and content of what it studies must be established beforehand in order to allow the positive science the opportunity to consider it. Otherwise, positive science would have nothing determinate to study, nor any viable approach. What positive science knows on its own is thus not the immediate truth, but a topic that it beholds by virtue of presupposing it as an object of examination, taking for granted the boundaries of its topic as well as its accessibility to study. Hence, the ensuing analysis addresses a predetermined content, already defined by the assumptions rendering it a specific object of inquiry. By the same token, the standpoint of the investigator is itself predetermined insofar as the positive science takes for granted its own relation to its object simply by taking that object as its given subject matter.

Consequently, positive science can only provide knowledge that is relative with regard to both its form and content. What its cognition addresses is not truth or justice without further qualification, but rather what it has postulated as its given object. Conversely, its knowing is not absolute, grasping concepts or objects as they are in themselves, but only a comprehension of what it makes accessible to itself by defining its terms, selecting its domain from the given array of facts, or otherwise taking certain matters for granted.

Determined in this way, positive science is by no means limited to empirical inquiry. Since its subject matter has no defining restriction other than that it be a given content, positive science equally includes such presumably formal disciplines as mathematics and symbolic logic. Although neither draws directly from objects of experience, each begins its analysis from an assumed subject matter comprised of defined terms such as number and logical operator.

Due to this open embrace of givenness in method and object, all debate in the positive sciences, be they empirical or not, ultimately rests on no more than common assumptions that can always be superseded by the adoption of a different set of terms establishing a new paradigm of science. Since the object of positive science is just as much an unjustified postulate as the cognition of it, positive science cannot establish truth or any valid conception of justice. At most, it can achieve the formal consistency of deriving conclusions from an assumed content according to some accepted procedure.

In effect, positive science is left with the very same inability to know reality and distinguish right from wrong that philosophy is ever more ascribed. Of course, there is nothing problematic in the endeavor of positive science so long as its relative character is acknowledged. Indeed, the limited approach of positive science may well be the only option available in certain fields. Nevertheless, it is problematic to reduce philosophy to positive science and advance the doubly conditioned standpoint of the latter as the inescapable predicament of all discourse. Those, such as Quine[1] and Kuhn,[2] who suggest such a reduction ignore that the acknowledged relativity of positive science leaves it incapable of ever establishing the exclusive universality they claim for it. Anyone who analyzes rational inquiry from the standpoint of positive science would better admit that whatever claims such analysis provides are mere opinion, depending upon the assumptions defining both the topic as well as the method by which it is treated. Then, one's conclusions about discourse have no authority over against any opposing views that do not issue from those same assumptions.

If the predicament of positive science is to have any lessons for the quests for truth and justice, it is that these quests, far from being precluded by the relativity of positive science, must rather be undertaken in radical departure from the latter's dependence upon givens. Whereas positive science involves description and analysis of a given subject matter, such that discrepancies between its scientific models and what they describe call for revolutions in science, the quests for truth and justice involve the prescription of valid reasoning and conduct. Accordingly, when the concepts of truth and justice fail to correspond with the given conventions of argument and existing customs and institutions, a revolution is called for not in theory, but in the current reality of discourse and action.

Similarly, if the positive scientist no longer limits himself to conclusions conditioned by a subject matter taken for granted, but claims absolute truth for his analysis, he falls into the pitfalls of what has since Kant been branded "metaphysics." Such thinking suffers from a two-fold confusion afflicting any attempt to move from opinion to truth on the basis of givens whose authority is assumed rather than established within philosophical inquiry itself.

If the term "metaphysics" can be used in this narrow sense to designate the approach to theorizing that operates with givens, as in positive science, but does not abandon the quest for unqualified truth, the confusion at hand can then be described in the following way: Although metaphysics begins with some given content or other, it fails to treat its object as something under view in virtue of the particular assumptions and standpoint of the investigation. Instead of regarding its subject matter as a stipulation of its own cognition with no other assured validity, metaphysics takes it to be something in itself, that is, to be true without the qualification of simply being that given content chosen as the starting point of inquiry. On the other hand, although the knowledge metaphysics arrives at refers to some assumed content, it is not held to be relative to that chosen point of departure. Because metaphysics takes its object to be immediately true in itself, and not something conditioned by the inquiry taking it for granted, metaphysics purports to have knowledge of it that is true knowledge without further qualification. In other words, metaphysical discourse presumes to have an absolute knowledge that corresponds to the true nature of reality and ideas. Actually, however, metaphysics' claim to absolute knowledge of what is in itself involves the fallacy of asserting direct truth for a given content and knowing both of whose unqualified validity are simply taken for granted.

Needless to say, ever since antiquity, many a philosopher has sought to conceive truth and justice by employing just such metaphysical knowing. Neither content to pursue the limited ends of positive science, nor able to dispense with all assumptions, such thinkers have perennially referred to the given content of their knowledge as true reasoning, true reality, or true justice and thereby canonized their knowing an absolute knowledge of things as they are in themselves.

Despite the patent problems of this whole approach, it has a lure that is not easily ignored, a lure to which once yielded spawns two correlative conceptions of truth and justice that must be identified and critiqued if a viable alternative is to be made comprehensible and convincing.

To avoid confusion, it should be noted that throughout the following discussions, the term "metaphysics" will be employed solely to designate the philosophical strategy that makes appeal to privileged givens as foundations for conceiving truth and justice. In using "metaphysics" to denote this strategy, no claim is being made that the term "metaphysics" has predominantly been used in this sense in the philosophical tradition, nor that thinkers who employ the term or have it applied to their thought follow this approach. Indeed, as subsequent chapters should make clear, "metaphysics," as here understood, is not equivalent to the science of being qua being, the system of synthetic a priori knowledge, or the theory of transcendent reality, any more than these are of necessity developed by appeal to privileged givens. Similarly, it would be wrong to suppose that what has counted as the metaphysical concerns of thinkers from the pre-Socratics through Whitehead can be reduced to the logic of the strategy here under consideration. Even when historical thinkers have pursued this strategy, by no means have all their arguments been faithfully limited to its path.

Accordingly, the following analysis of the metaphysical approach should not be understood as an account of the history of philosophy. Although historical figures will be drawn upon for purposes of illustration, what is at issue is the internal logic of one of the fundamental options of philosophical thought, an option whose promise in no way depends upon whether it be followed yesterday, today, or tomorrow.

1.2 *The Lure of Privileged Givenness and the Path of Metaphysics*

In order to understand the appeal of the metaphysical approach that made it the obvious choice for the originators of western philosophy, it must be recognized that metaphysics' recourse to givenness is tied to philosophy's perennial attempt to escape from the hold of givens that condemns positive science to labors of opinion. By setting out to transform opinion into truth, philosophy places itself in a predicament of radical independence where it bears the burden of being the freest of sciences, as Aristotle observed.[3] This freedom consists in a self-liberation from the authority of the given that can be characterized by two corollary prescriptions, one as purely negative as the other is purely positive. Since philosophy can take for granted neither its subject matter nor method if it is not to incorporate the reliance upon unjustified opinion it seeks to surmount, philosophy must free itself of all given foundations and achieve presupposition-lessness. If this liberation is to have any positive results, then philosophy must proceed to account for all its own terms and procedures so as to be fully self-grounding and self-legitimating. Obviously, these aspirations are intimately connected, for if philosophy has foundations, it rests upon something given outside itself and cannot be self-grounding, whereas if philosophy has no presuppositions, the only topics and standards of truth it can possess are those it has generated by and within itself.

Although philosophy may strive to commence its quest without assuming what it is seeking or how it will find it, it is no secret that philosophers end up always addressing one common object, the truth, with one common means, reason. This conjuncture of truth and reason may be so familiar as to seem self-evident, but if philosophy is to be self-legitimating rather than dogmatic, it must establish the appropriateness of its own employment of reason in seeking truth and so demonstrate that thinking the truth is what presuppositionless science comprises.

The completion of this task is bound up with the basic problem of justification addressed in the quest for truth. That is the problem of moving from opinion to knowledge, where knowledge signifies justified opinion. However the move actually be made, justifying an opinion always seemingly involves giving reasons establishing its validity. In this regard, the linguistic connection between "reasons" and "reason" would hardly appear to be accidental, particularly since what is ordinarily held to count as a reason in justifying truth claims are not feelings, beliefs, or some physical event, but products of reason, namely, propositions sanctioned by thinking in rational argument. These propositions may well refer to what is felt, believed and experienced, but only when argument grants these factors the status of evidential reasons can they figure as elements of justification. Of course, no matter how often common usage may connect reasons and reason, the existence of this practice cannot attest to its legitimacy. The problem is not removed by holding justification to be a matter of custom, where what counts as reasons are simply whatever agreed practice considers to be such. Such a view resurrects the self-referential dilemma of any absolute scepticism, for its own claim regarding the customary character of justification either is itself a contingent matter of custom, with no warrant preventing its repudiation by an adoption of different practices, or else a universally binding proposition whose privileged authority contradicts its own customary characterization of rationality. Instead of being dismissed out of hand, the right of reason to justify opinions and establish truth must be questioned. Obviously, the vindication of philosophy hinges upon the answer to this query to the extent that philosophers rely on reason to think the truth.

In dealing with the problem of justification thinkers have inveterately brought into play three related sets of categories to which the juridical role of reason is tied. They are the contrast terms of subjective-objective, particular-universal, and conditioned-unconditioned.

Justification seems to require that the reasons legitimating opinions be objective rather than subjective since what is true is so irrespective of the perspective of this or that individual. What is peculiar to the subject cannot figure as a reason transforming opinion into truth precisely because the demand for justification calls for something transcending individual viewpoint and having binding authority for all. For this very reason, when justifications are given, they are presented in arguments where individuals step beyond the confines of their single point of view and use language to present reasons that must be intersubjective in character simply to be expressed within that medium. If, on the contrary, reasons were merely subjective, no distinction could be drawn between opinion and truth that did not rest upon opinion.

The distinguishing between subjective and objective in justification directly entails that between particular and universal. If validity requires objectivity, that is, reasons that are not relative to a certain subject, but valid for all, then such reasons must be universal in character. Their authority is not limited to the particular subject who advances them any more than to the particular moment or locality in which they are presented. Even if the truth at issue concerns a subjective state of affairs at one time and place, what it is still possesses an objectivity transcending the limits of some particular point of view. In this respect, opinion is tied to what is subjective and particular, whereas justified opinion or knowledge involves what is objective and universal.

If, however, reasons justifying opinions must be objective and universal, they must be no less unconditioned. What is valid regardless of subjective standpoint and particular circumstance is none other than unconditionally valid, whereas what is unjustifiable is relative to, which is to say, conditioned by, factors that have no validity of their own, being as they are subjective and particular.

It can come as no surprise that philosophers have perennially ascribed to reason these very qualities that reasons must presumably possess in order to justify opinions and transform them into knowledge. Feeling, belief and perception have all been recognized to be subjective, particular, conditioned and thereby dependent upon given factors of some sort or other, such that they cannot be counted upon to provide justification in questions of truth and justice, let alone validate their own authority. By contrast, reason has been judged to have an objectivity, universality and unconditioned autonomy that qualifies it to judge between competing truth claims. Otherwise rational argument could play no role in the quests for truth and justice, and philosophy would be a vain enterprise even if its possibility could never be denied with the certainty absurdly claimed by sceptics.

Naturally, if the validity of reasoning and truth and justice all lies in objective unconditioned universal reasons, these reasons would seemingly have to enjoy the same support in order to possess their authority to justify reason and the candidates for truth and justice. In other words, valid reasons would have to be justified by reasons of their own satisfying the same requirements of objectivity and unconditioned universality. Indeed, if opinion is to be transformed into knowledge by reasons, these reasons must be true themselves, which is to say that they too must be backed up by reasons of like validity. This situation, however, results in an infinite regress of reasons in need of further reasons. That undermines the whole process of justification by leaving every reason conditioned by yet another and preventing any from having the unconditioned universality required to seal the validity of whatever reasons are reasons for.

What gives metaphysics its great appeal is that its defining approach seems to provide the only plausible solution to the impasse at which justification arrives. This solution to the problem of infinite regress consists in giving justification firm ground to stand upon by basing it upon a reason that has unconditioned universality by being immediately self-justifying and self-evident, while giving other reasons their support. Such a reason would be determined by no other, and instead would be the reason behind everything else that has validity, be it justice, true reality, or reasoning itself. This ultimate reason would therefore be an irreducibly given content neither relative to any standpoint nor particular to any circumstance. Resting on nothing else, such a reason would exhibit the presuppositionlessness to which philosophy must aspire and at the same time exhibit the positive feature of being the principle by which all that is valid is determined.

To secure justification by this means is the canonical route adopted by metaphysics, the route of understanding self-justification, unconditioned universality and presuppositionlessness to lie in some given. This approach of conceiving truth, justice, and the validity of reasoning to issue from a given content is naturally not equivalent to an indifferent embrace of all that is given. Metaphysics aims to solve the dilemma of justification by appealing to a privileged given, which is able to play its validating role as a first principle only by claiming that position to the exclusion of all other putative givens. Competing opinions, regimes and strategies of argument all have an aspect of givenness simply by existing. If they are to be judged valid or invalid by virtue of a given, that given must have a special kind of givenness that is objective, universal and unconditioned. By contrast, what is invalid, but given, must possess a givenness that is subjective, particular and conditioned.

This differentiation of privileged givenness that is self-justified from givenness that has no validity by itself can be represented by the distinction between nature and convention. What is given by convention possesses precisely the subjective, particular and conditioned character in which validity is lacking to the extent that the conventional is a product of arbitrariness prey to all the influence of subjective bias and particular circumstance. By contrast, what is given by nature exists independently of arbitrary conditions, provided that "nature" designates given determinacy that does not issue from any determiner, is impervious to all else, and is both the precondition and juridical standard for all that is conventional.

Employing this suitable distinction, metaphysics seeks the valid determination of truth and justice as well as the self-justification of reason by dispensing with reality, justice, and rationality as they are determined by mere convention in order to arrive at what they each are by nature.[4] This endeavor consists in directly asking what is reason, reality, and justice, and answering by directly apprehending some first principle or principles comprising the privileged given that defines their respective natures. In the case of reason and reality, this leads to conceptions having parallel forms and parallel difficulties.

1.3 The Problem of Grounding Reason on Privileged Givens

With its recourse to privileged givens, metaphysics views valid reasoning to consist in deductive argument resting upon the antecedent intuition of the given terms and operations with which deduction proceeds. Metaphysics elevates formal logic, buttressed by intuitive intelligence, to a normative canon of thought based on the understanding, so forcefully propounded by Aristotle, that reasons can transform opinion into knowledge only if there is a given self-evident principle upon whose prior apprehension justification can rest. Without such a foundation, justification would seemingly dissolve into an infinite regress of reasons needing reasons to support themselves. It would thus appear that rational argument must proceed from some given whose authority is completely independent and arrive at conclusions according to some given method whose validity must be equally self-evident and unmediated by any other. Only when the procedures of deduction have their own privileged immediacy will the move from the privileged given to concluded results have a form of valid demonstration that is not shaken by the same infinite regress that leads to a given content at the base of all argument. On these grounds, metaphysics concludes that the reason supplying reasons transforming opinion into truth has a structure characterizable in terms of a formal logic, where both the primitive terms and operations of reasoning are irreducible givens. They underlie all argument, such that they themselves are indemonstrable principles apprehensible only through the immediate cognition in which intuition consists.

The metaphysical attempt to salvage justification by appealing to given determinacy thus entails a dual doctrine of philosophical wisdom. It teaches that truth can only be known through the combination of an intelligence intuiting first principles and a subsidiary demonstrative reasoning deducing conclusions from them. Since the latter proceeds with premises and given operations neither of which can themselves be demonstrated without being taken for granted, the formal logic of rational demonstration can only consist in a deductive logic whose results are purely analytic in character, depending in their entirety upon the prior contents and procedures from which they issue. Insofar as deductive argument has a formal structure whose primitive terms and functions are not determined by demonstrative reasoning but given independently of its operation, all further concluded content must derive from the underlying intuition of first principles, or, failing that, from experience, imagination, language, or some other external source providing additional terms. As a consequence, deductive thought does not generate any new content by itself, but only arrives at what is in conformity with its premises and invariable functions. All its conclusions are properly contained in those premises, as supplemented by external stipulation and modified by the given operations of reasoning. As such, the ensuing demonstration is entirely tautological, providing only what is taken to be already at hand in the givens with which its argument operates. Accordingly, its demonstrative reasoning is governed by the principle of contradiction that ordains that justification is achieved provided the justified opinion does not contradict any of the premises and operations from which it is derived.

On these familiar terms, so "natural" from a metaphysical point of view, rational argument perennially relates universal, particular and individual in a way displayed by the structure of syllogism that aptly typifies a thinking stamped by given form and content, analyticity, and obedience to the principle of contradiction. To take the classic example of such syllogizing — "All men are mortal; Socrates is a man; Socrates is mortal" — one has a reasoning where the major premise advances a universal rule supplemented by a particular condition provided in the minor premise so that in conclusion, an individual is subsumed under the universal rule by virtue of its particular character. Certainly it is tempting to follow Kant and observe, as he does in his formal logic,[5] that this syllogistic relation comprises the very principle of valid rationality and necessity, showing how everything is determinable through universal rules and necessary under a certain condition. Prudence requires noting, however, that in this syllogism of demonstrative reasoning the universal, particular, and individual are all determined independently of one another and of the process of syllogizing that relates them. Each operates within the syllogism as a given term, as must be the case in a thinking whose form and content are independently given, and whose results are purely analytic in character. Such reasoning's independent determination of universal, particular, and individual is anything but a valid paradigm of rationality, for it leaves their connection resting upon some additional extrinsic factor, raising all the problems of "participation" decried by Aristotle in his attack on the Platonic theory of forms.

Even if the metaphysical approach to rational argument could surmount this problem, it must still contend with the entirely formal conception of truth entailed by demonstrative reasoning. Insofar as all deductive thought must operate with given terms and functions, and come to analytic conclusions in conformity with the principle of contradiction, its own reasoning can grant the truth it justifies nothing but certification that the thinking of it is self-consistent. By itself, demonstrative reasoning contributes to the quest for truth knowledge of one thing and one thing alone — the correspondence of thought with itself.

If one were to identify reason with deductive argument, then the logic of demonstration would comprise nothing but reason's self-understanding of how it can stand in conformity with itself. On these terms, where formal logic is taken as the exclusive arbiter of rationality, reasoning provides only the formal criterion of truth entailed in the coherence, or self-consistency of argument.

1.3.1 The Lesson of Logical Positivism

As common as this characterization of reason may be to a generation brought up in the shadow of logical positivism, it involves an insuperable dilemma. This is most plainly exhibited by none other than logical positivism's resolute acceptance of the formal consequences of characterizing reason in terms of given structures. Although the conundrum of logical positivism does not define the full plight of the metaphysical conception of reason, it points directly to the strategies of argument metaphysics is compelled to follow in its own attempt to salvage rational argument.

In contrast to the dual metaphysical conception of rational justification, logical positivism identifies reason and rational argument with deductive reasoning alone. Accordingly, logical positivism consistently concludes that all *a priori* knowledge is analytic, consisting in tautologies governed by the principle of contradiction, whereas all synthetic knowledge is empirical and subject to all the contingencies of empirical cognition. In drawing this analytic-synthetic distinction, logical positivism recognizes that the presumed analyticity of *a priori* knowledge, codified in formal logic, has by itself no relation to objective truth, and rejects as analytically indemonstrable and empirically unverifiable any assumption of the correspondence of thought and reality.

In the strict form advanced by Ayer,[6] logical positivism further refrains from claiming that the relations of analyticity expressed in formal logic comprise the essential form of meaningful speech, or the universally valid form of reason's correspondence with itself. If logical positivism were to make these claims, it would immediately fall victim to the dilemma of having to justify its candidate for the canon of reason. If appeal were made to any other principles to justify its canon, that canon would no longer be the universal form of proper argument. If, on the other hand, its exclusive authority were respected, then there would be no way of demonstrating its validity without taking it for granted as the privileged method of demonstration. To avoid this problem, logical positivists like Ayer take the analyticity of reason to be ultimately a matter of convention, reflecting the meanings of terms as they are pragmatically accepted in linguistic usage. This, of course, sets the stage for challenging the whole analytic-synthetic distinction, as Quine has done,[7] for it reduces analyticity to something that can only be descriptively, rather than prescriptively determined by observing the conventions of discourse.

The result is that logical positivism adopts the sceptical view that philosophy must be analytic in the sense of limiting itself to pointing out the consistency or inconsistency of the linguistic usage of the terms employed in articulating the synthetic knowledge obtained from experience. It thus might seem that logical positivism gives up altogether the enterprise of prescriptive logic, that is, of establishing the logic of true thought. This, however, is not the case for the fundamental reason that logical positivism does not offer its reduction of reason to deductive reasoning as a matter of convention and empirical happenstance. Logical positivism instead presents it as the irreducible fate of thought, excluding all theories to the contrary. By giving its blanket characterization of reasoning this juridical role, logical positivism cuts the ground out from under itself. It ends up in the self-annulling position of affirming a doctrine of reason whose own validity can neither be empirically verified nor analytically established.

What the plight of logical positivism underlines is the ultimate absurdity of claiming that all *a priori* knowledge is analytic, that deductive reasoning can be the principle of rationality, that formal logic can be the canon of reason and prescribe the rules of justification in philosophy's quest for truth. It is absurd to claim that all *a priori* knowledge is analytic because that very claim is itself synthetic, depending upon an antecedent acceptance of entailment that first makes it possible to rely on any analysis whatsoever. Similarly, deductive reasoning cannot be the one and only model of philosophical argument, for, as Plato[8] and Aristotle[9] point out, all deduction ultimately rests upon non-deducible premises and canons of deduction that would have to be justified by some other form of cognition. Even if one were to claim that the premises and procedures of reasoning are arbitrary, resting on tradition, linguistic usage, pragmatic agreement or singular stipulation, one would be at a loss to justify this very characterization of argument without stepping beyond its limits, and appealing to a non-demonstrative knowledge.

The dilemmas afflicting logical positivism thus indicate that the whole enterprise of metaphysical thought hangs on vindicating this other non-deductive, synthetic cognition where reason immediately apprehends the privileged givens providing rational argument with the primitive terms and procedures it seemingly needs to secure justification. Only if this foundation be provided can deductive reasoning play any role in the quest for truth, for without it, there is no legitimate content ready for analysis, nor any legitimate rules of demonstration.

1.3.2 The Impossibility of Justifying Any First Principles of Reasoning

From the outset, however, it appears impossible for metaphysics to validate any immediate cognition for reason and justify the choice of one set of privileged givens over any other.

Any attempt to provide reasons to justify a putative immediate apprehension of primitive terms and first principles of argument would be self-defeating. If the apprehension were to be supported by any such reasons it would be mediated by them and no longer count as the foundational immediate cognition it is supposed to be. The primitive terms and first principles to be defended would likewise forfeit their very primacy by having any reasons behind them. Conversely, no supporting reasons could count as valid, for they would not rest upon the primitive terms and first principles supposedly providing ultimate justification. As a consequence, it would appear that there would be no way of deciding between competing candidates for knowledge of the foundations of rational argument, for just as no adjudicating reasons could be supplied, each candidate would equally comprise an intuition immediately offering an intuited content.

In face of this impasse, metaphysical thought has little choice but to pursue an indirect approach. Instead of seeking reasons to provide mediating justification for what is supposed to be immediately given, metaphysics must somehow legitimate the privileged givens of reason without employing the mode of justification resting upon them.

One promising option consists of validating the putative given principles of reason by showing that everything rational does indeed rest upon them. This route would leave undisturbed the foundational primacy of the first terms of reason by showing that the totality of rational knowledge is determined by them. Nevertheless, carrying off this indirect proof is easier said than done. In order to certify that the immediately apprehended first terms and principles are indeed the given foundations of rational justification would here require an antecedent knowledge of both everything else that is valid and a principle of derivation to certify that everything else does rest upon those putative foundations. If, however, the given foundations of reason are necessary for justifying any truth claims, there could not be any sure knowledge of all else that did not already accept the authority of those foundations and rest upon them. Further, even if such knowledge were available without presupposing the foundations at issue, the need for a principle certifying the derivation of all other content from those foundations raises the whole problem anew. The moment the required principle of derivation gets introduced, it comprises but another fundamental given in need of the same ultimate justification that it is supposed to help supply. Consequently, there is no way this indirect route can accomplish its mission and salvage the metaphysical quest for truth.

This leaves one last option, pushed to the limit by Aristotle in Book Gamma of his *Metaphysics*. On the face of it, what Aristotle proposes seems to be an option impossible to reject. Its logic beckons with compelling force, up to a certain point. Since no ultimate givens of rational justification can be legitimated either by any anterior supporting reason or by reference to the derivative totality of what they ground, the only remaining strategy would be apogogic proof, that is, proof by refutation. Such a proof would have to show that every attempt to reason without employing the privileged givens under investigation refutes itself and ends up employing the very givens it intends to reject. In this roundabout way, the metaphysical quest for a viable foundation for reason would meet success, securing justification by arriving at principles of argument about which it is impossible to be mistaken.

What Aristotle proposes is that the principle of contradiction, the principle that nothing can both be and not be in the same manner, qualifies as just such an indubitable first principle of reason, feasibly defensible by apogogic argument. His proof by refutation of its validity operates at two levels, first with regard to meaning and then with regard to being.[10] Although Aristotle's argument concerns but one candidate for a privileged given for reason, it reveals the ultimate collapse of the entire metaphysical approach to justification.

If one does not adopt the principle of contradiction, it indeed appears that meaningful speech becomes impossible. Without the principle of contradiction, to speak of man would mean both man and what is not man, and so signify anything and everything. Even to refer to something that is not man, such as a door, would similarly signify what is and is not a door, and so present the very same totality of referents, each of which would mean something equally indeterminate. As a result, it would be impossible to mean anything definite, for every utterance would signify the same unlimited array of meanings, where each would be indistinguishable from any other.

In effect, nothing determinate could be meant whatsoever, least of all the claim that discourse can dispense with the principle of contradiction. Without that principle, this very claim means also its own contrary, or more correctly, nothing since every meant term comprising it ("nothing," "can," "be," "and," "not," "be," "in," "the," "same," "manner") would be completely indeterminate. The case already seems won. No position of any sort can be meaningfully held without adoption of the principle of contradiction. Every view to the contrary refutes itself by meaning something definite and thereby adopting the principle of contradiction despite itself.

When, following Aristotle's argument, one turns from meaning to being, the principle of contradiction again appears indispensable. In its absence there seemingly could be no objects of discourse nor discourse itself. For it anything that has being both is and is not what it is, there are no features whereby any being can be identified or distinguished from any other. Just as in regard to meaning, "man" would mean "man" as well as "not man," so now in regard to being, man would be both whatever is and is not man. Everything would thus share the same boundless array of characteristics, whose own defining qualities would themselves dissolve into undifferentiated unity with all others. Nature, thought, speech, art, and action could have no more reality than any other determinate being. Without the principle of contradiction holding true, being would collapse into the very same indeterminacy into which meaning would dissolve. Consequently, any theory of being that dispensed with that principle would undermine itself the moment it attempted to give being any determinacy. So long as there is being of any definiteness whatsoever, the principle of contradiction would already be ontologically effective. Therefore, to the extent that any individuals exist, let alone engage in meaningful speech, they cannot be mistaken about the validity of the principle of contradiction.

Of course, if metaphysics be granted this success, the question still arises whether the apogogic defense of the principle of contradiction allows for justification of any further reasoning or of any further truths concerning being. As Bertrand Russell has pointed out,[11] the principle of contradiction bears no fruit unless there be supplied some additional content ready for analysis. Such a content must ultimately be arrived at synthetically, for if it derives from something else, whatever stands as the ultimate given in the chain of derivation must be accounted for non-analytically. This, however, resuscitates the fundamental dilemma confronting metaphysics, namely, the problem of legitimating what is taken to be a given. Analysis of the principle of contradiction might give rise to corollary propositions such as the principle of excluded middle, as Aristotle maintains,[12] but that still leaves out of account all other content to which these principles could have actual application. By itself, adherence to the principle of contradiction might prevent the collapse into indeterminacy of previously given meanings, but not provide any help in justifying either them or any newly supplied contents.

Although this predicament applies to meaning, it might still be suggested, following Aristotle,[13] that the principle of contradiction still entails very definite strictures concerning the ultimate structures of being. Certainly, without the principle of contradiction, it does appear difficult to maintain any distinction between necessary and accidental features, or any determinate reality for the related notions of essence, nature and substance. For if everything that is both has and has not certain features, all ontological distinctions lose their character. Nevertheless, this does not mean that the principle of contradiction necessarily leads to any specific ontology, as Aristotle seems to presume by introducing his theory of substance on the heels of his apogogic defense of his first principle of reason. In order to arrive at any of the elements of Aristotle's theory of substance, much must be added to the principle of contradiction. By itself, the latter justifies no content of any sort.

Indeed, the same could be said of apogogic argument in general. Proof by refutation only testifies to the collapse of the self-refuted positions, and not to the truth of any alternative. In the case at issue, Aristotle tries to escape this limitation by suggesting that the refuted positions he has described exhaust all possible arguments, except for that which accepts the principle of contradiction. This claim, however, rests on the very direct presuppositions that there are no other alternative views and that there are both determinate meanings and determinate being that command self-evident truth as irreducible givens for philosophical inquiry. Needless to say, these assumptions themselves take for granted the nature of argument, meaning and being, all of which are key issues of debate. Presupposing them leaves what they are something determined prior to philosophical investigation, excluding them from rational treatment and reducing them to arbitrary assumptions.

Thus, when it is claimed that without acceptance of the principle of contradiction, all meaning and being collapses into indeterminacy, there is no reason not to answer, "So what?". For why should not indeterminacy be the starting point of the quest for truth instead of some privileged given? As shall become evident in the subsequent discussion, it is precisely indeterminacy that provides an alternative to the dilemmas afflicting the appeal to privileged givens characterizing metaphysical thought.

1.4 Problems of the Metaphysical Conception of Reality

The problems that surface in the metaphysical attempt to salvage rational justification reappear in all their tenacious difficulty when passive wonder gives way to the question, "What is?", and thinkers respond by conceiving reality through immediate reference to the putatively given. This question and direct response, so natural a starting point for inquiry into reality, provides the abiding guideline defining and condemning the metaphysical approach to reality.

Given its constitutive question and mode of answer, this approach inveterately conceives reality by first presenting some specific content and claiming that it is something given immediately *in res* independently of any reference to it. This content may comprise a single fundamental substance, a plurality of basic structures of reality, the totality of the universe in all its variegation, or a theological source preceding all else. No matter how the immediately given is characterized, the ensuing conception of reality will issue from a direct cognizance of what is, comprehending whatever mediation and relations are at hand in reality by directly discovering that which is most ultimately given.

Since whatever gets taken to be true reality is so in virtue of something identified as immediately given in itself, there can be no mediating principle by which the claimed reality of different contents can be judged. Any content can be presented as something immediately given in reality. Consequently, the history of metaphysical theories of reality is littered with completely disparate competing systems of reality, each identifying different ultimate givens for which equally unqualified immediate truth is claimed.

Naturally, such conflict between advocates of water, fire, earth, matter, substance, monads, and so on could not escape the attention of metaphysical thinkers themselves, and efforts were made to surmount the dilemma without abandoning appeal to privileged givens.

Paralleling the attempts to establish foundations for rational justification, some thinkers sought an absolute first principle of reality that would overcome the competing claims of different given contents by deriving them all out of itself in an ordered construction of the totality of reality. Once engaged, however, this strategy inevitably falls prey to disputes concerning not only what is the first principle, but what constitutes the criteria for the completeness and validity of its presumed grounding of all reality. An all too familiar vicious circle always arises, where in order to judge the truth of the stipulated foundation of reality, one already has to have true knowledge of the scope and interconnection of the entire content of the universe. This, however, should be unattainable without relying upon that foundation, if it be truly the basis of everything else.

A response to these difficulties is offered by Socrates when he argues that in order to answer the question, "What is?", one must first call opinion into question, purge oneself of all assumptions concerning reality and attain a state of knowing nothing at all, from which the quest for truth can genuinely begin. All this can be achieved without prior knowledge, provided one restricts oneself to questioning the claims of others, allowing their opinions to provide the topic of inquiry. By asking them to justify the knowledge they advance, one avoids the problem of already having to know any answers, including knowledge of what are the proper questions that philosophy should raise. Here, at the threshold of wisdom, no reasons are available to lead one forward on the quest for truth, for any rational grounds of inquiry would represent truths of their own that could not be known at the very outset of philosophical investigation. Instead, one can only be driven on by groundless impulse, by an inner voice suggesting that there is a difference between knowledge and opinion, warranting the examination of given beliefs. Lacking any knowledge by which to judge the truth or falsity of the opinions of others, one has little choice but to ask them to supply the reasons justifying their claims and bring them to judge whether the claims they affirm really support one another. Naturally, when discrepancies are recognized this does not establish the truth or falsity of any inconsistent claims, but only that those who advance them are unable to justify their opinions. If persistent questioning leads to this negative result, where individuals discover that they do not know what they thought they knew, it produces the radical ignorance providing the search for wisdom with its generic starting point. From that putatively presuppositionless perspective, for which no claims command any authority, one can immediately move beyond ignorance to know reality as it is in itself.

The problem with this alternative strategy becomes clear when Plato pursues the Socratic program in the discussion of the divided line in the *Republic*. Moving beyond the negative outcome of the dialectic of Socratic questioning, Plato there describes how upon reaching the radical ignorance rid of all assumptions one faces a content presupposing no other, a content on which all truth depends. This unconditioned given is the Good, and from it one can allegedly proceed without reference to anything else to conceive one idea after another of things as they are in themselves.

Admittedly, the features that Plato ascribes the Good give strong support to his claim that it has an irrefutable primacy. If truth consists in the known correspondence of ideas and reality, then it well appears that every truth philosophy uncovers presupposes that the knower and the knowable exist, that the knowable reveals itself to the knower, and that the ideas by which the knower comprehends the known correctly portray what they represent. Therefore, it would seem that truth cannot be known unless there be knowledge of something to account for the being of ideas and reality, as well as their correspondence. Plato offers the Good as precisely this needed ground of truth, a ground that not only gives being to reality and the knower, makes reality reveal itself and guarantees the conformity of ideas and their objects, but also grounds its own accurate presentation to the knower as an idea in its own right. After all, on this basis, if there were no reliable idea of the Good, philosophy could not know the ground of truth, nor trust any other idea. Consequently, the Good would have to underlie all being and knowledge, as something that can only be immediately apprehended as the privileged given on which the truth of all ideas depends.

Although Plato nowhere shows how the specific ideas immanently emerge from the Good, even if one allows that they do, the Platonic approach can never account for how one can decide what the

Good is and why it is the valid given beyond all assumption without already taking for granted what knowing and reality are in general, as well as what can and cannot be presuppositionless. So long as any specific content be ascribed immediate and unconditioned reality, there is nothing that can legitimate it against the opposing claim of some other arbitrary assumption. Appeal to anterior reasons or apogogic proof only resurrects the same dilemmas undermining every candidate for first principle of reason. Whether the privileged given be a particular fact, an all-encompassing first principle, or the divine determining source of everything real, whatever be immediately advanced as true in itself can comprise no justifiably true reality, but only the referent of a knowing that takes the fundamental content of reality for granted.

This remains the case, even if one were to follow Aristotle and preface the investigation of nature, mind and the humanities with a study of being qua being. Certainly, it seems very plausible that being must first be conceived in its own right since nothing real can lack being nor therefore be conceived without a prior understanding of being itself. The recourse to being qua being would seem to address the least determinate aspect of reality and thus avoid any of the determinate references to reality that plague alternative metaphysical theories. Precisely because of the unequaled indeterminancy of being qua being, all talk of specific real things would have to presume it as an established foundation that no conception of reality could avoid conceiving from the start. As much as this line of reasoning brings home anew the seductive attraction of the metaphysical appeal to privileged givens, the whole enterprise it promotes is yet again underlain and undermined by arbitrary assumptions. After all, how could the study of being qua being be pursued as first philosophy without already assuming in reality the primacy and elemental character ascribed to being? Although the science of being might appear to begin with indeterminacy, it actually starts with being that is very specificially determined as the irreducibly given, absolutely fundamental structure of reality. Consequently, it falls prey to the basic dilemma of rooting the quest for truth in the apprehension of privileged givens.

By asking, "What is?", as the first question of philosophy, metaphysics perennially commits the error of making immediate reference to reality. No matter what it gives in answer, metaphysical thought is always left presupposing the correlation between the content of its conception and that of the real, just as it was left presupposing the correlation between the content of its conception and that of valid thought when it turned to apprehend the principles of reason. The arbitrariness of such postulated congruence cannot be surmounted without abandoning the whole strategy of the metaphysical approach. Because metaphysics constitutively begins its inquiry with some presumed knowledge of what is given, it can never justifiably establish the correspondence between its thought and true ideas and reality, a correspondence on which its own immediate claims depend. As a result, the metaphysical conception of reality can never be more than a mere stipulation as arbitrarily posited as the foundations of reason it parallels.

Chapter 2

The Metaphysics of Justice

Once the metaphysical route is taken and justification is sought in the contemplation of privileged givens, it is natural for justice to be conceived by appeal to given norms that institutions and actions must embody to be legitimate. Just as the validity of knowledge would seem to lie in reasons resting upon an ultimate given foundation, so the legitimacy of conduct would seem to have its measure in standards antecendently apprehended by reason. Only by conforming to these forms of goodness, it would appear, can the will become the rational will possessing the unconditioned universal validity that reason determines and justice enjoys. Then human conduct relinquishes its arbitrary conventions and brings into being a second nature, a good life realizing the privileged givens in which the timeless ideal of justice resides.

This attempt to realize the good life by adopting given forms of conduct defines the metaphysics of justice. In order to understand its compelling logic and final impasse, it is best to consider the basic arguments developed by the classic originators of the position, Plato and Aristotle.

From the start, the metaphysics of justice is racked by a tension that is both its driving force and fatal bane. This tension lies in the attempt to unite what is unconditionally universal with what is determined by independently given norms. The moment justice is conceived as the Good, that unconditionally universal form prescribing rationally predetermined ends that action must achieve to be valid, legitimate conduct bears the challenge of somehow comprising

41

actions and institutions that are for their own sake while all the time remaining functional in character. With just action here having ends of a given character that action must achieve to be the rational willing of justice, instrumental action, or what Plato and Aristotle call *techne*, becomes the paradigm of legitimate conduct. Instead of exercising the autonomy of a free will following its own aims, valid action embodies those predetermined functions achieving the rationally prescribed universal goals of the Good. At the same time, such conduct must be an end in itself, for if what it does is just, its activity falls within the order of justice as something to be striven for without reserve.

2.1 Plato's Discovery of the Basic Logic of Praxis Theory

The shape of justice that immediately results from this exclusion of freedom in deference to the rule of reason is uncovered in all its firm logic by Plato in the *Republic*.

The starting point of this metaphysics of justice is the premise that reason prescribes goals for action whose fulfillment comprises the unconditionally justified conduct, the rational willing, constitutive of the Good. If this teleological view be admitted, paralleling as it does the metaphysical search for true reasoning and true reality in privileged givens, then justice will require performing those functions that fulfill the goals set by reason as universally valid features of the given form of the Good. Since these functions have fixed ends, they each require a corresponding expertise, disposition or character, and excellence or virtue in performance to assure their best possible completion.

Therefore, if the rational goals of justice are to be best achieved, then those best qualified by expertise, character, and virtue to carry out the functions attaining these goals must perform them. The community devoted to justice will accordingly divide itself into necessary classes performing the different functions required to fulfill the rational goals of goodness, classes to which individuals will belong not by choice, but according to their capabilities to perform the requisite functions, capabilities that will differ due to varying talent, training and attitude. Although Plato allots each individual to just one class, arguing that only such specialization insures the best performance of each task, it is not inconceivable that the same individual could be qualified for more than one occupation and perform several without prejudicing the rationally predetermined goals of justice. Strictly speaking, individuals could thus belong to several classes at once, provided they are fitted to carry out multiple functions with sufficient excellence.

Be this as it may, because participating individuals must have choosing wills simply to perform their designated occupations, it cannot be guaranteed that they will automatically join the appropriate classes and properly execute the functions they are best suited to perform. Even if they understand their own aptitudes and the needs of justice, they always have the ability to choose to ignore their duties. Consequently, a further function is called for, a function consisting in the ruling activity whose purpose is limited to safeguarding the realization of justice by making sure that all the functions achieving the rational ends of goodness are performed and performed well by those individuals most fitted to do so. An additional class of individuals is therefore needed to undertake this ruling activity, a class whose members must again be selected on ability and be required to serve their posts to guarantee the best possible rule. Plato is quite right to call this class a guardian class, for its task consists in maintaining an order already determined by reason's prescription of the goals and corresponding functions of justice.

On this basis, the ruling function of the guardians is a purely administrative activity of overseeing the given framework in which its own function operates. Like the action of other members of the community, the ruling action of the guardians remains an act of *techne*, enjoying validity only by conforming to the given norms of the Good. The guardians do not decide what organization the state should have, but simply implement the class organization eternally decided by reason. In this sense, the rule of the guardians does nothing but give each individual his due, for compelling everyone to perform the class activities they do best does produce the greatest justice for all, if justice indeed consists in the fulfillment of predetermined ends.

Under such a regime all freedoms that might interfere with achieving the set goals of justice would have to be precluded. If there be any rational hierarchy of economic needs and occupations, then market freedom must be restricted to prevent individuals from both satisfying whatever needs they please through commodity exchange and entering occupations through similar agreement irrespective of the tasks mandated by reason. Most importantly, all political freedom would have to be curtailed, since neither the goals of the state, its organization, nor the assignment of its different functions could be left to the will of all or any of its members, if the order of reason is to be automatically ensured. Democracy could thus not be tolerated, for there is no telling whether the majority will choose what is rational, when rationality in politics consists of fixed ends and activities.

Yet can political freedom possibly be so entirely excluded? Although the guardians may be able to use their power to restrict the political, market, and even household freedom of their subjects, can the guardians' own political freedom be curtailed without eliminating their necessary position as rulers? Does not the very structure of rule transcend the limits of *techne* by containing an irrepressible element of freedom that gives whoever governs a sovereign will knowing no limitation other than that which it imposes upon itself?

Plato, for one, addresses this problem by calling upon reason itself. He recognizes that there must be something to guarantee that the guardians do restrict their actions to achieve the goals of justice and will what is rational. His solution is to appeal to reason and require that the guardians be philosopher-kings. It is not enough that they be administrators expert in the administrative science consisting in right opinion of the ends of justice and the functions fulfilling them. All that can be apprehended without understanding why these ends should be followed. The guardians must therefore be philosophers of justice who also know the reasons justifying the ends of justice. Only then will they be compelled by the force of reason to recognize the legitimate authority of these goals.

This would be a solution if knowing what justice is in its full justification were identical with doing what is just. Yet Plato himself recognizes that willing and reasoning are different activities, that the philosopher must turn away from the particular phenomena of worldly affairs when he reasons, and therefore that the philosopher must be compelled to rule. But who will compel philosophers to rule or guardians to philosophize, when it is precisely the apex of command that must be rational? To be founders of the just state in speech or in deed guarantees nothing once the rulers are in place, lording over all others, as well as over themselves.

Plato's concerted attempt to secure the rational willing of justice by excluding freedom here collapses in face of the seeming bond between freedom and political rule. Although he seeks to conceive the just state as the embodiment of given forms of conduct antecedently apprehensible by the rulers imposing them, the structure of political dominion leaves justice to contend with a self-determining activity of rule imposing order upon the order of which it is a part. This sovereign activity of the guardians cannot be contained within the instrumental framework of *techne* where action, be it ruling or servile, has legitimacy by embodying prescribed modes of conduct. To the extent that ruling is a reflexive activity, determining the order of which it is the commanding element, it is not a passive material awaiting the imposition of given form, as in the paradigm of instrumental action. Rather, ruling seems to comprise a self-informing activity that has neither form nor matter prior to its own action upon itself and the order it governs. Although the individuals who rule must each have a given body, mind, and will in order to govern, their specific being as rulers would seem to be coevally determined by their own governing. Indeed, it well appears that whatever authority is sovereign within the state not only determines the policies it executes, but the very form of government in which it operates, including the character of its own ruling agency.[1]

Admittedly, this by no means makes the sovereign activity of rule self-evidently legitimate. Nonetheless, it does suggest that the conception of praxis, of action that embodies given form, yet enjoys the validity of being for its own sake, cannot provide for justice without going beyond its own limits and subverting the whole framework of given prescribed norms on which it rests.

What lays bare the full dilemma of the metaphysics of justice is Aristotle's concerted effort to salvage the legitimacy of praxis by remedying the problems afflicting Plato's argument.

2.2 Aristotle's Politics and the Internal Collapse of Praxis Theory

Accepting the defining framework of praxis, where justice is the realization of the predetermined Good through virtue, character and rational rule, Aristotle aims his ethical investigations at uncovering what is necessary to insure that the Good is actually willed. Well aware of Plato's difficulties, Aristotle recognizes that knowledge of the Good does not equal performance of good deeds. Habit, not knowledge, is the mother of virtue because it can train the will as knowledge never can. So too, the role of agreement and consent in political power must be paid heed, even if the best should rule. No matter how strongly reason argues in their favor, they can never get the chance to govern unless the many grant them the opportunity. Further, provision for the material prerequisites of the good life cannot be neglected.

2.2.1 The Good and the Shadow of Relativism

Conscious of these issues, Aristotle pushes the logic of the metaphysics of justice to the limit of its internal collapse. His starting point has all the compelling lure that the metaphysics of justice should possess, given the classic stature it has since come to command. Since justice concerns the domain of choice, where individuals voluntarily act to fulfill consciously represented goals, it is only natural to locate normative validity in the character of the chosen end. As in the search for reasons to justify knowledge claims, only an unconditioned principle could transform opinion into truth, so here with regard to conduct, only an end that is for its own sake can provide ultimate justification for action. Any goal that is not an end in itself, but merely a means serving something else, is only as valid as that to which it is subordinate. Consequently, the justice of any action must ultimately lie in the end that comes first as a fully independent and self-sufficient aim. The Good must thus be an end in itself, prescribing a goal for conduct that is for its own sake.

Yet, the Good does not possess the unconditioned universality justice requires simply by being something for its own sake. By itself, this quality of being an end in itself leaves room for a plurality of goods, where any aim counts as right provided it is pursued for no other reason than its own fulfillment. To prevent this fall into total relativism, the Good, the legitimating aim of valid conduct, must be both an end in itself and the final end to which all others are subordinated. Then, it will be the one exclusive first principle of all conduct. Under the sway of its privileged givenness, actions directed upon other goals will have validity only to the degree that the fulfillment of their chosen aims contributes to the realization of this supreme aim which alone deserves to be sought unconditionally.

If this recourse to an ultimate given end ruling over all else seems to secure justification by providing an exclusive norm eliminating relativism, the content of this Good still remains virtually undetermined. Indeed, if all that can be said is that it is the first principle and final end of all action, the Good seems to have no fixed content at all. Any ruling authority that succeeds in subordinating all actions to its governing aim would count as valid no matter what its aim might be. A radical evil pursued for its own sake by those in power would here be completely indistinguishable from any putative good. Unless further qualifications can be supplied, the argument for the primacy of the Good would be equivalent to the doctrine that might makes right, where whatever is all-powerful is valid in virtue of being the final ruling end of action.

What lies at issue is once again that perennial problem of metaphysics, the problem of justifying the privileged given in which ultimate justification is vested. It may be natural to root justice in some Good serving as the final end of action, but further argument must be supplied to determine what exactly it comprises. Aristotle does proceed to tackle this problem, but in so doing, he reveals just how insoluble the problem is.

In moving to concretize the Good and remove the relativity that still remains, Aristotle is logically compelled to characterize the Good as a form of activity, whose unconditioned validity challenges the instrumentality of *techne* that is equally bound up with praxis. What Aristotle realizes is that if the end of action is an end in itself that is equally a final end ruling over all others, it cannot be a product of action akin to an artifact produced by technical activity. An artifact cannot be an end in itself because a product is relative to its production, being conditioned by that antecedent act giving it its form. A product is thus not a privileged given, but rather a determined content issuing from a prior determiner. Further, an artifact does not subordinate action to itself as the Good should do. It rather remains an entity more subject to than master of action. Finally, the action realizing the Good is itself unconditionally valid, such that instead of being a mere means to an end, it shares in the justice whose work it is.

All this suggests that the privileged end of action, which is alone an end in itself, is not a product of action, but a form of activity. Namely, the goal of justice is none other than just action, or, in other words, the Good is the good life. Given the already established features of the Good, the activity in which it consists must be none other than action that is both for its own sake and the ruling aim of all other activities. If, following Aristotle, we call such valid conduct "praxis," then praxis signifies a non-instrumental activity that lords over all instrumental action, giving the latter the only end that it should unconditionally serve. Praxis, as the sole activity for its own sake, thus subordinates instrumental action to itself, granting instrumental action a secondary validity to the extent that the latter provides the conditions allowing praxis to be conducted.

These features should leave little doubt as to why Aristotle concludes that praxis is political in character. What else but politics could comprise that special activity conducted for its own sake, independently of any higher authority, ruling over all other practical affairs, subordinating them to its own pursuits and thereby affording them a legitimate purpose? If praxis is valid conduct, then the good life must be the life of the citizen, and the good must have for its total reality the just state.

Yet granted that the good has the added character of being the political activity comprising the just state, it still remains to be determined what precisely is the content of that institution and of the good life of the citizen who animates it. What makes this question particularly acute are the terms under which it must be answered. In light of the metaphysical approach to justification, the content of the Good must still reside in some privileged given comprising the proper nature of justice. Since this second nature prescribes the rationally apprehensible norm to which action and institutions should conform, the latter have their validity by embodying that antecedent form. Although what takes on that form are action and its institutional framework, rather than an artifact produced as a result of a prior act, the givenness of the Good still poses a problem for the new character that political action assumes once it is recognized to be an end in itself. The basic problem of praxis comes down to this: can just action be for its own sake, ruling over all other activity, and still be the embodiment of independently given form? In attempting to conceive the valid content of politics, Aristotle addresses this question and gives it a positive response. On all levels praxis is to combine both features at once.

At the level of ethics, where valid conduct is determined in general, independently of the specific political roles distinguishing citizens from one another, the parameters of action do indeed prescribe conduct that is both for its own sake and an embodiment of given determinacy. The particular content of action is not created by some autonomous act of will, but provided by the mean of conduct, whose determinacy is found at hand, contextually defined and ready to be followed. Virtue, comprising the excellence in the performance of the mean, is thus stamped with givenness as well, for it is mandated by the function the mean prescribes. Consequently, the virtues are each rooted in character, providing the given disposition from which their fixed excellence most naturally proceeds.

Yet, despite their stamp of given determinacy, character, virtue and the mean of conduct are still elements of conscious deliberative action. They cannot contribute to the Good without an intervening deliberation to choose the proper means to realize the prescribed end that conduct ought to achieve. Since this deliberation must take into account the particular situation in which action is contemplated, it must rely on perception, with all its subjective limitations, to grasp the present predicament and then employ discretion to determine how the universal aim of justice can be applied to the here and now of individual conduct. As Aristotle is famously aware, this judgment is not scientific, grasping what is necessarily true with the full autonomy of thought. It is rather a prudential decision, contextually bound by all the givens that determine both the situation at hand and the privileged aim to be realized. Nevertheless, the result of deliberation must still somehow be an act for its own sake and not simply an act serving as a means to a given end. By itself, the general structure of ethics, that is, of action taken in abstraction from the specific roles of citizenship, offers little to account for how this is possible. Already the requirement that the Good comprise an activity that is an end in itself ruling over all other pursuits indicates that the ethics of praxis is really inseparable from politics. Consequently, if there is to be any account of how action for its own sake can proceed from choice, it must lie in the analysis of the master activity in which political association consists.

2.2.2 The Praxis of Politics and the Appeal to Nature

At the outset of the turn to politics, two abiding questions light the way. Justice may well involve action for its own sake that subordinates all other affairs to its own, but this alone does not seem sufficient to distinguish justice from any conventional political power. On the other hand, the problem of justification may indeed suggest that justice consists in the realization of a privileged end antecedently prescribed by reason. But how can the second nature of such a good be distinguished from the givenness of operative practice or the normatively neutral nature given independently of voluntary action?

Because of praxis theory's metaphysical commitment to privileged givens, all it can do in its attempt to salvage justice is move back and forth from one aspect to the other, bringing in further "natural" features to distinguish action for its own sake from conventional might, while appealing to the self-sufficient independence of action for its own sake to distinguish the "nature" of justice from those givens of convention and nature having no privileged authority for ethics. Thus, when Aristotle opens his *Politics* with an investigation of the origin of the state, it is to concretize the ruling, subordinating quality of political action while establishing its special natural character. Both sides have a twofold character that is by no means accidental.

2 . 2 . 2 . 1 The Genesis of the State and the Relation Between Politics and Non-Political Associations

In discussing how the state arises from the household and village

society in Book I of his *Politics,* Aristotle depicts non-political associations that are preconditions of political life as well as institutions
incorporated within the state as subordinate elements. As preconditions, the household and village society can and do exist prior to the
state, so that it is possible to speak of the state arising out of them.
Insofar as they are distinguished from the proper political activity of
praxis, the household and village do not exist on their own for the
ethical concerns of the good life. By themselves, they instead provide
for the necessities of bare life and its procreation, and for the luxuries
of comfortable living that the market of village society provides. For
this very reason, they can certainly exist without a political domain
encompassing them. However, to the extent that neither life itself nor
comfortable living are ends in themselves, household and village
association have no normative validity until they do become incorporated within a political community where they can serve as prerequisite means for the good life, freeing citizens from the struggle for
survival and furnishing the state a surplus of social wealth allowing
political institutions to be financed.

Still, if the pursuit of goodness consists in the life of the citizen
within an existing body politic rather than in the constituting act
whereby a state is founded, the genesis of the state can no more be
rooted in political action than in activity directed to political goals. It
is thus reasonable to presume that the just state must be capable of
arising from pre-political associations on their own terms. The
grounds for this are not hard to find. Since neither households nor
village societies can protect their own pursuit of life and comfort
without a higher authority to adjudicate internal disputes and defend
against external enemies, political organization could be said to
emerge immanently from the concerns of pre-political institutions. In
other words, to paraphrase Aristotle, the state comes into being for the
sake of existence, the existence of life and convenience. Yet once
emergent, the state immediately transcends these concerns by being
a sovereign domain existing for the sake of its own good life of citizenship. Supreme unto itself, it incorporates under its sway the household and village society, granting them legitimacy as contributing
conditions for the good life.

This dual relation between pre-political and political association
does therefore concretize the meaning of action for its own sake by
indicating how praxis must involve a definite institutional connection
between politics and the affairs of household and society. At the same
time, it determines the natural character the just state enjoys as the
embodiment of privileged givens. Insofar as the relation between

politics and pre-political association is dual in character, so is the given "nature" of the state.

On the one hand, the state is natural because, as Aristotle notes, it arises from other natural associations.[2] Indeed, insofar as the state arises from preexisting households and village societies, it can be said to have a natural character signifying how political association rests upon foundations with natures of their own given independently and prior to it. However, the "nature" of these antecedent institutions is ambiguous. If it refers to their preexisting given character, the natural character the state obtains by issuing from them has no normative privilege, for all it refers to are ethically neutral foundations of life and comfort. If, on the other hand, it refers to their legitimate character as means of good living incorporated as material elements of an existing state, the nature of household and village society is actually not given, but posited by the ruling activity that shapes and secures their valid role.

In this regard, the state is natural in the very different sense of being the *telos* or final end of all non-political associations. Although temporally subsequent to household and village, the state is prior by nature, to the extent that the latter signifies not the nature consisting in what is antecedently given in existence, but the nature commanding normative validity as the privileged given end to which all else should be subordinate.

That the state is the telos of non-political institutions, such that the natural character of household and village society are relative to the privileged nature of politics, introduces a type of unity that is hardly identical to the natural unity exemplified by an organism. Whereas all parts of an organism reciprocally condition one another, without any one having a privileged role in securing the unity of the whole, the relation of state to household and village society is entirely different. By governing them for the sake of maintaining its own activity of political rule, the state achieves a self-sufficiency based on a very nonreciprocal relation between political institutions and the non-political associations underlying them. This self-sufficiency is not the same as self-creation, for the state can arise only by incorporating preexisting households and social institutions. Nevertheless, since the state makes these its subservient organs the moment it incorporates them, they lose their character as independent conditions that might determine the nature of what they condition. Instead they become elements of a regime whose determining political power is not defined by any household or social ends, but rather rules over their organization, securing their normatively valid nature while aiming at nothing but the perpetuation of its own special political activity. Only by exhibiting this unconditioned self-sufficiency, can politics rest on non-political associations without forfeiting its privileged character as an exclusive end in itself, coming first by nature.

Through this type of hegemony, it appears that the natural character of the state perfectly coincides with its character as an exclusive end in itself. Yet this coincidence is more a sign of an abiding formality than a token of an achieved resolution of the problem of justice. The subordination of household and society to politics might be an aspect of justice, but by itself it neither insures that all states achieving that subordination are just, nor what organization a just state should have. The mere hegemony of the state over family and social affairs can be no substitute for what qualifies a political order as the reality of the Good.

Again, the metaphysics of justice must provide some further precision to the privileged givenness of the Good to secure its legitimacy, and once again, Aristotle pushes forward the metaphysical approach in search of an answer.

2.2.2.2. The Constitution of the State and Privileged Givenness

It is no accident that neither Aristotle's account of the origin of the state nor his conception of the relation between politics and the affairs of household and society can provide the nature of justice.

The origin of the state cannot supply it with its valid nature simply because if the state is for its own sake, its nature must lie in itself and not in any antecedent source. Therefore, if the legitimacy of politics, as activity that is an exclusive end in itself, still lies in a privileged prescribed "nature," that nature is coeval with the actuality rather than the genesis of the state.

Similarly, the justice of the Good cannot be located in the relation between the state and non-political institutions if the only valid purpose of politics is realizing its own ruling activity. The legitimate nature of the state must rather lie within itself. Consequently, the quest for the justice of praxis must turn to the political constitution in search of the added features to render action for its own sake normatively valid.

The natural starting point for determining the state's constitution would seemingly lie in its most basic element, the citizen. Yet since politics is for its own sake and the constitution specifies its abiding internal order, the nature of the citizen would not be something prior to the state, but rather something relative to the constitution.

By itself, this insight could be taken as a merely descriptive observation insofar as constitutions, arising through convention, can take various forms. However, if it is understood against the background of the previous specifications of the Good, it does entail two normative prescriptions. First, it prescribes that no pre-political factors should determine citizenship. Only what is relevant to participating in political association and achieving its specific purpose should count, given the primacy of politics. Secondly, if the constitution has a privileged nature, distinct from the givenness of what simply exists, then citizenship equally possesses a nature distinct from the given forms of citizenship that convention historically imposes.

Although who is a citizen by convention will vary for each kind of constitution, who the citizen should be by nature can thus only be determined in reference to the constitution that is itself best by nature. Aristotle may define the citizen to be he who shares in administering justice and holding office,[3] but the normative character of this role remains unspecified until the content of the just state is defined in its own right.[4] For this to be done, the valid nature of the constitution must be uncovered.

Aristotle is quick to grasp the only alternative offered by the metaphysics of justice. Like the "nature" of praxis in general, that of the constitution has two faces.

First, with respect to mere existence, a constitution is by nature determined by who is sovereign. Since every state must be ruled by one, the few, or the many, constitutions must exhibit a corresponding threefold division.

Yet such a division cannot determine what the constitution should be. By itself the question of who governs says nothing of the state's goodness, if justice lies in realizing some privileged given form of conduct instead of in allowing a certain will or group of wills free sway. Any of these three forms of rule might or might not be directed at the proper ends antecedently prescribed by reason.

Accordingly, there must be a further division of constitutions taking into account this normative dimension. Once due heed is paid to the privileged nature that the just constitution requires, the threefold division of constitutions becomes doubled into a distinction between three legitimate and three perverted constitutions. As Aristotle rigorously points out, what differentiates them is naturally whether the one, the few, or the many who rule do so for the common good or for a separate end of their own.[5] In this way, monarchy, aristocracy, and polity comprise rule by one, the few, and the many for the common good, whereas tyranny, oligarchy, and democracy stand condemned as the illegitimate perversions of these forms.

Needless to say, such a distinction between legitimate and perverted constitutions has no significance for determining the privileged givenness of justice unless the common good can be further specified. Monarchy could not be distinguished from tyranny, any more than aristocracy from oligarchy or finally polity from democracy if the ruler in each legitimate constitution were sovereign. In order for the Good to be the firm end of their governing these rulers must be bound by law to realize that privileged aim, for only a supreme law's impersonal universal rule can guard against the arbitrariness of each and every will.

Of course, as Aristotle fully recognizes, such law cannot be positive law issuing from a legislator invested with independent legal authority.[6] In that case, the lawmaker rather than the law would be sovereign, leaving the pursuit of justice a matter of choice. Law may have a legal form, such that it must be posited to have effect. Yet if law is sovereign, legislators only discover and declare what the law is by nature, rather than exercising some privileged power of making law whatever they will. Since the justice of praxis lies in privileged givenness, and not in the acts of a privileged determiner, the essence of law should lie not in how and by whom it is enacted as a work of convention, but in the fixed content it prescribes as an impersonal rule of state.

If this signifies that the supreme law of the constitution is a law whose content is naturally given, it does not mean that the required law can be simply any given unalterable one. If justice is something other than arbitrary custom, the law in question must be a natural law whose nature has the privilege of being the one given body of rules possessing normative validity.

This is not to say that the metaphysics of justice rules out any role to positive law. As Aristotle observes, although the fundamental natural features of justice can be specified by an unchanging law, other matters, such as the length of prison terms, are inherently changeable and relative to the given situation.[7] If such affairs are to be decided in an impersonal way for the common good, then a law is called for which is local and changing. This then allows for two types of legislators: those declaring the immutable constitutional principles in which goodness lies, and those making positive laws of local application.

Similarly, as much as authority rests in the fixed principles of justice, the universal content of law leaves undecided how it should be applied in every individual case. Thus equity is needed as a further act of discretion to apply the law to particular situations, just as practical deliberation must enter into every act of praxis to determine how to embody the given means of conduct.[8]

With all these features in hand, it well seems that the metaphysics of justice is on the verge of finding its prey, especially once it is recognized how law, in the special sense of privileged natural law, entails several more consequences for politics.

First, since law, unlike decree, refers to legal subjects rather than particular individuals, it renders citizens equal in regard to its jurisdiction. Thus, if the law is sovereign in the just state, politics can be called an association of equals.[9] However, if what citizens are equal before is a law prescribing virtues rather than rights, their equality is a proportionate one, where equal merit is equally rewarded by allotment of those functions best fulfilled by those who are most virtuous.[10] This must be the case in the politics of praxis, for here what is legitimate is not the respected exercise of freedom, but the embodiment of fixed forms of goodness.

If the law is sovereign and prescribes an equality by merit, it is similarly natural for the just constitution to allow for rulers and ruled to alternate. To maintain its impersonality and the given primacy of its mandated ends, the law must not be the special charge of any individuals other than those who qualify according to the law itself. Therefore rulers can be permitted to retain power only so long as no better ones are found among the other citizens.[11]

In light of all this, it would appear that the nature of the just constitution is firmly and concretely rooted in the natural law which is sovereign over ruler and subject alike. Thus, what alone remains undone for justice to be securely grounded and defined would be specifying the content of that natural law itself.

Yet, as Aristotle properly observes, the just constitution is not simply a matter of law. It is rather a regime of justice that must contain the privileged natural law together with actual obedience to it. Only when both are at hand can praxis be said to exist.[12] This means that the metaphysics of justice must not only determine what is valid natural law, but what other features the constitution must have to be a regime of proper obedience.

In this regard, Aristotle seeks to temper what is best in an unqualified way with what is actually feasible. On the assumption that the best are few, it may well follow that the best constitution is aristocracy. However, political stability rests to some degree upon the consent of the citizens who are not among these few best. Consequently, unless they simply agree to be ruled by the best, the realization of justice may require incorporating some sort of democratic body within aristocracy.[13] Similarly, care must be taken with regard to the distribution of wealth in society to prevent the many from feeling at odds with their rulers.[14]

All these considerations, however, make sense only if the unqualified best constitution is already determined as a standard by which to judge what regime is the best one possible in any given situation. Aristotle's recourse to aristocracy is entirely formal so long as all that can be said about the best is that they are those most able to rule in accord with a privileged natural law that eludes specification.

When he attempts to spell out the functions of the ideal aristocratic state[15] in terms not entirely foreign to Plato's *Republic*, his specification of those functions and who should fulfill them still does not guarantee justice. Allotting farming and arts and crafts to a subordinate class, while assigning full-fledged citizenry to a leisured class whose young take care of military matters, whose middle-aged undertake the deliberations of government, and whose old minister to religion, may provide the conditions for the good life, but this does not prevent individuals from occupying their posts without doing what is right by nature. Once again the content of natural law remains a separate factor that is not intrinsically contained within the activities that should be its instrument.

Similarly, when Aristotle discusses the division of political powers[16] and the concrete ways in which regimes may change from one form to another,[17] none of the elements he describes guarantees the normative validity of the state. No matter how political functions are ordered and no matter how arrangements of wealth and equality are handled, the common interest of goodness may still go unattended, as the abiding distinction of legitimate and illegitimate regimes testifies. All these elements still need conform to some separate given nature, which makes them just only once embodied.

Perhaps the most acute example of this ineradicable formality is found in Aristotle's recourse to the paragon of an absolutely good man.[18] Such an individual would have to be a law unto himself, for he would be the perfect embodiment of self-sufficient goodness, so qualitatively superior to others that the only role he could play in a political community would be that of a permanent monarch.[19] Yet, precisely by being a law unto himself, this absolutely good man would overthrow the sovereignty of law and replace the system of justice resting on privileged givens with one resting on a privileged determiner. Although Aristotle elsewhere describes the absolutely good man as equal to the citizen of the best state who holds the office of ruler,[20] concealing the radical transformation of politics wrought by the introduction of realized goodness, the anomaly of the absolutely good man gives direct expression to the logical dilemma of the metaphysics of justice.

The final problem is this: so long as justice is taken to lie in the embodiment of some privileged given, the activities realizing that prescribed form of goodness can never exhibit in their own independent nature the given content that is supposed to lend them legitimacy. For justice to possess the unconditioned universality that validity demands, it must, however, consist in action that is an end in itself. Yet such action cannot be an instrument for the realization of independently given ends, since that would cancel its constitutive character as activity that is for its own sake. The example of the absolutely good man brings this contradiction to a head for the reason that such an individual could not be subject to any external prescriptions without ceasing to be a paragon in his own right.

The problem faced by the metaphysics of justice is thus identical to the dilemma afflicting the metaphysics of truth. Just as no privileged given can ground itself as a first principle of reason or reality, so no privileged given can possibly stand as the prescribed rule for justice. Not only can no natural law be defended without appealing to higher given principles in need of like justification, but the content of justice can never be an embodiment of antecedently determined forms without losing the intrinsic validity it requires. Nothing shows this more visibly than the highest point of praxis, the apex of rule, where, be it in Plato's republic or Aristotle's ideal state, those who govern exercise an activity that is ultimately subject only to whatever standards it gives itself. Aristotle's inability ever to discover the privileged nature of justice within the relations of political activity only testifies to the inner contradiction of praxis. Action cannot be both something for its own sake and the embodiment of independently given ends, any more than there can be foundations of reason or reality that are both irreducibly given and self-grounding. As the internal collapse of the metaphysical approach makes clear, the recourse to privileged givens must be abandoned if the quests for truth and justice are to meet success.

Part II

The Critique of the Given and the Appeal to a Privileged Determiner

Chapter 3

The Futile Temptation of Transcendental Argument

3.1 *The Move from Privileged Givenness to a Privileged Determiner*

The internal collapse of the metaphysical project of founding justification in privileged givenness does not signal the futility of the quest for truth and justice. By itself, the foundering of metaphysics testifies only to the inability of given determinacy to provide the unconditioned universality that truth and justice require for their validity. This does mean that reason cannot be prescriptively ordered by given terms and functions, that reality cannot be known by first asking "what is?" and responding with immediate reference to the given, that justice cannot consist in the embodiment of given forms of conduct, that one can never rely on privileged givens to justify the correspondence between thought and its object that all reference to givenness presumes. Yet if this leaves metaphysics without any knowledge of what is or what should be, it does not signify that reality and justice cannot be known.

Metaphysics' failure to know the real and the just rather casts in doubt the presumed correspondence between thought and the valid reasoning, reality and justice it seeks to conceive, while indicating that all immediate reference to the putatively given must be ruled out. In regard to the constitutive practice of metaphysics, this negative result teaches that whenever validity is rooted in some given determinacy, that determinacy enjoys its privilege not because of its given content, but by being bestowed with its normative status by whomever has ascribed it its foundational role.

As a consequence, the required abandonment of metaphysics is not without a positive outcome. Since no content can be valid in virtue of being given, and all assignment of privileged givenness rests on stipulation, it would appear that what makes something true or just depends not on its immediate content, but on whether it is determined by the proper determiner. This opens the door to an entirely new approach to truth and justice, an approach that supplants the metaphysical recourse to given determinacy with a turn to the determined determinacy issuing from a privileged determiner.

Given the compelling attraction of this move, it is entirely understandable that the metaphysics of truth and justice historically gave way to transcendental philosophy and liberal theory, the correlative attempts to secure the unconditioned universality of truth and justice in a privileged determiner. The appeal and dilemma of this alternate strategy are both exhibited by the train of its argument.

It should be kept in mind that the following analysis of transcendental philosophy and liberal theory is no more intended to be an account of philosophical history than was the preceding investigation of metaphysics. At issue is a basic strategy in theoretical and practical philosophy, which warrants investigation in its own right, independently of how historical figures may have developed its approach. Hence, what is discussed under the rubric of transcendental argument and liberal thought is solely the logic of founding truth and justice upon a privileged determiner. In appropriating the terms, "transcendental philosophy," "liberal thought," "social contract theory," and "practical reason" for the analysis of this strategy, no claim is being made that these labels have solely designated the approach in question, nor that historical thinkers to whom these labels have been applied either exhaust the possibilities of this approach or remain within its confines. Although, as in the preceding analysis of the metaphysical strategy, certain philosophers are considered, no attempt is made to provide an interpretation of the body of their thought. Their positions are examined only in so far as they illustrate the ramifications of appealing to a privileged determiner.

3.2 The Temptation of the Transcendental Project

With regard to the quest for truth in general, the move from privileged givens to a privileged determiner provides the defining project of what, since its initiation by Kant, has come to be known as transcendental philosophy. Confronting the failure of the metaphysical attempt to base truth in some given content, transcendental philosophy seeks to salvage justification by rooting rational validity in what is determined by some privileged determiner. This determiner is the so-called transcendental condition which plays the same role whether it be characterized as a noumenal subjectivity, intentionality, *Dasein*, communicative competence, language games, or the hermeneutic situation, to cite the favored terms of some of transcendental philosophy's most well-known practitioners. Whatever its guise, the transcendental condition provides for valid knowledge, meaningful speech, or, if one will, just the ongoing conversation of mankind by comprising a structure determining the object of knowledge in its relation to knowing so as to permit knowledge to conform to its object, whether that object be an actual thing or a conceptual or linguistic content.

The direct impetus for developing objective validity in these terms of determined determinacy lies jointly in a critical reflection upon the root dogmatism of metaphysics and in the basic objectivity problem of knowledge.

Due to metaphysics' direct appeal to a given content, its constitutive claim of having absolute knowledge of what is in itself perennially rests on the assumption that knowledge corresponds to its object, that thought adequately uncovers what is true and just, irrespective of the latter's relation to the knower. Consequently, it is natural to call into question the presupposed correspondence of thought and what is in itself, and with it, the possibility of making any absolute truth claims whatsoever. Since, further, all true knowledge must fall within knowing itself, it seems reasonable not just to suspend all knowledge claims, but to make knowing the object of investigation before examining what is accessible through it.

In this way, dismissing metaphysics' characteristic gambit of making immediate reference to reality by contemplating the given does not leave philosophy with just doubt and suspicion. Because all reference to reality occurs within knowing, the checkered experience of metaphysics bequeaths the positive task of first investigating the character and limits of knowing before asking, "What is?"

This now familiar transcendental turn to consider the conditions of knowledge as the foundation for all further inquiry is no less motivated by consideration of the seemingly insuperable objectivity problem of knowledge. So long as what is knowable is accessible to the knower only in the form of knowledge, and the object of knowledge has a given determinacy in its own right to which knowledge must conform to be true, there seems to be no way to certify any correspondence of knowledge and its object. No matter how carefully the knower proceeds, he can never directly address the object of knowledge as it is in itself, but must always refer to what he knows by means of knowledge. On these terms, all evaluation of knowledge is caught within knowing, with nothing other to rely upon than other mere knowledge claims, all of which remain shut off from the only standard that can justify one claim rather than another: the object of knowledge as it stands by itself, independent of knowing.

If, however, the structure of knowing, or reference, if one adopts a linguistic perspective, determines the object so that its very givenness is a content determined by that structure, then correspondence between that object and knowledge of it could be secured. For if knowing is not a passive contemplation of objects given independently to it, but a determining condition of what it knows, then the object would conform to the structure of knowing, and knowing would be in a position to know what it had put into the object in its capacity as that object's constitutive determiner. To borrow a phrase from Kant, synthetic *a priori* knowledge would then be possible, for the determined determinacy of the object of knowing would be a new content, rather than an analytic given, and yet be determined by a structure underlying and therefore prior to all particular acts of reference or "experience."

From this it is clear that once the transcendental turn is taken, the problem of conceiving objectivity, be it the objectivity of conceptual contents or of reality itself, is not simply put off till after knowing is certified ready and able to comprehend its objects. Rather, the conception of objectivity falls within the consideration of knowing on two accounts.

In the first place, since the knowing under investigation claims truth for its knowledge only by both distinguishing and comparing its concepts with the objects to which they are to correspond, the critical assessment of true knowing must involve considering what knowledge refers to and how it can be in accord with its concept. If the turn to investigate the structure of knowing left out of account the character of the object of knowledge, it would be in no position to determine whether knowledge claims have any validity.

Yet, since the motivation for first turning to knowing arises from calling into question the correspondence of thought and objectivity and proscribing all immediate reference to objectivity, the only way the critique of knowing can legitimately test the validity of knowledge against its objects is if objectivity is determined through the structure of knowing. Then, of course, the examination of the structure of knowing will include, rather than exclude, an account of the objects of knowledge, allowing the limits of true knowing to be ascertained.

Consequently, even though the turn to investigate knowing is made as a preliminary to obtaining true knowledge of objects, the critique of knowing should actually contain within itself knowledge of the essential features of objectivity. Thus, as much as Kant launches his *Critique of Pure Reason* as a propadeutic, paving the way for a system of a priori knowledge of the laws of nature and freedom, he admits that this subsequent system will only provide an analytic clarification of the concepts already established in the critique of pure reason.[1]

When transcendental inquiry proceeds to specify the conditions of knowing in their determining of knowable objectivity, in explicit rejection of all direct reference to what is given, it must naturally avoid making any immediate reference of its own to givenness, be it of the object of knowing or of knowing itself. At the same time, the transcendental investigator must avoid falling into solipsism where the object of knowledge and all standards of truth are mere postulates.

3.3 The Fundamental Dilemmas of Transcendental Philosophy

Despite all intentions, these very troubles arise the moment transcendental philosophy launches its explication of the conditions of objective knowing as something that must be executed before any actual knowledge claims can be justified. In the absence of such preliminary inquiry, all putative knowledge would seem to assume metaphysically that certainty guarantees truth, which is to say that knowing conforms to real and conceptual objectivity. Yet, once engaged, the transcendental turn involves metaphysical claims of its own concerning what knowing is in itself, claims that not only resurrect the dilemmas of immediate reference to the given, but construe knowing such that any objective knowledge is precluded from the outset.

To begin with, any transcendental inquiry takes for granted that knowing or reference can be examined by itself, prior to and independently of actual knowledge and its particular objects. This implies that knowing, whether based in the structure of consciousness, the context of ordinary language, an ideal speech situation, or any other condition, is determined in its own right, apart from what it knows.[2] Accordingly, transcendental philosophy would seem to assume that knowing be either an instrument or medium through which objectivity is encountered, or a structure of referring that constitutes the very object to which it refers.

In the first case, knowledge of objects as they are in themselves would be impossible since what would be obtained by the act of the instrument or the transmission of the medium would be something already worked upon and distorted by the process of knowing. If one attempted to get at the unaltered objects by somehow subtracting the effects of such knowing, one would only be left where one was before knowing, namely with no knowledge of objects at all.[3]

The outcome is no better when all reference to something in itself is rejected as metaphysical, and knowing is instead conceived as referring to an object generated in the act of knowing itself. In that case, where the transcendental structure constitutes what it refers to independently of any thing in itself, one is condemned to solipsism, where knowledge can never be of anything more than knowing's own subjective stipulation. After all, when the structure of referring generates its own referent, what is obtained cannot be true knowledge without further qualification, but merely what results *provided* the stipulated transcendental structure is itself taken for granted. If one nevertheless claims that that structure is irreducible, or the only form of knowing, or the special shape of rigorous science, it must be admitted that any such assertion is not itself transcendentally constituted as a subsequent result of reflection upon the conditions of knowing, but metaphysically presupposed as a given behind which one cannot go.

These difficulties present an acute challenge to transcendental philosophy's attempt to show how all that is objective in thought and reality can be determined without reliance upon any dogmatically accepted givens. If its generic striving be taken seriously, then transcendental inquiry cannot legitimately refer to the immediate givenness of a thing in itself or to any other content given independently of what is determined by the transcendental condition. Yet, if the transcendental approach is to succeed in distinguishing objective knowledge from opinion, it must somehow determine the object of knowledge without reducing it to an arbitrary stipulation of knowing. In other words, what is an object of thought must be immanent to knowing, as something constituted in terms of its structure, yet equally transcendent, as something which is nonetheless more than a subjective representation. This must be true whether the object of thought is a real thing or a concept, for in either case, the absence of distinguishable aspects of immanence and transcendence, or of reference and referent removes the possibility of establishing its objective validity.

If transcendental philosophy is to secure objectivity for knowledge, it must accordingly solve a problem first posed, if not satisfactorily answered, by Kant in his transcendental deduction of the categories. As Kant recognizes, once metaphysical reference be excluded and objective knowledge be seen as something to be determined in terms of the structure of knowing itself, then solipsism can be avoided and knowledge of reality redeemed if two conditions be fulfilled.

First, the knowing in terms of which all reference proceeds must be such that what it refers to as the object of its knowledge be not merely its own subjective stipulation, but something given independently of its reference to it. Of course, if the referent of knowledge be just knowing's own stipulation, then one is left with the solipsism of positive science, where the known object has no more reality than what the knower assumes it to have.

Second, even if the object of knowledge be something in itself, and no mere stipulation of the knower, there will be no knowledge of objects unless knowing be such that its knowledge does correspond to what it knows. Since, however, all immediate reference to reality is illegitimate, the correspondence at issue cannot be validated by any comparison falling outside the structure of knowing, that is, between it and some thing in itself. Rather, the only way transcendental philosophy can escape solipsism and achieve knowledge of reality is if it demonstrate that the conditions for the conception of what is given at the same time provide the conditions under which objects can be given in correspondence with those concepts. In that event, with the conditions of knowledge being one and the same as the conditions of the givenness of the object of knowledge, transcendental investigation could specify the principles of objective truth, since what would make knowledge or reference possible, would also supply the independent givenness of the referent of knowing, and do so such that knowledge could correspond to it. Thereby the possibility of synthetic *a priori* knowledge would be secured, for thought would be able to know in a justifiable manner objects that are neither stipulations of thought nor conclusions analytically deduced from such assumptions. If, further, this possibility extended beyond objects of experience to the concepts and procedures of reason itself, then transcendental inquiry would be in a position to supply the self-justification of thought perennially sought by philosophy.

In the "Transcendental Deduction of The Categories" Kant rightfully raises this general problem as the touchstone of his entire philosophical project. His own particular solution, however, is immediately self-defeating due to the complementary metaphysical assumptions upon which it depends. Through his openly "Metaphysical Deduction of The Categories," Kant supplies the content of these most essential elements of knowing's own structure by immediately referring to the cognitive reality of certain functions of judgment handed down traditionally from Aristotelian logic. Then, having determined the conditions of knowing through a metaphysical reference, Kant proceeds to characterize the conditions of the objects of its knowledge in the same manner. What knowing refers to as its object is claimed to be an appearance of some thing in itself which is not known in terms of the knowing under critique, but in virtue of an immediate reference to reality. Therefore, when Kant proceeds to show how the categories allow the conditions of a possible experience to coincide with the conditions for the possibility of the appearances to which knowing adequately refers, his argument is already undermined by the same metaphysical stipulation it seeks to avoid.

Clearly, if the problem of the transcendental deduction of the categories be resolved, with knowledge of reality secured, both the conditions of knowing and the conditions of what it knows must be determined independently of all immediate reference to reality or any other givens. In face of this challenge, thinkers such as Fichte, the young Schelling and Husserl have attempted to purge transcendental inquiry of every metaphysical vestige by seeking to eliminate all immediate reference to a thing in itself and to derive the entire content of the conditions of knowing from the transcendental critique establishing them.

Try as they may, transcendental thinkers cannot possibly succeed in this endeavor due to the inexpungible element of givenness that underlies all transcendental argument. This element is none other than the content of the transcendental condition. Because it is by definition the determining condition of objective knowledge, there is no way it can possess the character of being transcendentally constituted, which is what is supposed to render an object of thought valid in the first place. The logical reason for this is that a determiner determines what is other than itself, and thus has a character of its own antecedent to its act of determination. In both these regards the determination of determined determinacy by a determiner is distinct from the self-determination of self-determined determinacy. In the latter case, there is no difference between the determiner and what is determined by it, for anything self-determined determines itself. As a consequence, the character of something self-determined is not given prior to its act of self-determination, but arises from it. By contrast, a determiner can only determine what is other than itself provided that it has a given character preceding, rather than resulting from its action. Indeed, it is precisely this unconditioned givenness of its own content that allows the determiner to be the condition of what it determines. If, however, objectivity lies in being determined by the conditions of true knowledge, then these conditions cannot themselves enjoy objective validity.

By investigating the conditions of knowing as a necessary prelude to the attainment of objective knowledge, the transcendental approach therefore places itself in an insoluble situation. Although it rightly criticizes the dogmatic acceptance of privileged givens in metaphysics, transcendental philosophy cannot remove its own dependence upon givenness without forsaking its explication of the transcendental conditions of knowledge.

This dilemma is brought to a head when attention is focused on the vexing problem of legitimating the knowing of the transcendental philosopher whose knowledge has as its object the transcendental structure itself. Considered in its own right, the obtaining of this transcendental knowledge, which forms the very activity of transcendental philosophy, appears to contradict the whole transcendental enterprise. Since the constitutive project of transcendental philosophy consists in bracketing out all immediate true claims and instead investigating the structure of true knowing prior to any actual true knowing itself, the transcendental philosopher finds him or herself in the paradoxical situation of attempting to determine correctly the conditions of knowledge without providing any actual specific knowledge whatsoever. In other words, transcendental philosophy puts itself in the peculiar position, diagnosed so pointedly by Hegel, of attempting to know before knowing.

3.4 The Self-Elimination of Transcendental Argument

Insofar as the knowing tacitly practiced by transcendental inquiry is that of the critique of knowing in general, the problem here plaguing transcendental philosophy consists in resolving how the critique of knowing can be self-critical and forsake all metaphysical reference to its own object of investigation, the conditions of objective knowledge. The answer to this problem appears to involve but one thing: eliminating the distinction between the critique of knowing and the knowing under critique. To avoid metaphysically stipulating the character of the conditions of knowing, transcendental philosophy must somehow proceed so that knowing does its own critique, transcendentally constituting not just objects of experience, but every relation of the transcendental structure itself. In that case, the standpoint of the transcendental philosopher would be equalized with the knowing it examines, allowing transcendental knowledge to possess the same objectivity that it mandates for valid knowledge in general. Then reference to the transcendental conditions of knowledge would no longer be a dogmatic assertion of a given, unconstituted foundation.

If this could be accomplished, allowing the critique of knowing to become identical to the knowing under critique, then the element of givenness in the transcendental condition would be eliminated. Instead of determining something else, the transcendental condition would now determine itself, so that rather than being something given, it would be determined in accord with the same transcendental logic by which all objects of knowledge are determined. In effect, transcendental logic would become a self-determining logic of objectivity, whose own explication of the possibility of true knowledge would satisfy the identical requirements it establishes for valid objects of thought.

Starting with Fichte and Schelling, and continuing into our own century with Husserl,[4] thinkers have pursued this strategy in the hope of eliminating the uncriticized standpoint of transcendental argument. Recognizing the anomaly of Kant's metaphysical deductions of the categorial content of pure reason, they have attempted to radicalize the transcendental problematic to the point of having the entire critical apparatus be self-referring from the very start.

To be truly consistent, transcendental philosophy must tackle just such an enterprise. Nevertheless, no matter how persistently attempts be made to carry it out, they cannot possibly redeem any knowledge of reality nor any valid knowledge of knowing. The fatal reason for this is that once transcendental philosophy becomes self-critical, its own constitutive framework collapses.

To see this, all one need do is consider what would actually happen if transcendental philosophy were to abandon all metaphysical reference to its own object of inquiry. For this to occur, the knowing performing the critique of knowing would itself have to fulfill the conditions of the knowing under investigation. This means that if the transcendental philosopher is to avoid stipulating the conditions of knowing in a metaphysical manner, he must relate to his subject matter in just the same way that the knowing under critique properly relates to its object. Since what is to be known by the transcendental philosopher is the structure of knowing in terms of which all true knowledge of reality is possible, the transcendental inquiry can legitimately determine what such true knowing is only if its own discourse refers to true knowing just as true knowing refers to what it knows.

This requirement immediately offers its own solution, given the character of the whole transcendental enterprise. Because the knowing under critique is to be certified knowing whose knowledge corresponds to its object and is certain thereof, the critique of knowing is to have true knowing as its object. Consequently, transcendental philosophy is itself a knowing of true knowing. At the same time, its critical cognition of the transcendental structure must have that object's own character if its transcendental knowledge is to be true knowing and not just metaphysical dogma. In other words, the knowing of true knowing comprising the activity of the transcendental philosopher must have true knowing as its object in the same way that true knowing has its own object. This, however, can only be the case if true knowing is a knowing of true knowing. Then the transcendental knowing of true knowing will have the same relation to its object as does true knowing itself, for what both will have knowledge of is true knowing. In that event, what the transcendental inquiry performs is precisely what it investigates, just as knowing is itself self-critique.

However, when transcendental discourse thus becomes fully consistent, with metaphysical reference giving way to a knowing that does its own critique, the achieved equalization of transcendental argument with the knowing it investigates eliminates not just the difference between the critique of knowing and the knowing under critique. It also obliterates the basic distinction between knowing and its object. Knowing and the oject of knowing are here rendered indistinguishable because true knowing, the object known through transcendental investigation, is itself a knowing of true knowing, whereas the knowing exercised by the transcendental philosopher is nothing other than a knowing of true knowing as well. Since transcendental knowing is therefore no different from its object, true knowing, the former's identity with its object equally signifies that true knowing is indistinguishable from its object.

This resulting solipsism is of fatal consequence, for the ability to make a distinction between reference and referent, knowing and object known, is what first allows for true knowing as well as transcendental philosophy itself. If knowing and its object cannot be differentiated, knowing lacks the independent referent it needs to contrast against its knowledge to render the latter knowledge of something objective and not just a display of its own representation. In effect, the absence of such distinction leaves no knowing at all, for without any referent to refer to, there is neither any reference nor knowledge to be had.

The very basis of transcendental discourse is, however, nothing other than the contrast and difference between knowing and its object, for only insofar as knowing can be considered separately from its specific object can the conditions for knowing any object be investigated at all. The whole of transcendental philosophy rests upon this premise that the conditions of knowing can be antecedently investigated without introducing actual knowledge claims about particular objects of cognition. Then alone does it make sense to speak of transcendental conditions of knowing, whether these be characterized in terms of consciousness, language, culture or any other description. Yet no matter what content they be ascribed, these transcendental structures can only be juridical conditions of objective knowledge rather than conditioned objects of knowledge if the object of reference can be distinguished from the structure of reference. If, on the contrary, transcendental logic were to become self-determining, so that the knowledge it conditions were the same knowing exercised by the transcendental investigator, the distinction between knowledge and its object would disappear, making it impossible to investigate knowing prior to investigating its object.

Consequently, when transcendental philosophy becomes self-referentially consistent, with the knowing under critique assuming the same structure as the critique itself, the resulting collapse into identity of knowing and its object eliminates the possibility of any transcendental reflection or *epoche*. At one with its object, knowing can no longer be grasped by itself, for with its constitutive relation of reference eliminated, knowing not only has no structure apart, but none whatsoever. What one is left with is really the self-elimination of transcendental argument, where the underlying differentiation between knowing and its object collapses, leaving nothing but an undifferentiated unity in which there is neither anything in itself nor any relation of reference.[5]

This leaves transcendental philosophy at an impasse: either it accepts the given character of the transcendental condition and succumbs to the reliance upon privileged givenness it seeks to repudiate, or it eliminates that element and annuls its own foundational epistemology. However it proceeds, transcendental philosophy ultimately fails to secure just as much the conditions for its own quest as the conditions for objective knowledge of reason, reality, or justice.

For all the emptiness of the utterly indeterminate result of a consistently pursued transcendental philosophy, it is not without its lesson. What it shows is that whereas metaphysics can arrive at no knowledge of what is in itself, transcendental philosophy can arrive at no knowledge of knowing. In the end, recourse to a privileged determiner can no more fulfill the quest for truth than recourse to privileged givenness. Logically speaking, if justification is to be successful, then the unconditioned universality of truth and justice must be sought in something other than given determinacy or the determined determinacy of a given determiner.

Chapter 4

The Justice of Liberty

4.1 From Praxis to Liberty: The Rise of Freedom as the Principle of Justice

The problem of making freedom the principle of right has dominated the quest for justice ever since the legitimacy of prescribed forms of ethics and politics was called into question by the demand that individuals be beholden only to what issues from their own consent. The authority of set virtues, given means of conduct, and any fixed essence of goodness have all been subsequently cast in doubt in deference to this advocacy of the legitimacy of the autonomous will. It has set aside the metaphysical theories conceiving justice as praxis, wherein conduct is valid in virtue of embodying predetermined modes of action. In their place, it has given the quest for justice a new guiding problem, the problem of establishing what justice is, not by contemplating those given forms that action ought to realize, but by considering what relations emerge from the volition of the will itself. Paralleling the strategy of transcendental philosophy, liberal theory has adopted this framework, where the will stands as the privileged determiner out of which all right is to be derived. Accordingly, it has set itself the task of working out a theory of justice whose principle is freedom.

In making this move, liberal theory provides the original prototype of the attempt to conceive justice as something determined by a privileged determiner. Although other candidates for privileged determiner have been and can be advanced as a source of justice, nothing can reveal the logic of the position more clearly than the liberal strategy of choosing the will itself for this role. After all, if all ethical action issues from willing, and the validity of conduct is to be rooted in a given determiner, what more basic determiner of action

73

can be found than the will that every agent possesses?

Nonetheless, as much as the liberal recourse to the will provides the classic example of the attempt to ground justice in a privileged determiner, it also reflects the appeal of another strategy for conceiving just action, a strategy that locates the unconditioned universality of validity not in given determinacy or determined determinacy, but in the self-determined determinacy of freedom.

In certain respects, the collapse of the metaphysics of justice already suggests this recourse to freedom in so far as the praxis of politics always seemed to introduce an autonomous activity of rule. Although this ruling activity was confined to imposing the given form of justice upon the state and the non-political institutions under its sway, in doing so it imposed this form not only upon the subjects of rule, but upon the rulers themselves. Since they too stood within the state, their political role was just as much ordered by the act of rule as that of any other citizen. As a consequence, political rule had the peculiar character of imposing form upon itself, so that, instead of presenting a given matter awaiting the embodiment of an antecedently given form, it comprised a self-informing activity that could no longer be understood in terms of praxis. As a result, the theory of praxis seemed, almost despite itself, to indicate that the order of justice rested upon an activity of freedom, rather than upon an externally prescribed virtuous embodiment of goodness.[1]

4.1.1 Freedom and the Validity of Justice

Of course, concern with freedom is not something that only follows upon the collapse of the metaphysical project. From the very start of inquiry into right and wrong, justice has been understood to involve not what happens of necessity, independently of the wills of individuals, but only what lies within the power of voluntary action. Since, however, voluntary action is arbitrary, being no more ruled by reason than by nature, freedom has confronted the theory of justice with the problem of conceiving how actions and institutions can have validity even though they consist in activities of individuals who can just as well will something else. This would seem to leave freedom anything but a source of justice, for if arbitrariness provides the power to do both good and evil, it equally invites restraint. Nonetheless, freedom seems to command an undeniable legitimacy once it is considered how neither nature nor convention can determine what ought to be.

To begin with, since justice concerns what may legitimately occur through the voluntary actions of individuals, rather than what happens according to nature and its necessity, no natural relation can prescribe what is just. Whether natural relations proceed through causal necessity or a probabilistic quantum mechanics makes no difference on this score, for the absence of willing within natural events signifies the exclusion of voluntary action and all questions of ethics. Although individuals could neither exist nor have a world in which to act without the physical, chemical, and biological realities provided by nature, these are preconditions of all conduct, just or unjust. For this reason, contrary to the natural view of human rights, no anthropological fact of human species being can prescribe what men and women have a right to do. The human condition in its natural predicament may mandate what individuals are anthropologically capable of doing, but not which of their humanly possible actions should be performed.[2] What makes actions and institutions right rather than wrong is left utterly undetermined by the given universe of nature. All it offers is an ethically neutral, though indispensable environment for convention to enact a second nature of its own that is capable of being just or not.

Nonetheless, that nature is a material condition, but not a determining foundation of justice does not mean that right is merely a matter of convention, consisting in operative rules of behavior. Compliance with given rules signifies only that behavior is rule governed, not that it enjoys legitimacy warranting respect. Although justice is not given by nature, independent of willing, its constitutive normative validity does not permit it to be just a product of convention corresponding to whatever order a community happens to embody. This is manifest in the untenability of the doctrine that might makes right. This doctrine effectively claims that any prevailing practice is legitimate because it prevails. In so doing, it commits the fallacy afflicting any attempt to base justice in convention, the fallacy consisting in tying legitimacy to whatever is existing convention when legitimacy is not a question of fact, but of what ought to be.

Admittedly, as something that is not given, but willed into being, justice does exist only by convention. Nevertheless, when one focuses on the problem of justification, it becomes evident that justice can neither be relative to nor justified by the particular conditions of its enactment. The key to understanding this lies in noting that conduct and institutions are just and not merely given practice only when their existence is warranted regardless of any particular conditions that are not themselves elements of justice commanding equal authority. If a putative relation of justice were relative to any prior conditions that did not have legitimacy themselves, it would be relative to something unjust and disqualify itself as something that ought to be. In that case, justice would not be an end in itself, but for the sake of something outside justice, something thereby lacking validity and canceling whatever legitimacy justice itself should possess.

For this reason, what is just has universal validity, being justified under any circumstances, provided those circumstances do not already involve relations of justice that thereby fall within justice itself and should be paid heed. In this regard, the only particular features of a given state of affairs that enter into determining what ought to be done are those that already enjoy the validity of justice. Their prior possession of legitimacy is, after all, what first renders them worthy of being taken into account. Naturally, if there is any question of subordinating one relation of justice to another, this could only be legitimately decided in conformity with a principle that is itself a relation of justice. Otherwise, the subordination could have no valid basis.

Taken as a whole, the relations of justice cannot therefore be legitimately limited by anything but themselves. In this sense, the universality of justice is *juridically* unconditioned. Although the *existence* of justice may presuppose all the natural and psychological conditions that make voluntary action possible, nothing outside of justice can figure as a determining condition or principle for prescribing what justice is. For this reason, justice possesses unconditioned universality in respect of its validity, even if its coming into being and preservation remain conditioned by extraneous factors.

It is this feature of unconditioned universality, so crucial to the quests for both truth and justice, that ties freedom and justice together. Due to its unconditioned universality, the content of justice cannot be mandated by any factor given independently of just action. Otherwise, what is putatively just would turn into something conditioned by what does not enjoy equal validity. Instead of having its measure and ground in something else, and suffering this loss of legitimacy, justice must be its own ground and one and only standard. As the historical standardbearers of the metaphysics of justice, Plato and Aristotle, themselves recognized, this means that justice exists for its own sake and no other.

What the advocates of praxis theory did not fully realize is that if justice is to be an end in itself, free of all prior grounds, its content must be determined solely through its own workings and not in virtue of some separately given end or some prior determining procedure. In order to be for their own sake, the relations of justice must thus be entirely self-determined. Only then, when justice comprises an order of freedom whose constitutive activity orders itself, can it claim the unconditioned universality of being an end in itself, operating for its own sake, free of determination by anything outside its own self-grounded domain of valid action.

The lesson to be drawn from these considerations is clear: justice consists not in the embodiment of prescribed forms of goodness under the tutelage of experts in virtue, but in nothing other than the institutions of freedom giving self-determination objective reality. The basic reason why justice can have no other substance than freedom is simply that freedom alone possesses the unconditioned universality required for normative validity. Precisely by being determined by nothing other than itself, self-determination has this requisite character of not being relative to any given condition.

If rights be understood to consist in the legitimately recognized and respected exercise of freedom, it follows that the theory of justice is properly the theory of right, rather than a theory of the good prescribing restraints upon self-determination.

Furthermore, insofar as justice is the reality of freedom, possessing legitimacy by being self-determined, no independently given factors can prescribe its content. Hence, normatively speaking, justice has no foundations. Any theory that gives justice foundations, whether it be by grounding it in the privileged givenness of a natural law, or by deriving it through a privileged procedure of construction,[3] falls into the trap of letting justice be determined by something other than itself, rendering it relative to something outside justice and thereby illegitimate.

4.1.2 The Basic Dilemma of Liberal Theory

Starting with the traditional liberal standardbearers, Hobbes, Locke, and Rousseau, the theory of justice has been pursued as a theory of freedom in radical departure from the ethics and politics of metaphysics. Although this gives ethical philosophy its proper form, the classic liberal theoreticians and their contemporary followers[4] have treated freedom as a *foundation* of justice, as if freedom were a privileged principle from which the relations of justice should be derived.

This decisive move defines the liberal project and at the same time bestows upon it the fundamental dilemma that finally undermines any attempt to root validity in a privileged determiner. This dilemma is straightforward enough. By taking freedom as a principle, liberal theory contradicts the basic structure of freedom itself, for, instead of granting freedom its self-determined determinacy, it reduces it to a privileged determiner. This happens simply because making the free will a principle from which justice is derived turns it into something that determines what is other than itself. To be self-determining, the free will must, on the contrary, determine its own self and not something else. When the will gets treated as a principle, however, it is rendered a determiner whose character is given prior to its act of determination, while its act determines something other which therefore is not itself self-determined, but determined by what is prior to and other than it.

Thus, from the very outset, liberal theory puts itself in jeopardy of undermining the common validity of freedom and justice by depriving both of their requisite self-determined character. The moment it conceives the institutions of justice as structures derived from a principle of freedom, they are no longer self-determined, but determined by a freedom that figures logically prior to and separately from them. At the same time, the freedom from which justice is to be derived loses its own autonomy. Once again, by being a principle, freedom does not determine itself, but a derivative order which is secondary to it. Freedom's determining role as a principle adds nothing to its own character, for that already lies established prior to its act of determination, just as was the case with the transcendental conditions of knowledge. Since the principle of freedom thus fails to determine itself in its specification of justice, its own structure really has no self-determined character, for what it is precedes what it determines.

These fundamental features of any attempt to make the free will the privileged determiner of justice already provide a stark preliminary idea of the conceptual impasse awaiting liberal theory. By treating freedom as a principle, liberal theory reduces free agency to a determiner that, contrary to genuine self-determined agency, deter- mines what is other than itself by exercising a capacity to determine given antecedently to all its actions as their necessary precondition and invariable form. In so doing, liberal theory practices a brand of foundationalism completely parallel to the epistemological founda- tionalism of transcendental philosophy. Just as the transcendental turn to investigate the conditions of knowing involved appeal to a privileged determiner, so does the liberal reversion to a principle of freedom. In the case of liberalism, the reversion to foundationalism has the immediate result of reducing freedom to liberty, where liberty consists in a given faculty of choice common to all individuals by nature insofar as it has its defining essence prior to all particular acts of will and whatever conventions these acts establish.

This defining character of liberty is of key importance. To the degree that liberty is something every functioning individual possesses by nature, it is a universal feature of the self, bearing no particular qualities as part of its essence that differentiate one agent from another. By itself, liberty supplies only the form of choosing shared by each and every act of will performed by each and every agent. It does not provide the particular ends that distinguish real acts of willing from one another, nor any of the other features that make an act that of one individual rather than another. All of these aspects must derive from elsewhere, for if liberty is the omnipresent structure of every voluntary act, it leaves utterly undetermined what individuates agents and their actions. Consequently, in order for the will endowed with liberty to determine itself, which is to say, will something particular and thereby actually act, it must not only proceed as the will of an agent whose particular character is already determined by other means, but choose among alternative ends whose contents are independently given, be it by outer circumstance or some other inner faculty such as desire or the understanding. Although the choosing will is at liberty to will any alternative it wishes, it is still always bound to select from them if it is to will at all. Furthermore, it must do so as the act of an individual whose particular identity can never be the product of choice, but remains a given character always preceding it. Therefore, the choosing will simply cannot achieve genuine self-determination. Not only does it lack the freedom to will an end whose particular content derives from liberty itself, but it equally lacks the freedom to determine the particular agency whose will it is.

If, however, self-determination alone provides the substance of justice, the very freedom that liberal thinkers make the principle of justice lacks normative validity by failing to be self-determined. Although liberty may be common to all by nature who are not physically or mentally impaired, its willing is never free unto itself, but always relative to whatever array of alternatives stand given before it. As a consequence, what it wills can never have the unconditioned universality required of justice, so long as its legitimacy resides in its being an exercise of liberty.

4.1.3 *The Universal, Particular, and Individual Dimensions of Willing*

If all this points once more to how the project of liberal theory must be viewed in regard to the contrast between the positing of a given determiner and self-determination, what brings the issue into fuller focus is a consideration of the universal, particular, and individual aspects of the free will. This is especially pertinent in light of the insight that the will is free only to the degree that it gives itself its entire character so that the universal, particular, and individual features of its individuality are all determined through its act.[5]

To begin with, it should be evident that the free will has universality insofar as whenever it acts, it is not bound to the particular content it wills, but is always at liberty to set it aside and will another. Instead of being limited to any given set of ends, the free will defines itself by always exhibiting but one instance of its general capacity to determine itself, an instance that it can supersede with another at will. If, on the contrary, the will's character were bound to any specific aims, it would no longer be a self-determining, free agency, but a capacity of choice determined by external factors.

Although this quality of universality, of being unrestricted to any particular determination, thus underlies each and every example of free volition, the will's autonomy has no reality if it be limited to that. By itself, such universality comprises merely the negative freedom of liberty, whose power to resist choosing any given end leaves out of account the actual positive determination that self-determination requires. This must not be ignored, for the will fails to determine itself unless it actually wills something, adding a dimension of particularity to its universal character. In so doing, the free will gives itself new determination consisting in its willing some particular end. Yet in restricting itself to this end it does not cancel its unrestricted universality and turn into something unfree. On the contrary, the will remains at one with itself in its specific act, for it has here determined its own free self, which first wins its general character of being unbeholden to any specific end through its own act of willing something as a particular instance of itself. Since the free will must will to be what it is, and to will it must will something, the willing of a particular content does not cancel the will's autonomy, but realizes it instead. It does so by providing the will not just with determination, but with *self*-determination. The particular end it wills gives it its own particularity, for in willing something, the will determines itself in one instance of its general free agency.

In virtue of this element of particularity, the free will evidently cannot be conceived as a mere faculty or capacity that can be defined prior to and independently of its actual willing of something. Simply to be self-determining, the will must have particular determination as part of its essence. Therefore, the free will must be conceived as something inherently actual.

Its actuality is of a special kind, however, for it combines universality with particularity. As much as the free will has universality by being unbeholden to any given content, it must no less will a particular end in order to be self-determining. On the other hand, although the free will must restrict itself to a particular content in order to will something, it thereby remains self-determined precisely because what it has determined is an agency that is never bound to the particular content it has given itself, but can always cast it aside and will another.

As a consequence, the free will is not just universal or particular. Because its self-determination gives it a unique identity intrinsically bound up with its particular act, the free will's essence is irreducibly individual. Being at once universal and particular by having its unrestricted autonomy through the act of giving itself a specific purpose, the free will is not a universal capacity, definable prior to its actual willing, such as the liberty with which all men are said to be born. Instead, the free will has an individual structure whose character it gives itself in the particular self-determination building its unique development. Only in individuating itself in a specific act does the free will stand at one with itself, for it possesses its defining identity as a self-determining agency precisely by determining its entire character exclusively through its own activity.

Thus, in marked contrast to a will that figures as a determining principle, the free will actually wills nothing other than itself, for in its individual act, at once universal and particular, what it determines is its own self-determination.

Needless to say, these most rudimentary features of the free will tell nothing by themselves of how its autonomy is actually realized. What they do indicate in their own enriched terms is how the will's self-determination will be undermined if it be made a principle out of which the forms of justice are derived. When the will does get treated as a privileged determiner, it is now clear that the will is rendered something merely universal, in that its character is given prior to the form of justice it determines. Since the will's particular act of determination here falls outside its essence, as a derivative function that adds nothing to its character, the will is stripped of the dimensions of particularity and individuality that any real self-determination involves. Since the actuality of freedom is bound up with the individuality of the free will, any assertion of freedom as a foundation of justice deprives that freedom of its actuality by making it the prior principle of what it determines. By the same token, the derivative forms of justice cannot be actual realizations of freedom themselves, for they are not self-determined structures whose essence belongs to their particular existence, but relations owing their character to the prior principle of the will. On both sides, the liberal approach leaves the individuality of freedom unrealized.

Despite these basic problems, the overwhelming majority of modern thinkers of freedom have failed to conceive its individual character and fallen into the trap of treating the free will as a principle of justice. Avoiding their course without retaking the discredited route of praxis theory is no easier a matter than avoiding the pitfalls of transcendental argument without stumbling back into the cul de sac of metaphysics. Nevertheless, the search for a viable alternative is best aided by tracing the immanent logic of liberal theory. In doing so, one sees that the recourse to a privileged determiner of justice entails two successive paths of argument: the theory of liberty ushered in by Hobbes, Locke, and Rousseau, and the logically subsequent theory of practical reason introduced by Kant. By thinking through these two basic positions, one sees not only what is lacking with liberty and practical reason, but what is required to conceive freedom properly and conquer the challenge of nihilism.

Before proceeding further, it must be noted that although the various developers of the theory of liberty have come to conflicting conclusions on many matters, the divergence of their theories is due more to the inconsistent introduction of given factors extraneous to the will than to any systematic opportunity for alternate routes. Hobbes' appeal to the fear of death and the right of self-preservation, Locke's recourse to a divine source for natural law and right reason, and Rousseau's reliance upon civil religion and an expert legislator all involve holdovers from the metaphysics of justice, holdovers of a reliance upon given determinacy of one sort or another that stands at odds with the move to a privileged determiner, which alone gives their theories their novelty and genuine importance. Consequently, in order to evaluate the project of liberal theory that they historically initiated, it is best to leave aside the vagaries of their particular efforts and to concentrate instead upon the generic logic entailed in abandoning the metaphysical reliance on privileged givens and advancing the will as the privileged determiner of justice.

4.2 The Logic of Liberty and the Paradoxes of Social Contract

However misbegotten be the problem of making freedom the principle of justice, the problem both motivating and defining liberal theory, it is hardly fortuitous or arbitrary. The problem naturally arises once the lure of freedom casts in doubt the authority of teleological ends and the recognition grows that valid conduct cannot be subject to prescribed virtues but must be self-determined, that just government cannot be based on a division of ruler and ruled but must comprise self-rule, that in all spheres of public life what is valid must realize the autonomy of the will.

From the perspective of this break with the hold of convention and the tradition of metaphysics, freedom faces the given reality of ethical affairs as the one unconditional principle in terms of which that reality ought to be restructured. This critical opposition, historically experienced by the originators of liberal theory, immediately puts self-determination in the position of a given form, out of which the valid relations of justice are to be determined. Rather than letting self-determination stand as a freedom already situated in a world of its own, the challenge of its emergence sets it over and against an alien, unfree order of convention, as a revolutionary standard awaiting embodiment. Although self-determination is properly at one with what it determines, here it is cast in the role of a privileged determiner, having both its specific character and existence prior to what it determines.

The quest for an ethics of freedom thus understandably arises in terms of this conflation of self-determination with the determining of a given determiner. In so doing, it provides liberal theory with its starting point: the will conceived as a given agency, whose character stands defined prior to any actual volition, and whose right is to be realized as the first principle of justice.

4.2.1 The Natural Will and the State of Nature

As something given, the will is here a natural will, whose agency does not issue from any actions or enacted institutions, but rather precedes them all as an irreducible postulate. There could hardly be a more convincing starting point, for how could any voluntary action be undertaken if there were not already a will at hand able to act? The autonomy of this will accordingly exists not in virtue of any agreements or other conventions, but in a state of nature that is a "natural" condition precisely by existing independently of the will's activity. Since the will of every individual immediately exists in such a state of nature, being given, rather than determined and brought into existence through the will's own volition, the state of nature is logically prior to any instituted relations that could embody the freedom of the will.

Further, insofar as this natural will has its own form prior to any particular act, simply by being primordially given as the foundation of action, it is merely universal in character. Lacking particular self-determination as part of its nature, it is not an individual structure that is inherently actual to the extent that it cannot be defined apart from its particular acts. With its given universal form, the will in question is rather a natural *capacity* common to all individual agents. As such, the will is a universal faculty that all unimpaired individuals are born with and naturally possess in equal form. This provides liberal theory with its canonical first proposition: that all men are free and equal in the state of nature.

The freedom of such a will is accordingly a natural liberty, the mere capacity of unfettered choice that all enjoy by birth, granted the subsequent maturation of mind and body naturally providing each individual with the ability to make independent decisions. Because this choosing will has a given universal structure, with no element of particularity within itself, it is not only a mere faculty, but one that must choose from independently given alternatives in order to obtain any particular content to will. These alternatives may be supplied either by what exists externally in nature, or by separate subjective faculties, such as reason or desire. However they be furnished, the particular ends that the will chooses are independently derived, rather than determined by the will itself.

Consequently, although the natural will has the liberty to choose whatever alternative it wishes, it is still always bound to choices that are given to it rather than determined through freedom. This bondage is of fatal significance, for so long as liberty is relative to the independent alternatives before it, it remains ever tainted with an inability to act with the unconditioned universality required for normative validity. With regard to the logical structure of freedom, this means that the natural will can never give itself a particular content that is unique to its universal form and so attain the individuality of actual self-determination. No matter what choice is made, the content will be extraneous to the common structure of choosing by which the natural will is defined.

On this basis, what alone can provide an actual realization of the autonomy of such a will is an embodiment that is external and given, yet still comprises the express objectification of a will that must seek its particular content entirely outside itself. Since the character of the agent is no more a product of choice than the given alternatives from which the natural will must choose if it is to act at all, the choosing will can only exhibit its freedom in an objective fashion by choosing some given object as the explicit receptacle of its choice. Accordingly, the generic realization of the natural will consists in a natural appropriation of something or other whose possession provides appropriate objectification for that merely universal will of free choice, which can claim nothing more than some externally given thing for the reality of its own determination. If at the same time, the natural will is to be the principle of justice, then the possession by which it realizes itself should enjoy the rightful status of being an entitled possession, that is, property. It therefore follows that the liberty with which all agents are endowed by nature has its correlative extension in a natural right to property.

This rightful reality of liberty is, however, as much a problem as the basic conditioned predicament of choice due to the given character of the individual identity of each natural will. Because the liberty of choice is a natural capacity common to all, what individuates one agent from another must be particular factors extraneous to the structure of the natural will itself. This means that each such will stands differentiated from every other by nature. Individuals here face one another as bearers of a choosing will distinguishable from that of others not as a result of willing and in accord with its common liberty, but as inhabitants of a given natural state of affairs where what makes each particular is unmediated by freedom. In such a state, individuals, born free and equal, immediately confront one another as independent agents, ready to exercise their own separate liberty without any agreements, laws, or other acts of will concomitantly determining their relationship. By the very fact that their respective identity as particular agents is something given, their immediate plurality allows of no preestablished harmony. Since the choosing will of each agent has its individual character not in function and in realization of the common exercise of liberty, but as part of a given condition, the distinct agencies by which liberty is naturally exercised are not already integrated into any system of mutual respect and peaceful coexistence. On the contrary, each individual possesses the same capacity of choice without any inherent limits upon its arbitrariness.

Insofar as this leaves each individual at liberty to choose at will in total independence from the willing of others, there is nothing to prevent the separate volitions of different agents from conflicting with one another. Whether or not their aims be given by outer circumstance, inner desire, or rational reflection, what one individual wills may very well contradict the choice of another. Even if the external situation, the structure of desire, and reason were to offer the identical options to all, the liberty of each individual to choose which given alternative to will would preclude any guarantee of harmony.

Consequently, the state of nature, where individuals interact solely in terms of their natural wills, is under continual threat of discord, calling into question each individual's actual opportunity to exercise his liberty and embody it in property without opposition and interference from others. To the very degree that all agents are free and equal in regard to being endowed with a faculty of choice generically embodied in property, the state of nature of their liberty is no less a state of war where no will or possession is secure from the license of others. The will all individuals have by nature is not only just a *faculty* of choice bound to no given alternatives, but one which enjoys merely the *right* to its own liberty and property. Given the endemic possibility of a war of all against all, this natural right is not a natural reality, but an imperative, lacking the force of mutual respect that can supply right with the honored duty ensuring its exercise.

Under these conditions, no "natural law" evident to "right reason" can overcome the insecurity of liberty by mandating rules of respect for right. What is clear to reason may have binding force in rational argument, but not upon the natural will. It can always defy what reason ordains, as well as what others will, precisely because it has the freedom to choose its own particular ends by itself. Furthermore, once the legitimacy of all rationally prescribed, teleological ends has been denied, as liberal theory does in abandoning the project of the metaphysics of justice, no law can any longer command and oblige obedience just by being revealed by reason. When legitimacy is instead invested in a privileged determiner, law can only be valid by issuing from a will enjoying proper authority, whereas even such law will be universally obeyed only insofar as each individual has chosen to respect its authority.

These conditions of legal authority and enforcement are, however, just what are lacking in a natural condition. A "natural" law, whose validity rests in its given rational content, has no author to underwrite its legitimacy by enacting and publicly proclaiming it with the universally recognized authority on which obedience depends. Such an author would be a contradiction in terms, for in a state of nature there is no legitimate law-maker, but only a plurality of individuals each endowed with liberty and unbeholden to the will of any other.

No attempt to bestow validity upon natural law by ascribing it to a transcendent will of God can succeed in circumventing this problem. Although recourse to theological legislation might seem the perfect example of rooting legitimacy in a privileged determiner, liberty cannot be made to conform to divine commands without relinquishing its constitutive character of being free from any prescription it has not imposed upon itself.

4.2.2 The Perplexities of Social Contract

The predicament of the natural will, of freedom taken as a principle, mandates instead a very different course to secure the reality of liberty and make it the foundation of justice. This course is that of social contract, and it is called for in a dual way.

First, because the exercise of every individual's natural will in no way resolves itself into the common realization of everyone's liberty, there is need for some further agency to insure that the particular acts of different agents accord with one another. To overcome the incipient state of war natural to liberty, there must be a higher authority empowered to protect each will and its property by legislating and enforcing the unimpeached coexistence of all individuals in their exercise of their right to choose as they may.

On the other hand, given the plurality of natural wills and their natural right to exercise their liberty, the agency regulating their respective actions must issue from the consent of all if it is not to violate the very autonomy it is called upon to protect. If one were to argue that consent of the majority is enough to give the needed agency its authority, one would have to introduce some additional given principle to justify majority decision. Otherwise, the established power would be acting upon the minority without their consent in clear violation of their natural liberty. No principle of majority decision could have legitimacy, however, unless it was itself determined by the one and only privileged determiner available, namely, the natural will of each and every individual. Consequently, if the required agency is to have the authority to serve liberty, which cannot securely exist without it, then all individuals in the state of nature must unanimously will it upon themselves and agree to recognize and respect its validity. This leaves but one way to establish the new order required to suppress the license of the state of nature and secure natural liberty. It can arise only through a "social contract" where all agree to relinquish their unchecked arbitrariness by joining together as members of a "civil society," obligated to obey a "civil government" they impose upon themselves by consenting to its rule so long as it restricts itself to protecting their liberty and property.

Although such social contract provides the only route out of the state of nature, its agreement has a dual character of its own[6] that quickly casts in doubt its ability to provide freedom with an institutional reality.

Because the right of liberty and property is itself something natural, the public authority contractually instituted to secure it is something external and posterior to the freedom of the natural will. The civil government's ruling activity does not constitute liberty, but merely preserves personal autonomy and property as they are already defined in the state of nature.

Consequently, the social contract is not just a mutual covenant between equals, securing each the power to exercise his or her liberty by obligating all to respect that of others. Since the freedom herein secured is neither created by the new authority, nor specific to its institutional practice, but a liberty defined prior to it, this liberty does not involve any participation in government. Conversely, since civil government is contractually instituted for the sole sake of securing the antecedently given rights of the natural will, rights whose exercise is independent of all non-natural, institutional roles, the liberal state does not exist to realize political freedoms specific to its own governing activity. This means that when individuals mutually agree to join together into a civil society, they each simultaneously enter into an unequal, nonreciprocal relation to their new authority, a relation between ruler and subject consisting in their consent to abide by its law and regulation so long as it lets them enjoy their personal liberty and private property. In effect, no sooner do individuals enter into social contract, than they agree to hand over the monopoly of public action to the government itself in exchange for a "civil" freedom involving no more than the civil right to exercise their natural rights to liberty and property under the protection of public law and authority.

With legitimate government accordingly exercising a power entirely separate from the liberty of individuals, there is no need for political freedom to participate in self-government. All that justice here requires is that individuals have the freedom to institute and, if need be, replace the ruling regime before retreating to those essentially pre-political activities that the civil government allows to be pursued. So long as the government protects the natural rights of its subjects, it can take any form whatsoever. This is why Rousseau's attachment to democracy is much less consistent than Locke's sober recognition that civil government can be either a democracy, an oligarchy, or a monarchy and still be true to itself.[7]

The end result of all this is that not only is freedom deprived of any necessary political realization, but government is merely civil in character, having no ends distinct from those at play in the civil society it oversees. Instead of being a sovereign body politic existing for the sake of its own ruling activity, as any truly independent political self-determination would require, the instituted government has as its sole legitimate aim maintaining the liberty of the natural will. Its rule is consequently relative, receiving its fundamental law from elsewhere — namely, the pre-political sphere of the state of nature in which the privileged determiner of justice is to be found. Like liberty itself, the will of civil government thus has only a formal, negative freedom. It cannot determine its own ends, like a genuinely sovereign state, but can only choose the means for realizing natural right. Whereas the state of praxis had its legitimacy by embodying the given content of the good and not due to its genesis, the state enacted through social contract cannot be an end in itself precisely because its legitimacy is rooted in the procedure that both brings it into being and defines its valid purpose. Being determined by a given determiner, the regime arising from social contract cannot rule over civil society with any proper aims of its own, but must play the instrumental role of a civil government, administering the harmony of civil society against which it has no legitimate autonomy.

Nevertheless, because civil government is delegated to be the final arbiter among individuals, it has a will of its own. Since its jurisdiction extends to all individuals in their common character as agents in general, the first and foremost function of the will of the civil government is legislative. What it determines to be law is valid not by being an embodiment of the good or some given mean of conduct, but by being willed by that legitimate authority whose law commands obedience in virtue of the prior consent of the members of civil society. As such, the civil laws of justice do issue from a will and must be publicly proclaimed to the extent that they address individuals who are prepared to follow them only in conscious and willful recognition of their authority.

Although this might seem to make the will of civil government the real principle of justice, its legislation is only a formal determination of law, suffering from the same bondage to given content that afflicts liberty in general. Due to its instrumental character, civil government has no right to determine the particular statutes of law without restriction. It can legitimately enact only those laws that conform to the given "law" of nature prescribing the general preservation of the liberty and property of individuals. Since government legislation is thereby limited to a merely civil law, whose content derives from the liberty of the natural will, the rule of civil government cannot break the will's enslavement to particular ends that are not intrinsically its own.

Despite the fact that this adherence to externally given content is what alone provides civil government with legitimacy, it actually undermines the very authority and power it is supposed to confer. Due to the constitutive role of social contract, the standard of just rule lies outside the positive institutions of civil government in the implicit principles of natural right. As a result, there is no seat of authority *within* civil government that can certify the legitimacy of its measures in the binding way in which, for instance, the United States Supreme Court exercises its own politically mandated role by interpreting the enacted constitution and judging the legality of government policy on grounds that are political in origin and objectively valid for all citizens. Where freedom is a given principle and justice consists in no more than the realization of liberty, it must simply be left to personal judgment to decide whether government is properly enacting natural law. With no institutional seat of authority available, individuals have the prerogative to withdraw their recognition of the legitimacy of civil government as soon as they judge it to have violated its natural mandate. Their original consent agreement gives them all the right to do so, in default of any other non-natural source of authority competent to exercise an exclusive power of judgment. This means that the members of civil society are completely at liberty to throw off the obligations of the social contract and revert to a state of nature where no laws or agreements have any binding force upon them and where, consequently, any attempt by civil government to impose its rule may be duly met by war and rebellion.

Consequently, the authority of civil government is itself no more secure than individual liberty and property in the state of nature, insofar as respect for both is, in the final analysis, but a matter of personal judgment and choice. Although civil government is instituted to guarantee the exercise of liberty, its own instrumental character makes it just as inherently unstable as the right it is meant to uphold.

What adds further complication is that not only is the authority of civil government continually subject to challenge, but its power is continually prey to abuse for which there is no satisfactory remedy. So long as civil government is merely a means to an end distinct from its own political activity, there can be no guarantee that the state will fulfill its proper mandate. Whether the rulers be one, few, or many, there is no telling whether they will actually protect the natural rights of all. If, on the other hand, civil government had a form that was for its own sake, this problem would not arise, for the very existence of such a government would comprise the reason for its being. In that case, government could not fail to fulfill its purpose, for so long as it functioned it would have achieved its end, namely, its own governing activity.

With civil government, however, the possibility of abuse of power is endemic and the absence of any resources with which to judge objectively when violations occur only contributes to a situation where citizens have no reliable means to protect themselves from the government to which they have consented. Locke's appeal to the judgment of the people provides no remedy, for how will the people be able to convene, judge with authority, and act with an organized power? If unanimous consent of the people is required to pass judgment on the conduct of government, no judgment of censure could be counted on when the officials in question are members of the "people" themselves. If, on the other hand, majority decision be relied upon, civil freedom is made hostage to the tyranny of the majority. Finally, if each individual is free to rely upon personal judgment to determine when government no longer commands obedience, it is hard to see how there can be any concerted power of resistance which is not at the mercy of the same rule of individual arbitrariness that civil government was intended to supplant.[8]

Actually, it should come as no surprise that civil government ultimately fails to command a recognized authority or an effective, yet proper power any less contingent than harmony in the state of nature. The endemic instability of civil government is but a reflection of a basic dilemma casting in doubt the whole possibility of social contract. Although it is problematic enough that the authority and power of civil government has no guarantee without the unanimous respect of the members of society, the real difficulty is that social contract requires unanimity for its own existence. What makes this such a problem is that the unanimity upon whose basis social contract is made consists in the very same unanimous respect for right that is lacking in the state of nature and whose absence requires the founding of a civil government in the first place. With the natural will figuring as the privileged determiner of justice, the social contract can only come into being when the prospective members of civil society are already all resolved to honor each other's natural rights by taking the common measure of entering into agreement to institute civil government. Without this prior unanimous commitment, the social contract not only has no binding force, but cannot even be entered into by the inhabitants of the state of nature.

Even if one were to grant that only the contracting individuals would become duty-bound members of a new civil society, leaving behind all the rest in the same state of nature, the parties to the contract would still be under no obligation to respect their own agreement unless it were already a valid principle that contractual obligations should be honored. With all teleological ends discredited in favor of the privileged right of the natural will, no such principle could possibly have any prior validity. Furthermore, the principle of respecting contracts could not be established by an agreement among individuals, for that agreement would have no obligatory force of its own unless the principle it is supposed to found already had authority.

If this means that only a unanimous predisposition to enter and observe the social contract would allow for its execution, it must no less be recognized that only without such shared commitment, under a state of war where there is no common recognition of rights, does the need for a social contract even arise. When all individuals already choose to respect each other's liberty, something that can occur not out of necessity, but only due to everyone's simultaneous arbitrary decision to live in harmony, the state of nature is a state of peace, with no need of civil government. What this signifies is that wherever social contract is needed the conditions are lacking for it to be agreed upon, whereas, wherever those conditions prevail, social contract is superfluous.

Here the attempt to make freedom the principle of justice stumbles just as its gets underway, fatefully warning of the impasse awaiting it at the end of its travails. Freedom, reduced to the liberty of the natural will by being cast as a privileged determiner, must be sustained through a social contract precisely because the given liberty of agents in the state of nature leaves them free of any prior obligations to respect each other's rights. Yet, because social contract issues from the liberty of individuals, it cannot find support in any preexisting agreement or effective principle of justice (such as that contracts be honored) which might allow it to be convened and binding. Since, however, the primacy of liberty allows for no other source of higher authority than this contract, not only can such authority not be relied upon to legitimate and enforce the original covenant, but its civil government has no more respected authority and power than the given agents whose harmony it is designed to ensure. With the authority of civil government endemically problematic, the realization of individual liberty is itself thrown into question, given the abiding absence of any secured respect of natural right. As a result, instead of freedom determining an existing system of justice, all that is left is a condition of license leaving right just as unrealized in civil society as in the state of nature. The quest of liberal theory here grinds to a halt before a hopelessly hypothetical civil government, wherein freedom remains more an imperative than a reality, representing a formal capacity of only universal character, facing both the indifferent givenness of its alternative contents and the immediate opposition of the given plurality of agents.

Chapter 5

The Promise and Illusion of Practical Reason

The collapse of classical liberal theory may reveal the untenability of rooting right in the natural will, but it does not exhaust all options for developing freedom as a principle of justice. Instead, it prepares the way for a second approach, cognizant of the limits of liberty, yet still committed to conceiving the will as the privileged determiner of valid conduct. This approach is taken by the theory of practical reason, historically founded by Kant. It follows the path that beckons the moment an attempt is made to remove the blatantly conditioned aspect of the natural will, while maintaining freedom as the foundation of legitimate conduct and institutions.

The appeal of this undertaking is not hard to understand. Once it has become evident how liberty stands condemned to be a negative freedom lacking secure positive fulfillment so long as the content of its choice remains externally determined, it is only natural to expunge this externality in hope of attaining a genuine freedom enjoying the unconditioned character demanded for validity. However, if the will is retained as the given determiner of right, it still comprises a universal form shared by all agents and underlying all actions, no matter how purified it may be. Simply by being the privileged principle by which all subsequent acts should be determined, the will has a fixed autonomy to which none of its actions can add. Consequently, if the will's act of determination is to have a content internal, rather than external to it, all it has available to draw upon is its own universal form of choice. Making that the determining ground of its action would mean no more than willing actions so as to realize the universality of its own volition. Nevertheless, if the natural will were to will nothing but its own form in this fashion it would be exhibiting to some degree a dimension of self-determination absent in the exercise of liberty. The will would here manifest an autonomy giving the semblance of willing itself, which is precisely what self-determination should involve.

What defines the theory of practical reason is the project of taking up just such autonomy and developing it as the principle of ethics. Because its whole approach issues from an awareness of the problems inherent in reducing freedom to the arbitrariness of choice, the outcome of its argument provides a telling verdict on whether recourse to a privileged determiner can secure the justification justice requires. Since Kant develops the framework of practical reason with a rigor leading the argument to its inevitable conclusion, scrutiny of his statement of the position can readily uncover its governing logic.

5.1 Practical Reason and The Individuality of Freedom

Kant may well be considered the first modern thinker to recognize the inadequacy of liberty as a candidate for freedom and the principle of justice. His entire theory of practical reason is motivated by the need to salvage the possibility of normative validity in conduct by overcoming what he calls the "heteronomy" of willing exhibited in the exercise of liberty. This "heteronomy" consists in the determination of the will's purposes by factors other than itself, such as established custom, prescribed virtues, the decrees of supposed experts in justice, or, for that matter, the agent's own feelings, desires or prudential calculations of what happiness might result from particular actions. Kant properly realized that if the will is to engage in the normatively unconditioned activity in which justice consists, it must free itself of externally given ends, and instead supply itself with an aim that owes its content to the will itself. To be ascribed legitimacy, the freedom of the will must be conceived in terms of such actual self-determination, and this autonomy, rather than the negative freedom of liberty, must be advanced as the basis of justice.

In demanding the move from liberty to autonomy, Kant sets the theory of practical reason the proper task of giving expression to the self-determined individuality constitutive of freedom. Yet at the same time, he maintains the recourse to a privileged determiner by understanding autonomy to be the principle of ethics. It is the tension between these two aspects of autonomy that defines the course of practical reason. Although Kant rightly seeks to eliminate the external content to which the natural will is bound, treating autonomy as a given determiner of ethics leaves the autonomous will in a predicament all too similar to that of the natural will, whose liberty can add nothing particular to its given character. Certainly, the autonomous will does part company with the natural will by refraining from wiling any external content. Yet the question remains as to whether this leaves it with anything else to will than its own form of choice, certifying again and again its own identity without being able to introduce any non-external particular content that might provide needed determination for its self-determination. The theory of practical reason ultimately hinges on this problem, to which its own argument inexorably leads.

Certainly, it must be granted that Kant's prohibition of heteronomy in the determination of the will's ends presents a first step in the right direction. By mandating that the content of willing derive from the will itself, it effectively introduces the valid concern that the free will be individual in essence, giving itself particular determination in virtue of its own form of action.

Kant's affirmative account of the free will in terms of "practical reason," and not "practical understanding,"[1] makes this more explicit, for the differentiation between the two first makes possible a concept of autonomy that is not reducible to liberty.

Naturally, the distinction between practical reason and practical understanding rests upon Kant's conception of understanding and reason as distinct faculties of mind. What makes Kant's demarcation of reason from the understanding so important for ethics is that it lays the groundwork for thinking individuality, without which freedom cannot properly be conceived. How this is so becomes apparent when the basic formulations in Kant's *Critique of Pure Reason* are examined in light of the relations of universal and particular that hold in each faculty.

Kant describes the understanding as the faculty of rules that comprehends appearances as objects by unifying representations given in sensible intuition under concepts through an act of judgment.[2] Although the understanding exercises spontaneity in bringing the manifold contents of intuition under rules and so uniting them in one consciousness as objects of knowledge, its judgment refers a concept to sensible particulars that have been independently given. What distinguishes the concept in question from intuitions is that it is itself a representation of given representations, expressing what is common to them.[3] Although the concept is thus something general, its universality does not specify its own instances as in individuality, but is formal in character, having reference to particulars that are not immanent to it. Hence, the understanding cannot know anything particular by concepts alone, for the particulars to which they refer are independently given in intuition and therefore require the contribution of sensibility if they are to be known. Further, even with the benefit of sensible particulars, the understanding cannot know anything free and individual. Because the unifying law of the understanding subsumes given particulars under universals extraneous to them as well, it is a law of necessity. As a consequence, all objects of experience are causally determined, both by prior events and through the reciprocal interaction in which they stand related to other coexisting objects.

In contrast, Kant characterizes reason as the faculty of principles that thinks by syllogism, concluding something particular from a general premise.[4] Instead of understanding perceptions through judgment, where concepts are applied to given particulars to determine a nature ruled by necessity, reason conceives ideas by determining their particulars from out of the universal solely by means of concepts.[5] This effectively makes reason a faculty for thinking individuality, to the extent that individuality internally unites the universal and particular, such that they are immanent to one another. Since self-determination exhibits this same combination of universality and particularity, Kant accordingly grants reason the capacity to think the idea of freedom, which the understanding can never know.[6]

Already in the *Critique of Pure Reason* Kant draws the practical consequences which follow from these contrasting descriptions of reason and understanding. First, the understanding cannot be employed to determine justice, for taking the standard of right from understood experience amounts to deriving what should be universally valid from what is conditioned by the causal necessity of particular circumstances. Because justice must rather be *unconditioned* and *for its own sake*, what is right has to be determined from a principle of reason, whose ideas alone are unconditioned in virtue of their incipient individuality, which transcends the givenness of sensible intuition by determining the particular through the universal.[7]

If willing is to be just, it must not simply choose among ends given to it in experience by the understanding. All the understanding can offer when it tries to serve as a guide for conduct are maxims consisting in causal rules determining what actions will achieve the given ends of choice. The essentially technical, means-end calculus of such practical understanding cannot possibly prescribe what should be done, as Utilitarianism falsely claims. The simple reason it cannot is that it either leaves unexamined what ends should be sought in the first place, or else proceeds from empirical grounds and preferences, which, as such, are always conditioned and contingent, and therefore no more ends in themselves than aims that individuals will necessarily choose.

Any attempt to avoid these problems by advancing utility as an end in itself only falls into hopeless contradiction, precisely because what is useful is always for the sake of something else. If utility were of value because of its own utility, it would no longer be something for its own sake, whereas if its utility were not the source of its value, it would violate its own principle of legitimacy. In other words, the justification of utility cannot be sought in its usefulness, for this would not only take the authority of utility for granted, but equally deny it by subordinating the utility principle to that end for which it is a means. Conversely, making appeal to some other principle to justify utilitarianism would obviously undercut utility's very status as the final arbiter of conduct.

The outcome is the same if one argues for utilitarianism by suggesting that all values are matters of preference that can only be weighed against one another on the common ground of preference calculation. This leaves adherence to the utilitarian principle itself a matter of mere preference with no greater intrinsic authority than any other competing view.

The familiar refrain of each of these arguments should only underscore how it is just as nonsensical to make the instrumental calculation of practical understanding the foundation of ethics as it is to make pragmatic concerns the foundation of knowledge. In each case, the relative character of the postulated principle of pragmatic utility undercuts its own justifiability.

The only plausible alternative would seem to involve discarding practical understanding in favor of practical reason, and taking the route that Kant proposes. For there to be justice, reason must itself be practical and determine not means, but ends of conduct that have unconditional validity. In conjunction with the prohibition of heteronomy, this means that the will must give itself its end in virtue of an unconditioned principle specific to its own structure, thereby achieving an implicitly individual volition where the particular purpose of action is determined from out of a universal law rooted in the will's own character. However, that reason be practical further requires that the will be not just at liberty to choose among given alternatives, but free to exercise the distinct autonomy of determining itself independently of all extraneous particulars of experience and solely through the unconditioned, individual determination of reason. Consequently, practical reason ushers in a new positive determination of freedom, irreducible to liberty, and providing the foundation of normatively valid action.

These aspects of Kant's characterization anticipate the most essential feature of right: that justice consists in the self-determination of the free will, whose freedom is unconditioned and individual in character, in contrast to the conditioned choice of liberty, common to all agents. Yet, these same aspects render autonomy a privileged determiner with the result that practical reason cannot provide the individuality of free willing that it itself first poses as the genuine content of right.

5.2 The Impracticality of Practical Reason

In light of how freedom possesses an individual character, it can be said that the basic problem of practical reason lies in the way in which it relates the universal and the particular. Despite Kant's introduction of syllogizing reason and autonomy, the particular still remains something given to the universal in both thinking and acting. As becomes evident, this has as its consequence that Kantian reason remains dependent upon the understanding, while the will's autonomy fails to rise above the liberty of choice.

The core of the difficulty resides in Kant's conception of reason. Although Kant claims that reason generically seeks the unconditioned universal that determines the particular, the particular in question is actually provided independently by the understanding in the form of a given rule of experience that supplies the minor premise of the syllogism. To take the classic example of syllogism, "All men are mortal, Socrates is a man, therefore Socrates is mortal," the universal principle (All men are mortal) determines the particular (Socrates) only in virtue of being supplied with the minor premise (Socrates is a man), whose particular content can only be known in experience by the understanding. For Kant, this is true of all reasoning insofar as reason has nothing meaningful to think about unless it is provided with something known by understanding.

Furthermore, since the understanding has exclusive knowledge of objectivity, whose reality is grasped not from universal concepts alone, but with aid of the given particulars of sensible intuition, Kant is compelled to view the ideas of reason as concepts that are not real, but irreducibly transcendent. To the extent that reason thinks ideas of the unconditioned from which all else can be concluded, its ideas can never have any objective reality, so long as objectivity is itself something conditioned by the transcendental structure of knowing. Consequently, reason can here prescribe no law to reality nor contain any principles for either knowing it or determining anything real and particular. All such reason can do is provide a subjective regulation for the understanding, bringing its rules into consistent harmony under the ideal unity supplied by those ideas that reason thinks at the apex of all syllogistic inference. Although this regulative activity may certify the non-contradictory character of the rules of the understanding, this certification is something indifferent to both the particular content and the objective validity of those rules whose coherence is being judged.

Whereas Kant sees this predicament as the fate of thought, the impasse of transcendental philosophy suggests that it may just as well signify an abandonment of reason that reduces the unconditioned, individual determination of an autonomous thinking to the formal lawfulness of the understanding, whose rules apply to given particulars in an external way. The example of Kant might be taken to indicate that unless the concepts of reason be individual in character, determining the particular through the universal rather than letting particular existence fall outside it, neither can the real be rational, nor reason be actual.

Although these questions must await their resolution, what is immediately clear is the ethical import of Kant's conception. With the individuality of freedom barred from the domain of objectivity and with reason relegated to an external ordering of given particulars, practical reason cannot possibly provide freedom the self-determined reality it requires.

This could not be revealed more clearly than by Kant's conception of the categorical imperative. From the outset Kant binds himself to the structure of choice by having practical understanding play a role entirely analogous to that of theoretical understanding in its relation to reason. He has practical understanding supply practical reason with the particular content of action that reason is supposed to determine through a principle. This content is the maxim of the will, which is nothing more than a causal rule of the understanding determining what action will bring into being a given end.[8] In line with his treatment of reason, Kant makes the maxim the source of the particular end of willing and then asks what can be the unconditioned principle of its choice. By now, there can be little doubt as to what the answer must be. Given the structure of choice, where action is determined by instrumental rules of the understanding, the only thing that is not relative and conditioned, but necessary and dependent upon choice alone is the form of choosing. Taken by itself, it is none other than the lawfulness of the maxim of the will, since the generality of the maxim expresses how it commonly pertains to all agents.[9] This, however, is nothing but the same universal aspect of willing that liberal theory had previously isolated and made its principle. Consequently, practical reason has but one principle consisting in the categorical imperative to act so that the maxim of one's will be a universal law. In effect, what Kant has done here to eliminate the heteronomy of liberty is to have choice will its own empty form, which remains just as incapable as before of generating any particular ends of its own.

The problem at hand becomes painfully clear the moment any attempt is made to apply the categorical imperative. Due to the prior specification of the maxim, the categorical imperative does not determine the will by *concluding* its particular end from a universal principle. On the contrary, the categorical imperative can only operate as a moral law for *judging* whether the given choice contradicts the general form of choosing. In this respect, its function is tantamount to that of a rule of the understanding.

As Hegel has pointed out in his famous discussion of Kant's example of the depositum,[10] this leaves the categorical imperative with a purely formal universality preventing it from providing any particular criteria for determining which particular maxims can or cannot be a universal law. If, for instance, one were to judge whether it be moral or not to steal another individual's property, the test of universalizability mandated by the categorical imperative offers no grounds for condemning the theft. The resulting universal law that everyone steal the property of others would be invalid only if appeal were made to the principle that property warrants respect. If, however, the categorical imperative is the one and only unconditioned principle of morality, such an appeal would be entirely impermissible, bringing into play as it does a given prescription extraneous to the privileged form of autonomous willing. Since the same situation would occur in evaluating any other maxim of conduct, it is evident that no action can be judged immoral through practical reason without introducing additional principles whose own validity could never be categorical. By itself, the categorical imperative therefore sets no limits whatsoever upon morality. Consequently, the "kingdom of ends" it is supposed to found turns out to be a predicament of total license where autonomy has no definite objective determination to call its own.

In effect, practical reason not only restricts autonomy to an internal judgment of maxims, but prevents that judgment from arriving at any unequivocal conclusions. As as result, the autonomy that should overcome the heteronomy of liberty by inwardly obeying the categorical imperative is unable to give itself a particular end actually specific to the universality of the will. This leaves freedom without any reality, for the individuality of self-determination is nowhere achieved.

5.3 Civil Society in the Service of Practical Reason

In lieu of an applicable moral law that might testify to the existence of a freedom irreducible to liberty, the real relations between individuals are left captive to the arbitrariness of choice. Accordingly, when Kant turns to consider how the worldly existence of free individuals should be ordered, the theme of his *Metaphysical Elements of Justice* (*Der Metaphysik der Sitten*), he cannot help but revert to the same course taken by the theorists of liberty. Like them, he proceeds to conceive a hypothetical civil order of legality, issuing from the consent of individuals, with the single purpose of insuring the lawful coexistence of their choosing wills.

This move from morality to legality is as much a necessity for practical reason as is the corresponding departure from the state of nature for liberty. The categorical imperative itself requires it, not just because its formality leaves action prey to arbitrary choice, but because its own formula implicitly refers to an objective and recognizable reality of a plurality of free persons for whom the validity of maxims can be judged and applied. That reality opens a new terrain of justice, consisting in the coexistence of autonomous individuals relating to one another as such.

Although justice here has the proper form of being the objective reality of freedom, the freedom in question has its defining source in the autonomy of moral agents. As should be expected, this plants the seed of an irrepressible contradiction. Given the primacy of moral autonomy, whatever mutual obligation confirms the rights of individuals rests upon their application of the categorical imperative, whose unconditioned legislation provides the original determination of right from which all others should spring.[11] Since, however, the autonomy of each individual is a given, preceding their relation to one another, justice must contend with the factual presence of a plurality of free agents who immediately face one another without already being integrated under any other legitimate authority than their own exercise of moral judgment. Taken together, these specifications render justice what Kant consistently describes as the relation of inter-acting individuals that permits their mutual autonomy to be united through a universal law.[12]

Yet they also leave the reality of justice in an uncertain position. The first premise of practical reason, that agents be autonomous moral persons prior to entering into relation with one another, should leave the constitution of civil order a matter of complete indifference to a freedom that has its unassailable integrity in the ever possible inner application of the categorical imperative. On the other hand, the corol-lary premise, that agents act *immediately* upon one another in virtue of the givenness of their coexistence, should entirely exclude any objectivity of freedom since all direct causal action upon persons is incompatible with the reality of individual autonomy.

Practical reason may very well ordain that justice consists in the lawful coexistence of one person's freedom with that of every other individual,[13] but actually integrating the actions of different agents according to the universal law of freedom is another matter. Property, the most rudimentary relation in which right lies at hand, provides a first taste of the difficulty of erecting the order of justice upon the prin-ciple of practical reason. The establishment of an external Mine and Yours, the topic with which Kant opens his *Metaphysical Elements of Justice*, presents the central problem confronting autonomy, the ques-tion of how the free will can go beyond the inner application of the categorical imperative and give itself an objective existence valid for others within a community of autonomous persons. On this query hangs the entire project of practical reason to the degree that the insti-tution of property presents the most basic process whereby persons give their autonomy reality within the realm of experience, the realm in which they exist for others and others exist for them.

Kant, however, must admit that since property involves the reality of a respected determination of free will, rather than mere physical grasp, it presupposes a reciprocity of obligation that has force only through a communal will guaranteeing the security of ownership.[14] This means that property can possess an actual secure being only within an existing state of justice, regulated by the power of a civil legislation.

To bridge the gap between the person's appropriation of a rightless object through a unilateral act of will and the presence of mutual respect necessary to give this act objective validity, Kant follows the only route available to practical reason. With autonomy the privileged determiner of justice, preceding all valid institutions as their legitimating principle, persons are immediately able to take only physical possession. At best, they can seek in its natural Mine and Yours a provisory *comparative* rightfulness in expectancy of a civil order whose creation is an imperative for all, to the extent that it is needed to guarantee autonomy an unimpeached reality.[15] Consequently, the problem of realizing autonomy, which establishment of property first poses, cannot be resolved without advancing to the security of civil right where, in Kant's view, an actual sovereign emerges as the universal property owner, from whose ownership all particular property can be derived and preserved.[16]

This leads to all the difficulties encountered by liberal theory. Despite the failure of practical reason to give freedom objective reality, personal autonomy here still provides the sole unconditioned principle of justice. Therefore the needed civil order must derive from autonomy and restrict itself to maintaining the harmony of individual willing and with it, the respect of property. With this mandate, however, civil government only reenacts the formal universality of practical reason, since all it does is will the same non-contradiction of choice prescribed by the categorical imperative.[17] This deprives public action of any genuine freedom, for civil government cannot determine its own particular ends, but must accept them from the independently given structure of practical reason, just as, in the case of liberal theory, it accepted them from the natural agency of liberty.

What finally seals the failure of the Kantian conception of legality is the endemic inability of its civil order to come into existence and secure its own authority. Because it can arise and maintain its authority only if individuals actually choose to unite to realize their respective autonomy and honor their mutual agreement, the civil order really presupposes that all individuals do will in accord with practical reason in a way that brings their freedom into existence for one another. That, however, is just what can no more be guaranteed than done at all. It is the very absence of such a guarantee and the abiding formality of autonomy that provides the rationale for establishing a civil order in the first place. As a result, the justice civil legality should provide is here no more realizable than the moral law on which it is founded.

Kant himself virtually admits as much by pushing his quest for justice beyond the problematic domain of the single state and making appeal to the ideal of a perpetual peace to provide a final guarantee for the security of civil government and the reality of individual autonomy. His strategy, however, has an old ring about it. At the new all-encompassing level of international relations, Kant argues, the distribution of territory among nations stands in a provisory, comparative rightfulness in wait of the imperative union of all states under universal law that can remove the threat of war.[18] In their given plurality, individual states confront one another as moral persons in a state of nature, each bound by the categorical duty to strive to erect a league of nations by entering into their own "social contract."[19] The realization of this world order of international concord is an imperative because it alone can provide true law-governed security for person and property, and as such, it comprises the final aim of all justice.[20]

Despite all its widened reach, the familiar diction of "provisory right," "imperative striving," and "mutual obligation" betrays an ought brought to the highest point of contradiction. Just as Kant took for granted the given primacy of autonomy in order to determine civil government, so here the whole erection of a league of nations and the establishment of perpetual peace presupposes the very plurality of civil governments whose own existence has no security precisely because of the internal and external discord that calls for, yet renders unworkable any form of international "social contract." For this reason, the ideal of perpetual peace remains a mere imperative, just as problematic as the hypothetical ideal that civil government itself represents. At this stage, where recourse to the entire world of nations has been tried to no avail, practical reason has nowhere else to turn without falling into transcendence and abandoning the primacy of autonomy on which its own project rests.

5.4 The Miscarriage of Rawls' Rehabilitation of Social Contract Theory

Do the dilemmas of the theories of liberty and practical reason spell ruin for all attempts to conceive justice by appealing to a privileged determiner, or do they represent problems that could be avoided by more rigorous versions of the same strategy? John Rawls' attempt to rehabilitate social contract theory, *A Theory of Justice*, offers a telling answer to this question. Well aware of the problems created by Hobbes' recourse to psychological mechanisms and imperatives of survival, Locke's reliance upon a divine foundation for natural law, and Kant's differentiation of noumenal and phenomenal worlds, Rawls concertedly rejects all the metaphysical baggage that encumbered their efforts. In so doing, he transforms the social contract argument into a pure procedural theory specifying a process for determining norms that ostensibly proceeds with no theoretical commitment to anything but the most rudimentary meanings underlying all our talk about justice. On this most abstract and incontrovertible basis, Rawls recasts the privileged determiner of liberal theory, replacing the social contract with the choice procedure of a so-called original position. Under the restraints of its veil of ignorance, individuals choose common principles of justice with no knowledge of their own natural gifts, social situation, or future plans, and with no other guide than their rational self-interest. Rawls maintains that whatever norms these individuals agree upon will automatically provide the basic principles of justice, with which the institutions of the just society and state can then be determined. On his account, what makes laws and institutions just is not their given content, nor their conformity with human nature, divine law, or rationally prescribed ends, but solely whether they would be decided upon in following the choice procedure of the original position. It grounds what Rawls calls a pure procedural ethics in that it provides a unique procedure for choosing norms that arrives at an automatically valid outcome.[21] According to Rawls, when this procedure is given the determining role it deserves, two norms will be chosen as the fundamental principles of justice, governing the organization of society and state: the principle of equal liberty, that all individuals are entitled to the maximum liberty possible in harmony with the same liberty for others, and the difference principle, that social and economic inequalities should promote the advantage of the least well off, attach to positions open to all, and conform to the requirements of proper savings for future generations.[22]

Does Rawls succeed in rehabilitating social contract theory, or does his pure procedural justice merely translate into another idiom the fundamental dilemmas of any theory of justice founded upon a privileged determiner? Given Rawls' strategy, the issue can best be resolved by focusing on three questions: 1) Is Rawls' description of the original position free of normative assumptions, as it should be if its choice procedure is to be the source of all ethical norms? 2) Does the choice procedure of the original position successfully establish the two principles of justice that Rawls claims will there be agreed upon? 3) Is Rawls' turn to the original position a warranted move that can overcome the problems besetting the traditional appeal to social contract?

5.4.1 The Hidden Assumptions of Pure Procedural Justice

In turning to the choice procedure of the original position and investing it with exclusive privilege to decide the fundamental principles of justice, Rawls places himself in a theoretical bind that proved too much for his predecessors in the social contract tradition. Just as liberal thinkers were at pains to conceive the conditions of social contract without already determining them by independently given norms, so Rawls must characterize the original position without letting it depend upon any antecedent normative standards. Like the traditional social contract, the original position would forfeit its foundational role as the exclusive source of the principles of justice if its choice procedure were at all predicated upon any prior virtues, idea of the good, or rights and duties. In that case, it would retain the dependence upon teleological givens that it is designed to avoid.

To surmount this dilemma, which beset traditional liberal theorists the moment they postulated laws of nature given independently of the social contract, Rawls radically restricts the grounds of choice in the original position so as to exclude all normative considerations. He accomplishes this by making the choice procedure operate with little else but the prudential calculation of rational self-interest. Since such prudence attends to the strictly technical task of choosing the best means for realizing whatever ends self-interest happens to mandate, it would seem to be normatively neutral. As long as the veil of ignorance leaves rational self-interest the sole resource operative in the original position, it would appear that Rawls has succeeded in excluding all given norms that might prescribe either the ends or means to be selected.

Although, in this respect, Rawls' turn to the original position seems entirely in keeping with its Archimedean role as the source of normative principles, several difficulties remain that bring to mind the incoherencies afflicting transcendental argument and the appeal to a privileged determiner in general. Rawls may seem to have freed his argument from ethical presuppositions by rooting his choice procedure in the technical deliberations of rational self-interest, yet prudential calculations hardly mandate the veil of ignorance, whose restraints fundamentally condition the original position. The rationale for the veil of ignorance lies instead in a prior assumption that justice is fairness, where fairness is understood to consist in treating individuals equally in respect to their capacity as choosing selves, without regard for any other differences between them. The commitment to this interpretation of equality, and not rational self-interest, is what requires the veil of ignorance, whose whole point is to prevent individuals from using knowledge of their natural endowments, social position, and future goals to choose principles of justice that favor them by honoring unevenly distributed factors rather than the equal liberty of individuals. So long as this interpretation of justice as fairness represents a particular normative commitment conditioning the original position, it undermines the Archimedean role Rawls' choice procedure is supposed to have as the privileged source of ethical norms. Just as the participants in Locke's social contract arrive at a covenant predetermined by principles of right reason rooted in divine will, so the individuals in the original position end up choosing principles of justice that, far from being fundamental, actually derive from the interpretation of justice already informing their choice procedure.

Rawls, of course, maintains that interpreting justice as fairness is not an arbitrary assumption, but an inescapable feature of our understanding of the very meaning of justice. In so doing, he refrains from claiming that justice as fairness has an unconditioned universality, transcending whatever limits our perspective may have. Therefore, Rawls is content to label his conception merely *a*, rather than *the* theory of justice, acknowledging, much in the manner of his mentor Quine, that his prescriptive theory has a descriptive foundation, freeing it of metaphysical overstatement.

Nevertheless, it could seem that Rawls' interpretation of justice as fairness and his derivative notion of pure procedural justice are not the conceptual distillation of the ethical framework of our particular culture, nor the reinterpretation of one particular tradition within our heritage. Instead, they appear to be the fulcrums of a thoroughgoing effort to bar particular presuppositions from the field of ethics and fulfill the most general requirements of any theory of justice. Even if the original position is defined by a veil of ignorance conforming to the interpretation of justice as fairness, the constraints Rawls imposes upon his choice procedure seem to represent, as he himself suggests,[23] the limiting conditions for any conception of justice. Negatively speaking, the veil of ignorance insures that the principles of justice are decided upon by rational individuals who are compelled to make their choice independently of any accidental particulars about themselves and their society that would condition justice by contingent circumstances of no bearing upon ethics. Although this does not provide any positive direction to the theory of justice, Rawls adds additional guidelines that appear to capture the remaining desiderata for concepts of justice. As might be expected of any authoritative norms governing conduct in society, the principles to be chosen in the original position are to be general in content, universal in application, and publicly recognized as final.[24] The history of ethical thought only seems to corroborate Rawls' observation that these requirements are not peculiar to social contract theory, but indispensable for any reasoning about justice.[25]

Perhaps, then, Rawls can avert the common charge that his choice procedure is really predicated upon a deeper ethical theory, as Dworkin puts it,[26] requiring an entirely different justification than the contract argument can supply. This might be true if nothing else defined Rawls' choice procedure than the features just mentioned. However, the original position is marked by three other characteristics of signal importance. To begin with, the veil of ignorance extends not only to individuals' knowledge of their natural and social assets, but equally to knowledge of what they and others consider to be good.[27] Secondly, when these individuals choose the norms of justice, they employ rational prudence to arrive at principles advancing whatever ends may suit their preference.[28] Finally, they are all presumed to desire primary goods, which are defined to be resources necessary to fulfill personal goals of any sort.[29] The second feature follows from the first, insofar as ignorance of one's own and others' conception of the good leaves little else to be done but seek the promotion of ends in general. Similarly, the last feature follows from the second, since individuals guided by prudence in selecting principles furthering ends of any kind will also seek the resources necessary for achieving them. All three of these stipulations seem entirely in keeping with the general requirements of ethical theory. After all, if the theory of justice is to avoid assuming the principles it seeks to uncover and legitimate, its argument cannot proceed from any given privileged conception of the good. Accordingly, what else can the parties to the original position aim at but establishing norms that forward their ends, whatever they may turn out to be? Far from prejudicing his case, Rawls one more time seems to have hit upon the necessary conditions enabling the theory of justice to avoid begging its question.

In truth, however, the last three features of the original position are anything but general requirements of ethics. On the contrary, they represent particular assumptions peculiar to the social contract argument. Of course, this bodes no ill if social contract theory were the definitive theory of justice. As it turns out, these assumptions underline the weakness of the social contract argument, for they reflect a prior ethical commitment whose decisive role cannot be coherently justified.

Rawls may be right in excluding from his choice procedure all reference to given conceptions of the good. Yet, that exclusion is not equivalent to embracing rational prudence as the arbiter of ethical norms. It is one thing to take seriously the methodological imperative that ethics cannot take for granted its norms. It is something else entirely to confer the privilege of deciding the principles of justice upon the calculations of rational self-interest, constrained as these may be by the veil of ignorance. Only if reason cannot prescribe the good, leaving the ends of conduct without any rational hierarchy, does prudence win by default any chance of playing the role of privileged determiner of norms with which Rawls endows it. Nevertheless, Rawls considers it self-evident that justice consists in umpiring conflicting interests, where all deserve equal consideration. In so doing, he ignores that justice cannot become a problem of adjudicating differing opinions about the good, which is what interests here comprise, until ethical theory has abandoned as a vain undertaking the rational prescription of ends of conduct.

Consequently, Rawls' recourse to prudential calculation is predicated upon the basic move that gives liberal theory its point of departure. As we have seen, this consists in the repudiation of the appeal to privileged givens defining teleological ethics, an appeal represented by the latter's cardinal assumption that justice can only be ascertained by first conceiving a highest good from which all valid norms derive. Congruent with any move from privileged givens to a privileged determiner, Rawls' turn to pure procedural justice has meaning only if ethics can no longer prescribe what ends conduct should realize. Rawls himself admits as much, acknowledging that pure procedural justice, which aims at furnishing a procedure that is just regardless of what its result may be, is employable provided no independent criteria are available to mandate the valid outcome of a fair course of action.[30]

Given the breakdown of the appeal to privileged givens, which we have earlier documented, it might appear a mark in Rawls' favor that pure procedural justice follows the lead of liberal theory in proceeding from this rejection of teleological ethics. However, there is a further complication, which he shares with every social contract theorist. Although the denial of rationally prescribable ends removes the obvious obstacle to any appeal to prudence and its promotion of harmonized interests, it does not provide a positive ground for transforming ethics into a pure procedural theory. In order for rational self-interest to warrant the exclusive privilege of determining the principles of justice, the denial of teleological ethics must be supplemented by the affirmation of some alternative foundation that secures special standing to the role of prudence. For even if teleological values are ultimately groundless, recourse to rational self-interest would be just as arbitrary as submission to any prescribed end unless the appeal to prudence had an independent rationale. Of itself, the bankruptcy of the teleological appeal to privileged givens provides no compelling reason to embrace pure procedural justice.

What alone can supply the missing grounding is an affirmation of the normative primacy of liberty. If the freedom to choose and advance personal interests is accorded privileged validity, then the final arbiter of ethics will have to be a procedure giving the prudence of each individual an equal weight in determining the principles of conduct and the organization of just institutions. For once liberty is granted exclusive normative supremacy, so that all duties and obligations are recognized to derive from its privileged process of determining, then the pure procedural theory of social contract must be adopted. Otherwise, pure procedural justice remains an approach as arbitrary as any other. Consequently, when Rawls permits the principles of justice to be chosen by individuals deliberating under a veil of ignorance on the basis of rational self-interest, his strategy depends upon the same two assumptions underpinning all efforts of his liberal predecessors: the presuppositions that teleological ends cannot be rationally justified and that liberty alone has sovereign value.

This dependency extends to the second feature of the original position so important for the derivation of the principles of justice: the stipulation that individuals in the original position have a desire for primary goods and make that desire count in choosing the principles of justice. Given how the desire for primary goods is tied to the absence of any preferred interpretation of the good and the embrace of prudence, it should be no surprise that this desire, on which the difference principle directly rests, is not inherent in any discourse on justice, but specifically predicated upon the denial of teleological ethics and the promotion of liberty. The desire for primary goods can have no bearing upon justice unless reason is incapable of prescribing a highest good and liberty is granted exclusive legitimacy. Only when reason has left the ends of conduct to choice and justice is relegated to advancing the equal opportunity to pursue personal interests does the desire for primary goods warrant a guiding role. Then alone, where reason neither prescribes nor proscribes any goals of conduct and liberty has priority, does it make sense for all to desire the means for realizing ends of any sort and to agree to principles guaranteeing everyone as much primary goods as possible. If on the contrary, the realization of personal interests was secondary to achieving an antecedently prescribable good, the desire for primary goods would be shunted aside in deference to a preliminary determination by reason of which goals are worth pursuing, which means are thereby required, and which desires warrant satisfaction. Then there would no longer be any question of deriving the principles of justice as if what comes first is supplying everyone the means for achieving ends of any sort, so that personal interests can be promoted.

Therefore, Rawls' pure procedural justice can hardly lay claim to being pure in the sense of providing a method for determining principles of justice that makes no assumptions about the good. Far from providing a pure source for ethical norms, the Rawlsian choice procedure is just as dependent upon given stipulations as the traditional social contract. Like his liberal forebears, Rawls cannot set in motion his privileged determiner of justice without taking for granted the arbitrariness of teleological ends of conduct and the normative primacy of the right to liberty.

This undercuts the methodological privilege of pure procedural justice by grounding it upon normative theses that, as presuppositions of the original position, would require a different kind of argument for their own justification. Admittedly, it still remains possible that Rawls' theory could be supplemented by independent arguments justifying the denial of teleological ethics, legitimating the primacy of liberty, and thereby removing the dogmatism of these presuppositions. However, no such appeal to a "deeper theory" can save from collapse Rawls' derivation of the two principles of justice.

5.4.2 The Collapse of Rawls' Derivation of the Two Principles of Justice

With the choice procedure of the original position predicated upon the two above mentioned assumptions, the constructions of the principle of equal liberty and the difference principle are fatally undermined. Since the description of the original position depends upon a prior affirmation of the primacy of liberty, any procedural argument for the principle of equal liberty runs in circles, employing a framework containing its conclusion as the basis of the derivation. This circularity is apparent when Rawls argues that the principle of equal liberty is agreed upon by the parties in the original position because it provides the best guarantee that they can realize their interests and enjoy the self-respect that is a psychological prerequisite for achieving any goals.[31] Even if this were true, it would not alter the fact that these reasons are calculations of rational prudence that only warrant their deciding say if the right to equal liberty already counts as the paramount value.

It might appear that the derivation of the difference principle can escape these difficulties. For, as Alasdair MacIntyre has suggested, the difference principle seemingly rests on an appeal to the legitimacy of equality of need that is incommensurate with the appeal to entitlements entailed in the affirmation of liberty. Hence, Robert Nozick's objection that the difference principle's formula for regulating social inequality violates the property entitlements of individuals is off the mark, ignoring that considerations of liberty are not what are at stake.[32] Here, however, MacIntyre ignores the significance of the fact that the needs addressed by the difference principle are needs for primary goods. These needs warrant fair consideration, so that social inequalities be reduced in the interests of the least advantaged, not due to some independent entitlement, but precisely because liberty has primary value. As we have seen, only if the right to liberty is already acknowledged as the positive counterpart of the rejection of teleological values, can the desire for primary goods play any role in determining principles of justice. Then alone is it imperative to furnish everyone with as equal access to primary goods as possible, since these goods are the means for realizing interests of any sort and the primacy of liberty makes justice center around promoting the harmonious fulfillment of personal ends. Yet, if the difference principle is predicated upon the desire for primary goods, which itself presupposes the right to liberty, the choice procedure of the original position cannot establish the difference principle without once again taking for granted the key foundation of its deliberations. In sum, since the difference principle ultimately rests upon the principle of equal liberty, and pure procedural justice cannot justify the latter, the derivation of both principles of justice collapses.

This problem applies equally to Rawls' justification of the difference principle's toleration of inequalities that promote the welfare of the least advantaged group of society. Rawls' account of how a certain level of social inequality can be to the benefit of the least advantaged seems to presuppose markets as the background condition permitting incentives to channel resources in a beneficial manner. For unless individuals are at liberty to choose their occupation and how to invest their assets, while equally requiring goods from others to satisfy their own needs, incentives cannot function as aids to fair distribution of primary goods. If this is true, then the difference principle presupposes the existence of markets. Yet if markets are contingent social arrangements, rather than necessary features of social life, as history and anthropology testify, the difference principle forfeits its status as a universally valid norm of justice unless markets

have an independent normative validity. Given Rawls' choice procedure, the only remaining resource for justifying markets would be
the principle of equal liberty, which could conceivably be employed
insofar as markets give individuals the freedom to choose their occupations and the goods they wish to acquire. However, even if markets
are institutions of freedom, appeal to the principle of equal liberty is
of no avail when pure procedural justice is incapable of justifying that
principle without begging the question. Hence, Rawls is left with no
means of deriving the difference principle's toleration of inequality.

5.4.3 The Incoherence of the Move to the Original Position

These difficulties reflect the root dilemma afflicting pure procedural justice, a dilemma that stands in relief the moment recourse
is made to the original position. This dilemma involves not just the
dependent character of the description of the choice procedure. It fundamentally applies to the very right of that choice procedure to play
its foundational role.

For even if the original position were characterized without any
ethical presuppositions and the two principles of justice followed consistently from it, an account would still be required to legitimate its
unique stature as the source of ethical norms. Why should its choice
procedure enjoy the exclusive right to decide the principles of justice?
What gives common agreements grounded in rational self-interest any
authority to mandate the anatomy of just laws and institutions? And
why should agreements reached under the veil of ignorance have
authority in situations where individuals are fully aware of their own
endowments, social position and conceptions of the good?

These questions parallel those that Hume, Bentham, and more
recently H.L.A. Hart have raised to cast doubt upon the authority of
the traditional social contract. The social contract can have no binding
force unless it is already an established principle that contracts should
be honored. However, if such a rule already has normative validity,
the social contract loses its privileged role as the source of ethical
norms. Yet, without such a preestablished rule, the provisions of the
social contract have no legitimacy of their own.

The choice procedure of the original position is in the same
embarrassing predicament. To be true to its character as the privileged
determiner of ethical principles, it cannot possess its special authority
in virtue of any antecedently given norms. For if any aspect of the
original position were predicated upon an independent ethical term,
the defining Archimedean character of its standpoint would be con-

tradicted. However, the move to the original position cannot be justified by its own choice procedure, for that would take for granted its authority when that is precisely what is in question. Either way, Rawlsian theory stands at an impasse, unable to justify the primacy of its privileged procedure.

The underlying problem, which is the common stumbling block of social contract theory and procedural ethics generally, resides in the same logical difficulty which we saw undermining the transcendental turn. Just as the appeal to conditions of knowledge rendered unaccountable both the description and privileged role of the alleged transcendental condition, so the turn to a privileged determiner of ethical norms precludes any coherent justification of either its characterization or its exclusive status as the source of ethical principles. It makes no more difference whether the privileged determiner be described as a covenant among free and equal individuals inhabiting a state of nature, the exercise of practical reason by noumenal selves, or the choice procedure of self-interested individuals subjected to a veil of ignorance, than whether the transcendental conditions of knowledge be described as the structure of consciousness, the practices of a linguistic community, or the hermeneutic self-reflection of the inhabitants of a common tradition. In every case, there is an unbridgeable discrepancy between the terms of normative validity and the status of the privileged determiner. The logic of the appeal to a privileged determiner makes this inevitable. The moment the turn is made to a privileged determiner, normative validity becomes identified with being determined by that determiner. Yet, because, by definition, the privileged determiner has its own character prior to its act of determination, neither its description nor its exclusive status can possibly conform to the standard of validity it establishes.

Hence, when Robert Nozick observes that any theory grounding norms in a privileged process begins with something that is not itself justified by being the outcome of that process,[33] he has hit upon the Achilles' heel of both Rawls' rehabilitation of social contract theory, and the liberal principles Nozick himself defends.

Admittedly, Rawls might seem untroubled by the logical impossibility of legitimating the pure procedural approach. After all, his professed aim is simply to present a theory of justice carrying through a "reflective equilibrium," clarifying how our given moral assumptions can be made to cohere with our intuitions and considered judgments about social and political justice. In this respect, Rawls abandons the Kantian quest for an ethics of categorical imperatives and settles for a construction of hypothetical norms relative to our shared views. Yet, if the "reflective equilibrium" of *A Theory of Justice* is to confirm our considered judgments about justice, guide us in those gray areas where these judgments are incomplete or insecure, and lead us to revise our ethical intuitions, as Rawls also maintains,[34] how can it do so without freeing itself of its bondage to given opinion and justifying the Archimedean aspirations of the original position?

Merely constructing a coherent system of moral sentiments is insufficient. It can neither exclude the possibility of other competing coherent systems nor establish that ethical theory has no other alternative to resigning itself to the doxology of coherence. And even if these problems could be solved, there would still be no defense against the nihilist objection that our ultimate entrapment within a unique framework of coherent ethical claims is no compelling reason to accept its authority. As Dworkin asks,[35] how can Rawls' derivation of the principles of justice not just conform but lend support to our ethical judgments if it fails to ground itself? As we have seen, pure procedural justice is incapable of achieving this fulfillment of social contract theory. As such, it is equally unable to satisfy the critical demands of Rawls' own reflective equilibrium. On neither count can Rawls succeed in making the appeal to a privileged determiner a viable strategy for ethics.

Part III

Freedom from Foundations and the Validity of Self-Determination

Chapter 6

Self-determination and Systematic Philosophy

6.1 The Perplexity of Abandoning the Appeal to Privileged Givens and Privileged Determiners

The difficulties derailing the attempts to ground truth and justice in the determination of a privileged determiner hardly come unexpected when viewed in light of the problems undermining the metaphysical project of rooting justification in some privileged given. Although transcendental philosophy and the corollary theories of liberty and practical reason make appeal to their respective privileged determiners in order to avoid the foundationalism of metaphysics, their recourse to a given determiner involves the same error of making immediate reference to a given content and asserting it as the foundation of truth or justice. Precisely because a determiner of determined determinacy has a given character antecedent to its act of determination, it remains burdened with a givenness of its own. Therefore no determiner, not some transcendental condition of knowledge, nor a will endowed with liberty, nor the autonomy of practical reason, can be made the ground of truth or justice without reinstating the arbitrary appeal to some privileged given.

Although the underlying dilemma is pointedly simple, it is hard to fathom how the quests for truth and justice can overcome it and

118

proceed any further. The challenges of scepticism and nihilism loom very large indeed.

In face of the relative character of positive science and the failures of metaphysics and transcendental philosophy, the quest for truth seems to have nothing to go on but a purely negative proscription. The experience of metaphysical and transcendental inquiries appears to teach but one lesson: that the search for truth cannot begin with any immediate truth claims either concerning reality or knowing. No appeal can be permitted to any privileged given or privileged determiner to establish what is, for that would involve immediate reference to their own privileged reality and thus take for granted both the adequacy of knowing and the content of what is given. Similarly, philosophy must not rely on either given or determined determinacy to supply reason with its order and validity, for if it does, it bases its own method on an assumed foundation, foregoing all opportunity to be presuppositionless and self-grounding. So long as reasoning is stamped with any residue of givenness it stands conditioned by a content taken for granted, depriving it of the unconditioned universality it needs to provide justification and transform opinion into truth.

Yet how can philosophy proceed at all without reverting to the strategems of positive science, metaphysics, and transcendental argument? In view of the encompassing character of these three failed approaches, it would be difficult not to embrace some form of scepticism in weary resignation. If philosophy is not to stipulate any content, nor make any immediate reference to what is, nor finally determine objectivity in terms of some conception of knowing, what is left but nothing at all?

The plight of the quest for justice appears no more sanguine. If there can be neither a valid good, comprising the given form of conduct prescribed by reason, nor a valid determiner, whose determining provides legitimacy, where can justice lie? To the extent that both these options base justice in some privileged given, be it the rational form of virtue, the liberty of the natural will, or the autonomy of practical reason, they each provide justice with a foundation allowing talk of there being natural right, counterpoised to the arbitrary products of convention. If, however, all appeal to privileged givens be precluded, it appears that the only resource left the quest for justice is convention. Yet how can convention spawn anything but one equally unjustifiable creation after another if justice has no fixed nature that can serve as a prior standard of legitimacy? With the collapse of all natural right, there seems to be no defense before the onslaught of nihilism.

6.1.1 The Futile Route of Holism

In recent years the program of theoretical and practical holism has been winning adherents as a solution to the foundational dilemmas of metaphysics and transcendental argument. Advanced in different versions by such thinkers as Hans-Georg Gadamer,[1] Alasdair MacIntyre,[2] Richard Rorty,[3] and Hilary Putnam,[4] the holist strategy seeks to cure philosophy of its longing to know what is true and what is just. Holism takes on this endeavor after reflecting upon the failures of metaphysics and transcendental argument, and judging that their recourse to privileged givens and privileged determiners exhausts the possibilities for philosophical justification. Since neither metaphysics nor transcendental argument can ever succeed in eliminating the arbitrariness of their chosen foundations, holism offers what it considers to be the sobering conclusion that all truth claims and ethical prescriptions rest upon pragmatic decisions that stipulate norms for justification. Without the prior adoption of such assumed standards, no "rational" evaluation is possible. However, once some such norms be accepted as an agreed-upon practice by those in conversation and community, they provide the commensurable framework first permitting any meaningful argument and ethical judgment.

The pragmatic decisions so underlying all theoretical and practical justification may already be enshrined in the normal discourse of a shared culture and tradition, or they may frame a new paradigm of science challenging the old. Whatever the case, holism argues, claims of objectivity always ultimately rest in agreement on some favored conceptual scheme rather than in any accurate mirroring of nature or in the constituting activity of a transcendental condition. With all questions of justification so rooted in arbitrary acceptance, discourse is rendered an open-ended conversation where no terms have any privilege beyond what agreed practice confers on them. Accordingly, the holist reasons, philosophy must abandon all attempt to be presuppositionless and self-grounding, and humbly restrict itself to interpreting and contrasting the different conventions of discourse, without imposing any preferred set of terms of its own. Instead of seeking true knowledge of reason, reality, and justice, philosophy can only resign itself to fostering a self-conscious awareness of the practices through which objectivity and ethics are construed by one framework or another.

In limiting philosophy to such edification, the holist presumes not only to have unmasked the pitfalls of all direct reference to either reality or transcendental conditions, but to have avoided those errors in his own discourse. However, precisely by supplanting the quests for truth and justice with edifying deconstructions of the conceptual schemes underlying any given theory, holism hardly advances its own pragmatic characterization of knowing as a mere matter of agreement, just as arbitrary as any other description. On the contrary, holism asserts it juridically as the conception that correctly represents the universal predicament of rational discourse and that accordingly is qualified to preclude the legitimacy of any systematic philosophy seeking knowledge of truth and justice. In so doing, holism ends up making a metaphysical claim of its own about the reality of conversation, namely, that that reality is accurately mirrored by the holist description of discourse. Then, holism just as soon reverts to transcendental foundationalism by treating this putative reality of conversation as the ultimate context in which justifications are constituted. In this way, holism's affirmation of the exclusive universality of its pragmatic description of discourse renders the latter a preferred set of terms. As a result, the holist reduction of philosophy to edification ends up reinstating the very same dilemmas of foundational argument it properly seeks to overcome. Instead of providing an alternative to the problems of metaphysical and transcendental theories, holism thus offers but one more example of their fatal recourse to privileged givens and privileged determiners.

6.2 *Indeterminacy, Self-Determination, and Freedom From Foundations*

How then can the quests for truth and justice go forward without falling into the foundational dilemmas that give scepticism and nihilism their most effective ammunition?

Strange as it may sound, if there is anything that can lead to a true determination of reason, reality, or justice, it is nothing: nothing that is stipulated, nothing that is real in itself, nothing that can be claimed about knowing, nothing that is either a privileged given or a privileged determiner. The travails of positive science, metaphysics and transcendental philosophy leave this one alternative, an alternative of simply considering the utter indeterminacy that is left when all stipulation is ruled out and all immediate truth claims about reality and knowing have shown their bankruptcy and been discarded. To forego metaphysical and transcendental arguments and dispense with all foundations whatsoever, philosophy has no choice but to take this novel route of beginning without any specific preferred set of terms regarding either the method or subject matter of its inquiry. Only if it begins with indeterminacy, that is, the total exclusion of all assumed topics and procedures, can the quest for truth enjoy the presuppositionlessness from which a genuinely self-grounding, unconditioned argument could ensue.

As it turns out, eliminating the dilemmas of foundationalism by starting with indeterminacy amounts to the very same thing as supplanting the recourse to privileged givens and privileged determiners with the exposition of self-determined determinacy. How beginning with indeterminacy is identical to beginning with self-determined determinacy, how both further supply the unconditioned universality justification requires, and how both finally provide the quests for truth and justice with the sole approach able to defeat the challenges of scepticism and nihilism — all become apparent no matter whether indeterminacy or self-determined determinacy is first addressed.

6.2.1 Self-Determination as Immanent Development from Indeterminacy

Why recourse to self-determined determinacy, or, in other words, self-determination, should be the proper alternative to all appeals to privileged givens and privileged determiners is something already manifest from the central dilemma of the transcendental turn. As preceding discussion has shown, the only way transcendental argument can avoid dogmatically describing the conditions of knowing is by becoming self-determining, such that knowing does its own critique, rendering the conditions of knowing identical with the objective knowledge they determine. Transcendental argument, however, cannot do so without canceling itself, for once it becomes self-critical, equalizing the knowing performing transcendental investigation with the knowing under critique, and determining the transcendental structure according to the very strictures it prescribes for objective knowledge, what gets immediately eliminated is the givenness of the transcendental conditions, the givenness that alone allows them to be what they are, namely, the antecedent determiners of objectivity. What this suggests is that the logic of objectivity must be conceived as self-determined determinacy if dogmatism is to be avoided, and that this can be achieved only when reason has neither any privileged given nor determiner at its root.

In this sense, the impetus for taking up self-determined determinacy is wedded to the endeavor to work out a logic with no primitive terms or principles. Indeed, the connection is so radical that it augurs nothing less than that presuppositionlessness, self-grounding, and unconditioned universality all consist in self-determination. This may appear to be a very bizarre equation, since developing self-determined determinacy or self-determination as a candidate for all that normative validity involves is a novel if not unheard of strategy in face of the traditional alternatives of foundationalism and scepticism. Nevertheless, its plausibility beckons once self-determination is examined in light of these qualities that reason must possess to justify its own special role in seeking truth, that objectivity must bear in order not to rest upon arbitrary foundations, and that justice must enjoy so as to have its constitutive legitimacy.

That self-determination not just enjoys, but is identical to presuppositionlessness is evident to the extent that what is neither given nor determined, but self-determined, rests on nothing antecedent to itself. Although self-determination gives itself determinacy simply to be what it is, it contains no element of givenness whatsoever. Unlike a determiner such as some transcendental condition or the choosing will, self-determination has no predetermined nature, for it possesses neither any content nor form until it has proceeded to determine itself. If, on the contrary, self-determination had any given character, it would be characterized by something it had not given itself and cease to be self-determined determinacy. For this reason, self-determination involves a freedom from givenness so radical that it can only be conceived to issue from nothing at all. This means that self-determination must begin from sheer indeterminacy. After all, if self-determination were not at the start utterly indeterminate, it would be burdened with givenness of some sort or other. Then self-determination would rest on a foundation that it has not determined, leaving it dependent rather than free.

Similarly, self-determined determinacy is totally self-grounding, or, more accurately, identical to self-grounding. Because whatever form or content self-determined determinacy has is a product of its own self-determination, it might be said to possess the quality of being self-grounding. However, this is not its nature, in the sense of a given character, for that would violate the indeterminacy from which self-determination presuppositionlessly unfolds. Rather, the self-grounding "character" of self-determination is something it becomes as a result of its own process, which determines itself to be nothing other than the process of self-grounding.

How this is entailed is readily apparent. Precisely because self-determination proceeds from nothing and generates its own order and substance without reliance on anything else, all its features rest upon what it has determined itself to be, which is, of course, self-determined determinacy. Accordingly, what self-determination actually is can only be had at the conclusion of its own process of determination. Until then, the "content" of self-determined determinacy is not yet at hand for the simple reason that the self-determination remains incomplete, still engaged as it is in bringing into being its own integral self. Conversely, the "form" or, if one will, the "logic" of its determining is equally unspecifiable before the conclusion of self-determination. This is because the ordering principle of the content of self-determined determinacy is none other than what has here given itself its own determination, namely the resultant subject of the whole process: self-determination itself. If anything else provided order for the sequence of determinacies following from indeterminacy, there would no longer be the self-ordered development that self-determination signifies.

Indeed, to speak of self-determination having a "form" and "content" is really inappropriate inasmuch as neither aspect can actually be distinguished from the other. The content of self-determination consists in nothing but its own self-ordering, whereas its form is this very same self-ordering content. If, on the contrary, form and content fell asunder, the ordering would be distinct from what it orders, rendering the ordered content a determined, rather than self-determined content, while leaving the ordering form a determiner of something other than itself. As a result, if there is to be any talk of form and content in reference to self-determination, it must be understood that here, as with indeterminacy, form and content are one and the same.

As for self-determination possessing, or properly speaking, comprising unconditioned universality, this is something part and parcel of its freedom from foundations. Although self-determination gives itself a determinate content, what is particular about it is neither limited with regard to any given circumstance nor relative to anything other than itself. The determinacy of self-determination therefore instantiates only itself, just as its unity, the "self" of self-determination, has its own identity exclusively by being the abiding subject that is at work constituting itself in all its determinations. On both these counts, self-determination exhibits the particularization of a universal that is independent of all external givens. This universal, which stands free of all conditions, is the unity or common self of self-determination whose being consists in incorporating each of its particular determinations within its own unitary self-determination.

As such, the unity of self-determination has a very unique relation to the particular content of which it is the "self." It is universal with regard to each and every one of its own determinacies insofar as the latter are nothing but its complete and exclusive instantiation. Moreover, the self-identical subject of self-determination has a universality indistinguishable from its particular content, for it comprises the latter's unity by being the very same self-determined determinacy in which that content consists. Accordingly, self-determination's universality is a concrete universality, containing its particularization within its unity, just as its particularization is a universal particularity, containing the very process of self-determination that it instantiates.

If this interpenetration of universal and particular expresses the same inseparability of form and content that renders each something unconditioned by any extrinsic factors, it also introduces a further term to the equation of self-determination, presuppositionlessness, self-grounding, and unconditioned universality. This is individuality. It enters in to the extent that individuality consists in that same unification of universal and particular where the uniqueness of its particular content comprises the self-same general identity of the individual. In that event, the unconditioned universality of self-determination exhibits the structure of individuality. Furthermore, since the determinacy of self-determination involves nothing other than its unconditioned universality, it would be better to say that self-determination is individuality itself.

However plausible be the conjunction of all these features, it might well be objected that self-determined determinacy can be considered the proper candidate for presuppositionlessness, self-grounding, and unconditioned universality, and thereby the bearer of normative validity, only insofar as one presupposes what self-determination is, not to mention what counts as justification in the quest for truth. It turns out, however, that if all assumptions be excluded, all privileged givens and determiners be discarded, and all metaphysical and transcendental arguments be foresworn, what results is self-determination and with it, everything that justification seems to require.

6.2.2 *The Advance from Indeterminacy as Self-Determination*

That the exclusion of all presuppositions should resolve itself into a self-exposition of self-determination seems a most unlikely prospect at first glance. If to begin without any assumptions is to begin with nothing at all, this means proceeding with just indeterminacy, rather than something so richly defined as self-determined determinacy. After all, nothing but this very indeterminacy can possibly remain when ontological and epistemological truth claims are given up as untenable starting points for philosophical inquiry. With their abandonment in wake of the foundational dilemmas of metaphysics and transcendental argument, what is left is an absence of all reference and referent and not any reality or knowledge. Since there is no stipulated content, nor anything in itself, nor any specification of knowing, their exclusion results in an indeterminacy with no internal distinctions, no relation to anything else, and no quality of any kind. Otherwise a specific determinacy would lie at hand, which, coming as it does at the start, would amount to an assumption.

Therefore, the indeterminacy in question does not comprise indeterminacy *in res* or a category of some knowing, but unanalyzable, undifferentiated, uncontrasted indeterminacy about which nothing specific can be said. In contrast to the indeterminacy of being to which metaphysics traditionally refers, this indeterminacy has no ontological status, nor any status as a primitive term that either obtains further determination through other terms or provides the privileged principle for their specification. It can play no such foundational role, for it would cease to be indeterminate if it were further qualified as a foundation of something else, be it epistemically as a category of thought or ontologically as the totality of all that is. Even if one were to take indeterminacy to be merely indeterminate reality, as being qua being, this would still involve more than just indeterminacy due to the added reference to the real. Only when all such extraneous qualification is strictly avoided, is indeterminacy at issue. What allows its consideration to escape the pitfalls of positive science, metaphysics and transcendental philosophy is precisely the utter indefiniteness it involves, an indefiniteness that simply can contain no stipulated content or claims about reality or knowing.

Nevertheless, it is tempting to object that any attempt to begin philosophy's quest for truth with indeterminacy only reintroduces foundationalism under a new, if very vague, guise. Does not beginning with indeterminacy amount to stipulating it to the exclusion of other terms and thereby presuppose that the category of indeterminacy is the privileged starting point of philosophical investigation? What this objection fails to recognize is that indeterminacy is not the same thing as stipulated indeterminacy. Considering indeterminacy by suspending all claims concerning method and subject matter is not identical to considering indeterminacy taken as the immediate given addressed by the quest for truth. If one were to begin with stipulated indeterminacy, and view it as such, what would lie at hand would be a knower's stipulation of indeterminacy as what is immediately given for true knowing.[5] Such a beginning cannot qualify as the starting point of philosophy, for it instead comprises the most elementary shape of a cognition whose knowing remains burdened by reference to some content in itself that it posits as the given standard of its knowledge. By contrast, indeterminacy in its own right involves no stipulated content, nor any assumption concerning its relation to philosophy or reality. If it contained any such further relations, its own indeterminacy would be violated. For this reason, beginning with indeterminacy does not involve beginning with any notion of how indeterminacy comprises the first topic of philosophy, nor any notion of how indeterminacy is a beginning at all. If indeterminacy is genuinely all that lies at hand, one simply cannot speak of philosophy or of any other specific topic in any valid way. In order for all assumptions to be precluded, the point at which philosophy begins must involve no preconceptions of what it is a beginning of, no indication that it is a commencement, nor any given whatsoever. At its start, philosophy can only be an empty word, which is precisely why indeterminacy is all with which the quest for truth can begin.[6]

Once this total poverty of content is taken seriously, it is not hard to anticipate how any development from indeterminacy would comprise self-determination. If anything were to follow from indeterminacy without illicit introduction of any independently given terms or given procedures of determination, it would have to arise out of indeterminacy in a completely self-generated way. Since nothing else would be available to give it character, what it consists of would have to be self-determined. Yet, because it would not be the self-determination of any given substrate, but a self-determination issuing from indeterminacy, incorporating nothing to start with and obtaining nothing extraneous along the way, it would have to be self-determination without any further qualification. In that case, what follows from indeterminacy would possess the radically self-grounding, unconditionally universal and individual character already indicated through the analysis of self-determination per se.

Of course, even if the only thing that could arise from indeterminacy were self-determination, this would not guarantee that anything can in fact follow from it and it alone. The very indefiniteness of indeterminacy would seem to render it a dead end for all inquiry since it appears inexplicable how anything could arise from it. Because indeterminacy can only be addressed if nothing else be admitted, any further determination would have to emerge from it alone, independently of any outside reference, be it to some given method or given content. Otherwise the foundational problems afflicting metaphysical reference and transcendental constitution would be reintroduced. Yet, since indeterminacy lacks all quality, difference, and relation just to be what it is, it cannot be a ground or cause or determiner of anything, any more than it can give rise to something whose own character involves relation or difference to something determinate. Consequently, it appears that there can be no reason for anything to follow from indeterminacy. Moreover, even if anything did follow without reason, it could not have any determinate character, so long as indeterminacy remained the sole resource at hand.

The most cursory examination of indeterminacy thus seems to suggest that despite the ensuing dilemmas of foundationalism, discourse must begin with privileged givens and a privileged determiner if it is to have any content whatsoever. It is therefore hard to refrain from objecting that any attempt to begin the quest for truth from a presuppositionless starting point really invites theoretical anarchy, and that without given premises and arbitrary stipulations nothing at all could ever possibly result.

Certainly in order to meet this objection in a completely satisfactory way it is ultimately necessary to show how something, namely self-determination, does follow from indeterminacy without appeal to any extraneous factors. Yet, before addressing this task, it is worth pointing out that proceeding from indeterminacy by developing self-determination need not, and indeed, could not amount to conceptual chaos. To forego all assumptions regarding methodology and subject matter is not equivalent to giving free reign to the arbitrariness of the theorist. Allowing either method or content to be decided by the unguided caprice of the latter would hardly be congruent with presuppositionless inquiry and the development of self-determination. It would rather result in a science issuing from a privileged determiner, being none other than the theoretical anarchist who here determines what to investigate and how to proceed. Instead of consisting in a development of self-determined determinacy, this science would present a determined subject matter owing its form and content to the arbitrary stipulating performed by its author. Beginning the quest for truth with nothing but indeterminacy would thus have to comprise a theory of a very different character from that which relies on the given theorizer to determine its subject matter and order.

Nevertheless, even if this is so and the dilemmas of basing the quest for truth upon any given are patent enough, it is still difficult to imagine how a development of self-determination issuing from indeterminacy would not either collapse into nothing due to the absence of any foundation to support it, or involve an utterly accidental, open-ended series of determinacies.

Why these alternatives do not apply becomes understandable once due note is taken of how what determines itself from indeterminacy could only be manifest at the conclusion of the development. This is because only at its own completion would the self-determination have fully determined its subject, which is none other than itself in its entirety. Therefore indeterminacy would not be the substrate of development, ever acquiring new content for itself in the manner of the omnipresent being presupposed by fundamental ontology. On the contrary, indeterminacy would not even stand as the beginning of what finally results until the very conclusion of the entire development. Then alone would what indeterminacy is a beginning of first come into view.

What this signifies is that the development of self-determined determinacy does have a non-collapsing structure, even though it has no foundation. What gives it its unique character, is that its structure is not immediately given, but entirely produced through the mediation of its own self-determination. This structure is no more accidental than arbitrary, for it does not issue from the happenstance of any externally given circumstances any more than from the arbitrariness of any given determiner. Precisely by being a self-determination starting from nothing, it is subject to no given conditions, no matter whether they take the form of arbitrary orderings or external accident.

By the same token, the self-development of self-determined determinacy could not be open-ended. If self-determination is to have unity, that unity must be self-imposed as part and parcel of self-determination's very own identity. Otherwise its integrality would depend upon something else, robbing it of the wholly self-determined character by which it defines itself. Consequently, what self-determined determinacy determines itself to be necessarily provides closure for its development from indeterminacy. It does so by giving the development its unity as self-determination, something that can only occur when the development has come to a definite end and produced that self-determined unity as its conclusion.

If this suggests that presuppositionlessness and self-determination are not synonymous with conceptual anarchy, it is nonetheless true that there can be no positive criteria with which to judge whether a particular candidate for the development from indeterminacy has had its putatively foundation-free self-grounding subject matter properly presented. Any application of positive criteria must be barred because it would involve appeal to standards of method and content that would not be generated within what is to be judged, but instead be independently given. Such criteria could have no validity, for by the very fact that they are not elements of the self-determination from indeterminacy which presuppositionlessness could alone entail, they would either have to be assumptions themselves, or rest upon other unwarranted premises.

That there can be no positive criteria for judging philosophy's move beyond the starting point of indeterminacy to develop self-determination does not rob it of necessity and leave it unsusceptible of critical validation. Far from ushering in mute observation of a blind advance, the absence of prior criteria is just what allows for theoretical necessity in the first place. After all, the reason why all criterialogical knowing falls victim to sceptical challenge is precisely that it commits the fallacy of evaluating truth on the basis of given criteria, which, as such, must lie outside the purview of truth as unexaminable assumptions. This predicament itself prescribes a purely negative way for evaluating the philosophical rigor of a candidate for the presuppositionless development of self-determination from indeterminacy. Since all appeal to criteria must be excluded, the necessity of development can be certified by making sure that none enter into its unfolding. So long as examination shows that not one of the development's determinations owes its character or order of presentation to introductions of extraneously given material or the stipulating of an extraneous determiner, the development can be said to exhibit the radically independent immanence that alone can signal its freedom from arbitrary direction and dogmatic foundations.

Admittedly, as much as these points suggest how self-determined determinacy could be developed presuppositionlessly without succumbing to theoretical anarchy, they do not themselves indicate how the quest for truth can move beyond indeterminacy to something determinate. The presuppositionlessness of indeterminacy may be as unchallengeable as its role as the starting point of philosophy and of the development of self-determination, but the question of how and why there should be determinacy is not yet answered. Nevertheless, that question can only be asked by foundation-free philosophy since any theorizing that operates with given determinacy takes determinacy for granted. Thus no metaphysical or transcendental philosophy can account for this most common and basic of assumptions, which, so long as it is assumed, seals the dogmatism of the discourse in which it figures. The stakes could not be higher. If no answer can be given to the problem of how and why there is determinacy, indeterminacy will remain a dead end for philosophical investigation, leaving little option but to choose between scepticism and faith.

6.3 Moving from Indeterminacy to Determinacy without Foundations

A plausible resolution to this problem is provided by Hegel in the opening sections of his *Science of Logic*, a work that still today represents the only comprehensive attempt to conceive a presuppositionless, self-grounding development of categories consisting in the presentation of self-determined determinacy. Although interpreters starting with Schelling, Marx and Kierkegaard have judged and dismissed Hegel as the last great metaphysical system-builder who conceives reality as it is in itself from an absolute standpoint of subject-object identity, there is a central, if neglected current in Hegel's thought that attempts to forego metaphysical and transcendental arguments and instead begin philosophy without any favored conceptual schemes whatsoever. This radically anti-foundational course is given its inauguration in the discussion of being, nothing, and becoming with which Hegel opens his *Science of Logic*. Although Hegel here and elsewhere makes many a remark that can be taken metaphysically in accord with prevailing interpretations, he nevertheless presents the basic outline of an account of determinacy that takes no determinacy for granted.

Hegel's use of "being" as a term for indeterminacy has led many to presume that the development at hand has an ontological character, where being receives further determination as the substrate of the totality of existence, such that the logic proceeding from being is a metaphysical ontology presupposing the correspondence between thought and reality. That Hegel's usage of "being" has no such metaphysical significance, but rather denotes the utter indeterminacy resulting from the exclusion of all foundations, has been argued elsewhere, and need not be dealt with here.[7] What is relevant to the problem here at issue is simply the non-metaphysical account of determinacy that can be distilled from Hegel's argument. The solution suggested by his treatment of being, nothing, and becoming offers the following line of argument.

First, it must be remembered that the fatal bane of metaphysical and transcendental philosophies amounts to their failure to account for determinacy. This failure is expressed in their generic basing of argument in some given content, whose determinacy provides a foundation the veracity of which is presupposed rather than established. Their examples have demonstrated the obvious point that philosophy cannot be fully self-responsible if it takes any determinacy for granted. In so doing they have equally suggested that accounting for determinacy is unavoidably the first problem philosophy must address. That this is so need not be based on any preconception concerning the subject matter or method of philosophy. Accounting for determinacy requires abandoning all preconceptions precisely because reliance upon any given term automatically begs the question. It does so by employing a determinacy when the very right to appeal to determinacy is precisely what is at issue. For this reason, no foundational theory can possibly address the question of determinacy. On the contrary, an account of determinacy must somehow be provided without reference to any determinate content. There is no choice but to begin with indeterminacy, the same absence of givenness providing the only alternative to succumbing to foundationalism or abandoning philosophy.

Yet, a development of something determinate from indeterminacy cannot be caused or grounded nor have any reason behind it whatsoever. To search for one would amount to imputing to indeterminacy the very definite character of being a determining principle. That would, of course, violate the constitutive nothingness of indeterminacy and reintroduce an element of givenness, namely the ascribed character of being a given principle, something that would preclude presuppositionlessness and reinstate the dilemmas of foundationalism. What this means is that if anything were to develop from indeterminacy, it would have to arise utterly immediately without any basis for doing so. Since there would literally be nothing determinate underlying it to serve as a mediating reason, whatever followed would have to do so completely groundlessly.

Accordingly, the only answer that can be given to the question, "Why is there determinacy?", is that there is and can be no reason. This is simply because any attempt to provide one presupposes determinacy by treating indeterminacy as if it were already a definite determiner, determining the determinacy following from it. All that can be offered instead is an account of how indeterminacy gives rise to something else.

With respect to this question, it is clear from the outset that what follows from indeterminacy must do so immediately, that is, without reason, and without being determined by anything. Otherwise, it bears repeating, what develops would follow from something that is no longer indeterminate.

By the same token, what issues from indeterminacy must not just be uncaused, ungrounded and undetermined in any way, but must equally be whatever it is without containing any element of givenness or involving contrast to anything determinate. Since all reference to internal or external terms would have no basis in indeterminacy, they could only be present through some illicit introduction.

Thus, if anything were to develop from indeterminacy it could only do so in an utterly groundless fashion and be just as uncontrasted, undifferentiated, and unmediated as indeterminacy itself. In other words, the only thing that could follow from indeterminacy without appeal to some given or given determiner is nothing, whereas nothing could only arise from indeterminacy immediately. This most meager possibility does not signify that there can be no non-foundational development from indeterminacy. Instead, it offers the very terms of advance, indicating that nothing does arise from indeterminacy without any ground at all. Rather than precluding further development, the indeterminacy with which foundation-free philosophy must begin allows as its only possible successor a second indistinguishable indeterminacy that follows without any cause or reason. When Hegel moves from "being" to "nothing" in his *Science of Logic*, he is presenting just this groundless passage from indeterminacy to an indistinguishable nothingness.

Admittedly, the groundless presence of nothing can hardly signify an emergence of determinacy when nothing is just as unmediated and indeterminate as the indeterminacy that it succeeds. Although nothing could be said to comprise a "second" category, it has no determinate standing opposite indeterminacy (or "being," as Hegel calls it). Since nothing lacks all quality just as much as does being, it cannot coexist beside the latter as a distinct entity. For this reason, it well appears that the purported advance to "nothing" is really not any development, but merely an arbitrary reiteration of the very same emptiness with which one "began." Indeed, to claim that any beginning has been made with being seems nonsensical, for if all that can "follow" is an indeterminacy indistinguishable from being, the supposed move to nothing is no move at all, but a perennial braying of the same vacant term.

What these objections ignore is that the "nothing" that alone can follow immediately from being must be both indistinguishable from being and immediately different. It must be immediately different, for only then can it figure as a second indeterminacy. Yet it cannot contain any quality distinguishing it from being, for then it would introduce determinacy before determinacy has been legitimately established. How nothing can figure in both these capacities must therefore lie neither in itsélf nor in being, but elsewhere, and the only place available to look is the very succession of being and nothing. This succession is immediately at hand the moment nothing is articulated, without any intervening reason or support, as a second indeterminacy. Entitled "becoming" by Hegel, this succession is what makes intelligible how being does entail something more than itself and the sheer indeterminacy from which it cannot be distinguished.

This can and must be seen by restricting attention to what little indeterminacy and nothing offer by themselves. As pointed out earlier, since nothing cannot be differentiated from what is indeterminate, the two cannot coexist in distinction from one another. Rather, nothing immediately passes over into indeterminacy, or, to be more precise, nothing is at once indeterminacy without any passage at all, for it is immediately the same absence of all determinacy that indeterminacy comprises. For its part, indeterminacy no less "passes over" into nothing with no transition at all, insofar as it is utterly identical to the nothingness that alone can immediately follow from indeterminacy without further foundation. In its entirety, then, the groundless succession of nothing from indeterminacy involves at one and the same time the immediate transitions of indeterminacy into nothing and nothing into indeterminacy (or, to use Hegel's terms, of being into nothing and nothing into being), within which each is groundlessly identical and different from the other.

Although each term cancels its difference from the other by immediately becoming what the other is, this same process of becoming contains the dual indeterminacies in the only way they can be distinguished — as successive terms whose equivalent lack of content makes them immediately pass into one another. Their succession thus operates in two directions at once, as a ceasing-to-be and coming-to-be signifying no more than the respective immediate successions of nothing from being and being from nothing. In each of these movements, the identity and difference are both at hand, for if the two indeterminacies were just identical there would be no sequence, whereas if they were only different, not only would they coexist as contrasting entities, but some resource other than indeterminacy would have had to have been illicitly introduced to account for their abiding diversity.

Similarly, ceasing-to-be and coming-to-be are both indistinguishable and different from one another within the unitary movement of becoming they comprise. They are identical to the extent that the identity of being and nothing renders the passage of being into nothing indistinguishable from that of nothing into being. Yet they are equally distinct, insofar as ceasing-to-be proceeds from the first indeterminacy to that which follows, whereas coming-to-be proceeds from the second to the first. This may amount to a very fleeting difference, but it does provide for something more than just indeterminacy and nothing.

How this could be might appear suspect, for it is certainly true that the process wherein indeterminacy and nothing immediately pass over into each other contains nothing determinate among its component elements. Nevertheless, it does comprise something that, as a whole, is distinct from them, the twin indeterminacies figuring within it. With the rise of nothing from indeterminacy, what has here further arisen is the process of a contrast that is no contrast at all, of indeterminacy that is nothing, and nothing that is indeterminacy, where each is the groundless emergence of the other. With this passage that immediately cancels itself as a passage insofar as indeterminacy and nothing are indistinguishable, indeterminacy has given rise to something other than itself, namely, this very process within which indeterminacy and nothing continually resolve themselves into one another. Consequently, it can be appropriately given its own discrete name, "becoming," as Hegel has baptized it, and designate something distinguishable from being and nothing, which nevertheless owes its character to no privileged given nor privileged determiner. To the extent that this becoming is contrastible to the aspects of indeterminacy and nothing contained within it, it comprises a definite determinacy whose presentation occurs without reference to any determinate foundations. In this respect, the move from indeterminacy to nothing to becoming that Hegel's discussion suggests offers the first deed of the one and only positive alternative to the foundational argumentation of metaphysical and transcendental thought. What it presents in an unheralded and largely ignored way is a development of determinacy that takes no determinacy for granted, a development that thus provides an account of how there is determinacy without begging the question by assuming given determinacy of one sort or another.

Chapter 7

The Theory of Determinacy and The Quests For Truth and Justice

7.1 The Nature of the Logic of Determinacy

If the emergence of becoming indicates how indeterminacy can be a starting point of further determination, and how thereby a foundation-free philosophy might at least get off the ground by presenting determinacies through which self-determination constitutes itself presuppositionlessly, it still leaves unclear how reason, reality, or justice are to be determined. In fact, when one considers the character and terminus of the advance, it becomes apparent that the development from being has a radical formality such that all it offers is a foundation-free, presuppositionless science of determinacy having no immediate bearing upon reality, conduct, or even thought.

As we have seen, inasmuch as what develops from indeterminacy does so in complete absence of all stipulation of given contents, all reference to reality, and any preconceived notion of true knowing, it must follow from that starting point in an entirely immanent manner that precludes any consideration of extraneous factors. Instead of arising through the application of some given method or the direct introduction of what is claimed to be, the development from indeterminacy must be determined through nothing other than itself. Consequently, it comprises a self-determination, which, proceeding from indeterminacy rather than from any given substrate, is nothing other than self-determination per se. This means that the foundation-free theory of determinacy that starts from indeterminacy turns out to be a theory of self-determined determinacy with no immediate ontological or epistemological application. These applications are entirely wanting since, by itself, the development of self-determined determinacy presents self-determination and nothing else. Because of this, it is no more an ontological theory demonstrating that the fundamental structure of reality is something self-determined, than it is an epistemological doctrine ordaining the manner in which reason can arrive at each and every truth.

In just this sense, it is merely a theory of determinacy, whose categories must not be misinterpreted as either categories of thought or categories of being. The moment this is done, the categories following from indeterminacy become encumbered with the same foundational assumptions afflicting metaphysical and transcendental thought. If philosophy were to begin with indeterminacy and view it and the emergence of becoming as a succession of categories of being, it would be making immediate reference to reality and thereby be taking for granted the correspondence of its categories and objects in themselves. If, on the other hand, philosophy views its first determinations as categories of thought, it would be presupposing the framework of thought that itself must be investigated if reason is to justify its own role in philosophy. Either way, the identification of categories with something more than mere determinacy involves taking certain determinacies for granted, reinstating all the dilemmas of foundationalism that have earlier been diagnosed. Only a theory of determinacy issuing from indeterminacy makes possible any talk of categories that avoids these foundational identifications. Since all theories that begin with categories of thought or reality take determinacy for granted simply by referring categories to either respective domain, it could be said that their inability to rise beyond assumptions rests on their failure to undertake beforehand an investigation of categories per se, an investigation that is precisely what the theory of determinacy provides.

For this reason, the radical formality of the development from indeterminacy is more a virtue than a vice. What it bodes for the quests for truth and justice is something that can already be gleaned from the few basic features nascent in it.

Although the ensuing development of self-determined determinacy is such that not till its end can it be fully manifest what the determinations following from indeterminacy are determinations of, the general character of the conclusion can still be anticipated. Since no independently given content or knowing can be employed to establish either the relation between the stages in the development from indeterminacy or what certifies its completion, the development must itself generate the terms to accomplish these functions. The relation between the various stages of development cannot be determined prior to the completion of the development, for it is that completion that first makes available all the stages, as well as the entirety of their relations to one another. This means that the very same term that certifies the completion of the development also determines the relation between its different stages. Accordingly, the presuppositionless development of determinacy must arrive independently at a determination that presents the interconnection of all the categories including itself while at the same time grasping them all as a totality determined in and through the very development they together comprise.

Only then will our exposition and reflection play no constitutive role in placing the different categories in relation to one another as constituents of a whole. It may be that the theory of determinacy cannot be undertaken without the theoretical labor of conscious individuals living in a common world and making use of a common language to express their thoughts. Yet if what is expressed has the radically self-ordered character that has here been outlined for the theory of determinacy, that theory will not be determined in any juridical way by these preconditions. Naturally, if it were, that would resurrect all the foundational dilemmas undercutting transcendental theory. Those problems can be avoided so long as the conditions under which determinacy comes to expression figure as mere vehicles of its self-exposition.

What all this means is that if the self-development of determinacy is to arrive at any conclusion at all, this will have to comprise a final determination so structured as to relate all the preceding ones together as the constitutive components of the self-determined totality that is their result as well as their encompassing unity. In so far, however, as this final category consists in the entire retrospective ordering of all that has preceded, an ordering wherein every category figures as a constitutive stage in the concluded self-determination containing them all and to which they have led, it becomes their totality itself.

This resultant self-ordering whole is therefore the actual subject of the development following from indeterminacy. Not surprisingly, it forms a most unique subject matter. Because it brings the development to conclusion only by incorporating all the other determinacies as components of a self-determined totality of determinacy, it provides the ordering principle of its own developed content. This final determination thus comprises the method by which all the categories are determined. If there were any other ordering principle at work, the development would no longer be self-determined, but rather depend upon something other than its own complete self for its character and order.

Conversely, since this concluding totality forms the ultimate subject of the development, it builds that of which each and every determinacy is a self-determination. Therefore, if, as the foundation-free development of determinacy from indeterminacy first makes possible, the term "category" is used to designate a determinacy as such, without imputing the added qualifications of thought determination or ontological structure, it can be said that the final category with which self-determination concludes is categorial totality itself, or, in other words, the category presenting the self-specification of the entire development of categories.

For his part, Hegel calls this categorial totality the "Absolute Idea" and appropriately closes his *Science of Logic* with it, characterizing it as the method of the self-determined development of determinacy that it itself comprises. If this description brings to a head the unification of form and content so unique to self-determination, it equally indicates the special significance of the development that closes with itself in such a wholly immanent manner.

What is evident from the constitutive character of categorial totality is that both method and subject matter have here emerged at the very end of the development from indeterminacy. Neither has been presupposed at the start as is always the case in positive science, metaphysics, and transcendental philosophy. Because such a development of categories instead proceeds with no primitive terms, no logical operators, no conceptual schemes, and no foundations of any sort, it is genuinely self-grounding. By arriving at its method and subject matter as the final result of its own investigation, this categorial development has the unprecedented character of establishing its own procedure and topic, its own form and content without taking anything for granted. In just this way, it exhibits a self-ordered content needing no exogenous criteria to justify its sequence and material.

For this very reason, the development of categorial totality involves no referral of its categories to anything distinguishable from them as reality, a knowing subject, or a thing in itself. Indeterminacy, or being, to use Hegel's terminology, is not a determinacy existing *in res*, nor something thought as a category of reason, but simply the indeterminate without any further qualification than that it retrospectively be revealed to be the component starting point of the self-determination of categorial totality. Even as a whole, categorial totality refers to nothing given in reality, nor anything thought, but only to its own system of categories.

7.1.1 The Theory of Determinacy as a Science of Logic

Consequently, what results when all privileged givens and determiners are cast aside, and all positive science, metaphysics and transcendental inquiry are left behind, is a development of categories more formal than any formal logic could be. Although formal logic may abstract from the particular content of propositions, it nevertheless assumes certain logical operators and functions, as well as the logician who manipulates them. In this sense, it begins with a preconceived topic, namely, the forms of thought, for which it stipulates a most concrete content. Since this topic already has a given character stipulated by the logician, the form of its presentation is necessarily different from the content presented. The various logical topics cannot be treated in an order consisting in their own forms of entailment, for the very fact that they comprise given forms signifies that they have an axiomatic character rather than a content "proven" in accord with the rules they provide.

Yet, the whole project of philosophical logic requires that this separation of form and content be eliminated. After all, if the study of logic consists in establishing the forms of correct thinking, it is not a completely formal science abstracting from all content, but rather a science addressing the very specific content of valid reasoning. Then, however, its own establishment of what correct reasoning comprises can only be valid if the method it employs is correct reasoning. The method of philosophical logic must thus be identical with its subject matter. In other words, for logic to achieve its constitutive aim, the form in which it determines valid reasoning must coincide with the content of valid reasoning. If, however, logic is not to take for granted what it is supposed to establish, its coinciding method and content must be legitimately determined as the result of its labors, labors that will not consist in any external act upon some given material, but in valid reasoning's own self-establishment. For this is to be achieved, what is first for thought must no less be first in the process of thinking.[1] Otherwise form and content will fall asunder, and the thinking of valid reasoning will fail to be valid thought. This leaves logical investigation but one option to avoid illogically developing the logic of thought: to conceive logic as the self-determination of valid reasoning, something that is only possible when all preconceptions concerning method or topic are discarded.

This should indicate why Hegel has good reason to develop the theory of determinacy under the rubric of "The Science of Logic." What philosophical logic demands is precisely what the development of categories from indeterminacy provides. Unlike the fixed, externally ordered functions of formal logic, the categories following from indeterminacy would have to develop themselves without dependence upon any given knower or any given content. Thereby they would achieve the unity of form and content that has its ultimate expression in the way in which categorial totality at one and the same time crowns the presuppositionless development of determinacy with its resulting method and subject matter. Just as the project of logic requires that what is first for thought be first in the process of thinking, so the development from indeterminacy would exclude all determinate thought from playing a role in determining the indeterminate with which philosophy begins. Admittedly, this does signify that the ensuing theory of determinacy is not a logic of thought categories in the traditional sense of a logic of determinacies as conceived by a given structure of cognition. It is instead simply a logic of categories, considered in their own right without reference to any predetermined thinking or speech. Nonetheless, as the preceding reflections on logic should suggest, a science of logic that does not beg its own questioning by taking for granted the form of valid thought amounts to just such a logic of categories as the theory of determinacy affords.

7.1.2 The Argument of the Theory of Determinacy

Even though the project of philosophical logic may resolve itself into the same presuppositionless inquiry that begins with indeterminacy, it is by no means clear in what sense the ensuing development of categories could contain an "argument," let alone the argument of self-justifying reason. One thing that is clear is that if the theory of determinacy could be said to present any argument at all, it would not be in the manner of the deductive reasoning of formal logic or the constitution of meanings provided by transcendental logic. Although it would be improper to state that the theory of determinacy is predetermined by any antecedent motivation, what does provide the historical motive for taking it seriously is the recognition that philosophical argument cannot consist in either deductive reasoning or transcendental constitution because both rely upon unjustifiable premises. The theory of determinacy may indeed employ propositions in explicating self-determination, just as it may require acts of consciousness to be thought out and understood. Yet these aspects of its expression in no way determine the validity of its form or content, for what the theory of determinacy presents cannot be guided or legitimated by any propositional calculus, rules of syllogism, logic of discovery, semantic analysis, or doctrine of intentionality. If they entered in, the theory of determinacy would end up being ordered by terms taking determinacy for granted.

In face of this, the argument of the theory of determinacy would be neither analytic nor synthetic in the customary sense in which these concepts are used. The theory of determinacy would no more analyze what is already present in a given subject matter than judge synthetically how given concepts are connected to one another in virtue of something outside them. As Hegel has suggested,[2] the theory of determinacy would instead proceed analytically and synthetically at one and the same time. This is because everything it presents would be both contained in the ultimate determinacy (namely, categorial totality or self-determined determinacy) that is under way determining itself, and not yet given in the preceding determinacies that are stages in the self-determination proceeding through and incorporating them.

As such, the theory of determinacy is necessarily systematic in character in the rigorous sense that for it, no topic can warrant consideration until it has been generated immanently within the self-development of categories. Whereas foundational theories move from one topic to another according to the stipulation of their author, the philosophy starting with indeterminacy can only address contents when they emerge as stages in the self-determination that follows.

This does not mean that the reason for presenting a topic lies in the determinations preceding its introduction. That would invert the character of the advance, turning the preceding determinations into causes and grounds of the succeeding ones. The whole course of self-determination would then be disrupted. Instead of allowing each determinacy to be an element of a continuing self-determination whose determining subject only arises at the end, the preceding categories would figure as determiners given prior to the subsequent categories whose emergence they determine. If this understanding were applied to the entire advance, it would render the starting point a given foundation whose own presence could never be justified without reintroducing all the problems afflicting first principles.

The systematic character of the theory of determinacy instead entails that each successive topic be included in what follows, not as a determining ground, but as a constitutive element whose own being finally resides in the whole encompassing them all as features of its self-determination. Although every category would indeed incorporate what precedes it, it would also contain an irreducible added character defined by the resultant totality of which it is a part.

7.1.3 Systematic Philosophy versus Coherence Theories of Truth

This might make it appear that the systematic philosophy beginning with the theory of determinacy entails a coherence theory of truth. Certainly the example of Hegel's system easily gives rise to such suspicion given the frequency with which he claims that the truth of a determinacy lies not in its correspondence to some object or concept, but in a subsequently developed content incorporating it. In his scheme of things, the categorial domain of the concept is the truth of that of being and essence,[3] just as spirit is the truth of soul and consciousness,[4] and the state is the truth of family and civil society,[5] to cite but a few of the more prominent examples. If this signified that truth resided in coherence, and applied not just to Hegel's own work but to the theory of determinacy in general, then systematic philosophy would be afflicted with the fundamental incoherency undermining all coherence theories of truth.

That incoherency is due to two perennially overlooked limits of coherence-based knowledge that inevitably trap the coherence theory of truth in self-referential inconsistency. These limits consist in the impossibility of ever obtaining by means of coherence either the knowledge that truth lies in coherence or knowledge of whatever be the context in coherence with which truth is held to be located.

The former limit is patent enough, for one would obviously be begging the question if one were to rely on coherence to establish that truth lies in coherence. Since that would involve employing as the basis of the demonstration precisely what must be proved, the principle of the coherence theory of truth is caught in the unenviable predicament of either lacking justification or being based on knowledge obtained through other means. Naturally, if the latter alternative were the case, this would contradict the coherence theory of truth's constitutive claim that all knowledge lies in coherence.

That claim fares no better when attention is directed to the ultimate context in coherence with which knowledge supposedly has its truth. The only way knowledge of this ultimate context could be obtained is by an immediate reference to it that violates the coherence principle by reintroducing the direct metaphysical reference against which coherence theorists rightly rebel. The ultimate context cannot be known in coherence with itself, for that would presuppose the very knowledge of it which is here being sought. If, however, that context were known in virtue of being coherent with something else, it would cease being the ultimate context it is alleged to be. By the same token, that in terms of which it is knowable would be just as unknowable through coherence unless it too were not the ultimate context. This leaves two alternatives, each as pernicious to coherence theory as the other. Either there would be an infinite regress wherein the framework of coherence remains ever unattainable, or an ultimate framework would be discovered which is known not in terms of anything else, but through precisely the immediate reference that must be avoided.

Systematic philosophy is spared these problems to the extent that its theory of determinacy refrains from developing any content in terms of a given framework. What allows it to escape this variety of foundationalism is its constitutive restriction to following the advance of self-determined categories, an advance that results in, rather than presupposes, what it is that comprises the whole at issue. Nevertheless, this resulting whole can be considered the truth of its previously determined components for the simple reason that their complete character is not at hand until they stand incorporated within the whole of which they are constitutive elements. Before then, their actual status as parts of a self-determined totality is not fully determined.

In this regard, the final category of the theory of determinacy, categorial totality, could be said to be the very determinacy of truth. Whereas all other categories have their character as elements in its self-determination, it has its character in virtue of nothing but itself. Categorial totality has this unique status precisely by being self-determined determinacy, and as such it possesses the same unconditioned, self-grounded universality that philosophy has traditionally sought in its quest for truth and justice.

7.1.4 The Limit of the Theory of Determinacy

This suggests how the "argument" of the theory of determinacy would reside in the completely self-grounded character of what it presents. Since all foundations have been discarded in virtue of their own untenability, the justification of the ordering and content of the development of categories must lie in nothing other than that they owe their form and content entirely to themselves. To the degree that they do, the presentation of categories achieves the perennial aim of all philosophical discourse — radical self-responsibility, achieved by accounting within itself for every aspect of its own inquiry.

Furthermore, because the theory of determinacy turns out to consist in the specification of self-determination, one could even say that its development of categories attains self-justification by establishing self-determination to be the very "logic" or determinacy of self-justification itself. Nevertheless, as pregnant with application as this logic may seem, it must not be forgotten that it is not a logic of thinking or a logic of reality. Categorial totality refers to nothing but its own domain of determinacy, which is so far the only content available that is not the product of illicit metaphysical reference or transcendental constitution. The development of categories from indeterminacy may establish what is self-determined determinacy as such, but it provides no answer as to whether reality corresponds to its categories or, for that matter, in what way what is real might differ from them.

How then can the theory of determinacy contribute at all to reason's self-justification and the conception of worldly things and valid norms of conduct? Even if the development from indeterminacy does reveal self-determination to be the structure of presuppositionlessness, unconditioned universality and self-grounding, how does this allow philosophy to turn to reality and address the problem of justice?

By itself, the theory of determinacy can offer but a partial and seemingly paradoxical answer to these questions. Through developing self-determination as presuppositionless, self-grounding determinacy, it indicates how the whole enterprise of philosophy remains misguided so long as philosophers seek the determinacy of true reality or true knowing without first investigating determinacy itself. Failing this most elementary investigation, any theory of reason or reality falls victim to the dogmatism of taking determinacy for granted. The theory of determinacy avoids this error by taking the problem of presuppositionlessness and self-responsibility to its radical extreme, and providing a self-exposition of categories in which no givenness is assumed. In so doing, the theory of determinacy does not prescribe rules of thought or principles of reality, but instead conceives the true categories of determinacy. Their truth resides not in any correspondence to reality or thought, nor in any coherence with some given framework, but rather in the presuppositionlessness and unconditioned universality they possess as elements of self-determined determinacy.

Only with such categories is it possible to advance to a conception of reality and justice whose incorporation of determinacies need not rest solely on opined assumptions. Nevertheless, the conception of these non-categorial domains lies beyond the reach of the theory of determinacy to the extent that reality and justice involve more than just determinacy. For this reason, the categorial development from indeterminacy is but a first, yet necessary step in philosophy's quest for truth and justice.

7.2 The Move from the Theory of Determinacy to the Theory of Reality

Despite the special formality that bars any immediate application of the theory of determinacy, the latter still has a positive role to play in conceiving all the non-categorial realms, such as nature, mind, and justice, that reality can be broadly understood to encompass. Besides providing the categories that may be incorporated in the concepts of these domains, the theory of determinacy also has a hand in determining the character that makes these realities what they are in distinction from mere categories.

This role is ordained by the situation created by the completed development of self-determined determinacy. Because the self-determination issuing from indeterminacy manifests itself as the only content to which reference can legitimately be made without recourse to presupposed foundations, its system of self-ordered categories will have to provide the sole resource for accounting for what is, in general, more than just categorial determinacy. This anti-foundational requirement may seem a paradoxical demand, in so far as it appears to summon categories to transcend their own limits. Nevertheless, what is clear is that no retreat can be made to what have been traditionally the two favored options for advancing from categories to an understanding of reality: realism and idealism.[6]

7.2.1 The Dogma of Realism and Idealism

The preceding critique of foundationalism has already shown why it is fruitless to take the familiar realist route of a "logic of discovery" where one turns to what one accepts to be given and then conceives reality by finding categories as they are there purportedly embodied. This approach would only resurrect all the dilemmas of metaphysical reference, for once again, one would be taking for granted the correspondence of categories and reality. The realist falls into this dogmatism the moment he attempts to map reality by taking the content of his knowledge as a direct reflection of what is. With every step he takes, the realist addresses what he finds given as something independent of his thought, yet transparent to it. In so doing, the realist presumes that our conceptual determinations can reliably be applied in comprehending what is, and thereupon makes immediate truth claims about the content of the given and its particular categorial character. Such claims cannot possibly be coherently adjudicated, since the only criteria by which they could be judged in realist fashion would be some other set of immediate assertions concerning the "real" content of what is. Any attempted verification would thus beg the question, relying as it would upon claims in want of like investigation.

The remedy to the realist appeal to "the given" cannot, however, consist in the alternative strategy of idealism, where reality is conceived not as a given correlate of categories, but as something determined by them. Although in one famous instance Hegel seems to follow this path by characterizing the Absolute Idea as God before Creation,[7] the whole argument of the theory of determinacy runs counter to any idealist suggestion that categorial totality be the determiner of reality. If the system of categories were to be treated in an idealist fashion as the intellectual foundation of what is, categorial determinacy would immediately assume a primacy foreign to its own special uncontrasted formality. Instead of being left as the *self-determined* whole it is, categorial totality would here figure as the determiner of something other than itself. On these terms, it would be transformed into a transcendental structure contrasted to "reality" just as a positor stands in relation to what it posits. With this idealist treatment of categories, all the dilemmas of transcendental argument would return, leaving "reality" no more than a solipsist construction, rooted in concepts which are themselves subjective stipulations.

7.2.2 Beyond Realism and Idealism

A viable alternative to realist and idealist conceptions of reality can be provided by the theory of determinacy only if its system of categories establishes what is non-categorial without appealing to anything beyond the categories whose legitimacy it has determined. How this can be achieved is something that Hegel has outlined in the transition from his *Science of Logic* to his *Philosophy of Nature*. His primary insight is basic enough: although the theory of determinacy no more assumes than founds the identity or difference between categories and reality, it does comprise the content in contrast to which the non-categorial is defined. Furthermore, since the system of categories is the only content to which legitimate reference can be made, no external standpoint can be introduced with warrant to contrast categories with what is other than them. Instead, this contrast, if it is to be made at all, must be accomplished through the categories themselves. In other words, the self-exposition of the system of categories must arrive by its own means at what is other than itself, and thereby stand in what Hegel calls "self-externality." If we adopt Hegel's terminology and designate the totality of categories as the "Absolute Idea," then the most basic characterization of what is non-categorial, that is, real, will have to be the self-externality of the Absolute Idea.

Admittedly, this appears to foster a new foundationalism, where the system of categories figures as the defining ground of reality. Nonetheless, an immanent transition from the categorial to the non-categorial need not fall into that dilemma due to two features of self-determination already displayed in the development of categories from indeterminacy.

First, if the system of categories were to develop immanently into what is non-categorial, where thinking the categories through according to their own self-determination resulted in something irreducible to them, this would involve no immediate reference to anything in itself. Since the transition would occur entirely in virtue of what the system of categories itself comprises, the non-categorial domain would be arrived at without any appeal to givenness or any external intervention. As a result, the conception of reality would not be burdened by the problem of metaphysics.

Secondly, it must be remembered that what results from immanent development is not determined *by* that from which it arises. On the contrary, a fully independent development is a *self*-determination, and what determines itself is not already given at the start, but only comes to be at the end as its own result. If this be applied to a conception of reality immanently proceeding from the conception of the system of categories, it signifies that the actual subject of the self-development will not be the system of categories, but rather the reality conceived by virtue of conceiving them. Arrived at as a result of the development, the concept of reality will be what has actually determined itself in the process, whereas categorial totality will stand not as reality's determiner nor as God before creation, but as the component starting point from which the concept of reality develops itself. In this way, reality will be conceived to be as free of foundations as the theory that conceives it.

On these terms, the possibility of a non-positive, non-metaphysical and non-transcendental conception of reality lies open. However, possibility is one thing, and actuality another. In order for there to be a systematic conception of reality it must still be determined how categorial totality can immanently result in the concept of something other than itself that is.

To address this problem, it is worth reviewing why the only non-categorial content that can legitimately follow from the system of categories is, to paraphrase Hegel, the self-externality of categorial totality. To begin with, any non-categorial content following from categorial totality would have to be irreducible to all and any of the latter's constitutive categories. Otherwise, the putative candidate for real determinacy would fall back within the system of categories as one of its purely formal determinations. Irreducibility would have to be achieved, however, without introducing any stipulations, be they immediate references to reality or to acts of knowing. Because the only content that is legitimately available is categorical totality, the only non-categorial term that could warrant consideration would have to be a pure "other" of categorial totality — "pure" in that its otherness refers to nothing but categorial totality for its specific character.

. Furthermore, since no extraneous determiner could be relied upon to introduce it, this pure other would have to have its specific character in the form of a self-development from categorial totality. As such, it would incorporate the system of categories as its own structural element, yet do so as the first, most rudimentary aspect of what can comprise itself as an irreducible reality.

As we have seen, these conditions are all met provided that the system of categories develops into what is its own content external to itself. If the self-exposition of the sytem of categories results in the entirety of categorial totality related to itself as something other, then one will have what is specifically other to categories, without introducing any extraneous content or falling back into any particular category.

The question, then, is whether the system of categories resolves itself into this result. At the very end of the *Science of Logic*, Hegel attempts to show that just such a transition immediately occurs once categorial totality emerges as the concluding determination of the development from indeterminacy.[8] His argument consists as it should in simply noting what is at hand in the fully developed self-determined determinacy that categorial totality comprises. To be total and concluding, this final category is itself a retrospective ordering of all preceding categories, relating them to one another as component stages in the self-determination that incorporates them all by determining itself through them. Thus the moment categorial totality is arrived at, providing closure for self-determined determinacy, the entire preceding development stands as something given that has already run its course and entered into being. Admittedly, this development is identical in content to what categorial totality contains. Nevertheless, it is still something other to the degree that its development, if not logically prior to categorial totality, is genetically anterior. In this sense, as soon as categorial totality is exposited, it stands external to itself, related to a given content otherwise no different from it. Thus, despite the total abstention from introducing extraneous content, thinking through the system of categories immediately presents something that is no longer categorial totality in all its radical formality, but rather the self-externality of categorial totality, or the self-externality of the Absolute Idea, to use Hegel's expression.[9]

Although this new structure incorporates nothing but the features of categorial totality, it does so as something given, standing in an immediate otherness to the system of categories. As such, it does not contain categorial determinacy in a manner that is itself a category, as was the case with the purely formal ordering comprising the concluding category of the system of categories. Since what lies at hand is other to the entirety of categorial determinacy, its otherness cannot be reducible to any particular category, but rather represents what is non-categorial without any further qualification.

As a result, for the first time there is not just determinacy per se, but non-categorial, or if one will, real determinacy to which categories stand in contrast. This real determinacy is given not over against some presupposed structure of knowing, as in the representational model of traditional epistemology. It instead stands in contrast to the groundless, presuppositionless totality of determinacy it contains within itself as its structural element. Because such non-categorial determinacy is neither metaphysically affirmed nor transcendentally constituted, it provides a reality free of the dilemmas confronting all past candidates for what is.

Needless to say, the self-externality of categorial totality does not exhaust the concept of reality, but at best supplies the minimal threshold of non-categorial determinacy required for conceiving any further real structure, be it nature, mind or the reality of justice. Hegel himself accordingly characterizes it as the most rudimentary and immediate content of nature that all other real entities must presuppose and incorporate.[10]

7.3 *Normativity, Rational Reconstruction, and the Theory of Justice*

Hegel's argument for arriving at a foundation-free conception of reality may provide access to non-categorial determinacy without falling into the traps of idealism and realism, but it does not directly indicate how any further results can be obtained. In particular, it leaves unanswered how a systematic theory of justice should be developed.

Nevertheless, the move from the theory of categories to the conception of non-categorial domains does offer two basic guidelines for conceiving justice. These consist in the concept of normativity established by the theory of determinacy and in the correlative method of rational reconstruction.

7.3.1 *Freedom as Normativity*

As has been noted, the theory of determinacy is neither a logic of reality nor a logic of knowing. Nonetheless, the development of categories from indeterminacy makes manifest how presupposition-lessness, unconditioned universality, and self-grounding are achieved by self-determined determinacy. In so doing, the theory of determinacy indicates that the demands of normativity perennially raised by philosophy's call for theoretical self-responsibility are met by nothing other than self-determination. If this provides meaning to the autonomy of reason sought by philosophers since antiquity, it also suggests how the parallel demand of practical justification can be met only when conduct attains the same radically self-determined character. To the extent that justice consists in valid conduct, the theory of determinacy indicates through its own foundation-free validity that justice is equivalent to the reality of free action.

This equation would be an empty formula of little applicability were it not for the very concrete character that the theory of determinacy establishes for self-determined determinacy. The category of freedom, as opposed to the reality of freedom, may be a formal determinacy involving no aspects of nature or mind, yet it is still the most concrete of categories, containing as it does the entire system of determinacy as its own constitutive self-determination. For this reason, if conduct is to achieve validity by being free, the reality of free action should be expected to comprise a self-ordered system of conduct that is a totality in its own right.

Determining how this totality of justice is internally composed is not something that can be done by simply grafting the logic of self-determination upon the given matter of the will. Any attempt to do so would repeat the idealist error of taking for granted that the structure of reality is merely a translation of categories into flesh. If this signifies that the reality of freedom cannot be deduced from the logic of freedom, it does not mean that the system of justice is to be found in realist fashion by appealing to the given reality of conduct. That would involve the very same stumbling block on which idealism founders: the taking for granted that the real is rational. This can be avoided by following the non-idealist, non-realist path of rational reconstruction as it is defined by the program of foundation-free systematic philosophy.

7.3.2 The Rational Reconstruction of Justice

Rational reconstruction functions as a viable tool of philosophical thought by taking given contents and recasting them as components of a conceptual development satisfying the systematic immanence in which validity consists. The givens in question may be terms of natural language, empirical phenomena, or concepts developed by prior thinkers. Whatever their source, they can serve as a touchstone for valid thought provided they are not used as privileged terms whose truth is taken for granted. Rational reconstruction instead establishes their truth or falsity by working back from them, determining their prerequisites and ultimately revealing whether their constitutive elements are themselves ungrounded assumptions, or contents that result from the presuppositionless development of categories of the theory of determinacy. In undertaking this investigation, rational reconstruction places the given contents it "reconstructs" in an order of constitution, where each term is directly preceded by those that comprise all its necessary constituents, and followed by those that incorporate it as a necessary component. In this fashion, the order of terms is determined by their own content, a content that places them as particular components of a conceptual development where no term is introduced without prior account of its constitutive elements.

To the extent that a real content is incorporated in the reality of others that follow it in the order of conception, the prior content exists in two related fashions. First, it may exist independently of the terms that follow upon it, provided that its own prerequisites are at hand. However, since it is itself part of some further structure, its own existence is fully captured only with the coming to be of the latter terms that incorporate it. In this sense, its own existence is mediated by the whole of which it is a necessary element, as well as a genetically anterior condition.

If such rational reconstruction be employed in working out the theory of justice, the task of determining the totality of freedom takes on the following form:

First, the theory of justice will begin with the minimal structure of freedom. What qualifies for this starting point will do so by presupposing no other structures of self-determination and by being incorporated in the reality of all further structures of freedom. Naturally, the prerequisites of this most indeterminate relation of freedom will have to be accounted for previously, or else be pointed to as presuppositions awaiting their own theoretical treatment.

Second, further relations of justice may then be introduced provided their own structures of freedom involve no constituents beyond what the more minimal modes of self-determination have already made available. Institutions such as the family, society and state may here figure so long as their given contents are reconstructed as structures of freedom whose prior conditions and components have been established.

Since a candidate for a structure of justice will qualify simply by being a mode of self-determined conduct, the theory of justice will achieve closure only when all modes of freedom have been given account. The relation between the different modes is not, however, simply a numerical one of indifferently existing entities. Due to the requirement that all conditions be provided for, the various relations of justice stand in a more qualitative connection. Each structure of freedom may come to be once its own components are at hand, but its existence will not be the same as that it achieves as a component of a more inclusive relation of justice. Only when the most complete structure of freedom is at hand, incorporating all the rest, will all structures of freedom have their existence determined and secured by freedom, and not by the hazard of external circumstance.

This already indicates the way in which political institutions of freedom provide closure to the system of freedom. Although it might seem enough that the most concrete institution of justice qualify as such by incorporating all the rest, one more requirement must be met for justice to enjoy the self-grounding character validity demands. Not only must all relations of freedom be components of the most determinate structure of freedom, but the relation between the different elements of justice must be determined by that highest structure itself. If it were not, and the relations of justice had to depend on some external agency for their unity, the system of justice would not be self-determined, but ordered by some factor outside it. In that case, justice would be founded on something that is not itself just, and forfeit its validity in the same way as does any theory that bases its truth claims upon some given foundation. For this reason, the system of freedom must be crowned by a structure of freedom that not only determines its own activity, but in so doing, orders all modes of freedom into a self-determined whole. This crowning institution of freedom must unite the entire system of freedom in the very exercise of its own constitutive freedom, for otherwise, its ordering activity would be imposed upon it by something else, rendering the reality of freedom a reality subordinated to a power lying beyond the institutions of self-determination.

The requirement for political institutions of freedom as the crowning sphere of justice is here mandated. What this suggests is that the totality of justice will ultimately be political in character. Whereas the theory of justice must be the theory of the reality of freedom, the reality of freedom must lie in the reality of the free state, incorporating within its realm all the non-political institutions of freedom. These non-political institutions of freedom may exist antecedently to the just state, which requires them as its component elements. Nevertheless, they will exist in virtue of freedom, that is, in a condition of justice, only when there are political institutions of freedom to guarantee and rule their life in common.

The preeminent political character of freedom's reality indicates one last feature to guide the rational reconstruction of justice. The maintenance of non-political institutions of freedom must not conflict with the autonomy of political freedom. If it did, political freedom would have to be restricted so as to protect non-political relations of justice. This, however, would require some agency standing over the state with power to limit its sovereignty. If the free state contains within it all other institutions of freedom, then this higher agency would act from outside justice, and thereby undermine its normativity.

The only way this problem can be avoided is if the non-political institutions of freedom are indeed prerequisites of political freedom. In that case, the state's protection of their reality would involve no imposition upon political freedom, but rather be part and parcel of its realization. Accordingly, the rational reconstruction of justice will not only have to ascertain what are the different types of self-determination, but show how the non-political modes are required for the activity of political freedom. Naturally, this will have important implications for the internal constitution of the political order.

It should be evident that developing the theory of justice on these terms bears no resemblance to the Rawlsian strategy of reflective equilibrium. The latter strategy is satisfied to construct a theory of justice by arriving at a procedure for determining public institutions in consonance with certain accepted moral and political values. Reflective equilibrium thus cannot possibly deliver a genuinely normative theory of conduct, for all its conclusions issue from views whose authority is never questioned. Rawls himself admits as much by carefully titling his theory "A Theory of Justice," instead of "The Theory of Justice." In this way, he veers from Kant, who still aspires to develop an unconditionally prescriptive theory of ethics, as evident in his demand for categorical, rather than hypothetical principles of morals.

Rational reconstruction, in contrast to reflective equilibrium, seeks a systematic determination of justice. Instead of ascertaining what conforms to any given views, it searches out in given institutions and given theories those structures of conduct which fit within the reality of freedom as component preconditions and encompassing guarantors of one another. With the possibility of systematic philosophy established and freedom invested with normative validity, rational reconstruction can now contest the challenge of nihilism.

Part IV

The System of Justice

Chapter 8

The Elementary Structures of Freedom

8.1 *Justice as the Reality of Freedom*

The examples of metaphysical and transcendental philosophies have shown how truth and justice can only be attained if the norms of theory and practice are freed of all taint of givenness. In the case of theory, philosophy can escape dependence upon unjustified assumptions only by becoming entirely self-grounding. To achieve radical independence from all claims that have not already been philosophically established, philosophy must somehow proceed without resting on any determinate foundation. As we have seen, philosophy can do so only if it begins from indeterminacy, an indeterminacy signifying the exclusion of all presuppositions concerning reality and knowing, including all preconceptions about the subject matter and method of philosophy. From that empty starting point, philosophy can succeed in grounding itself so long as it remains systematic, generating its entire content and ordering solely in virtue of what follows from its indeterminate beginning. Instead of moving from one topic to another through arbitrary reflections upon what is claimed to be given, philosophical discourse must be self-determining, for only by unfolding with the total immanence of rational autonomy can it avoid relying upon extra-philosophical assumptions to define its subject matter and the order of its consideration. Since the immanent development of systematic philosophy proceeds from indeterminacy, its self-determination will not be that of some given content, but self-determination per se. Although this establishes freedom as the logic of normativity, satisfying the requirements of presuppositionlessness, self-grounding, and unconditioned universality, the normativity of practice is another matter.

This is because in practice, unlike in philosophical theory, a specific content is already at hand. Whereas philosophy begins without appealing to any givens, practice irreducibly involves a given field consisting in the relations among willing individuals. It may be true that among these relations, the theory of justice addresses solely those falling within the reach of normative conduct. Further, as the efforts of classical and liberal theorists have revealed, the validity of these normative relations cannot be derived from any prior conditions without falling prey to foundational dilemmas. Nevertheless, justice still has as its necessary material condition the existence of willing selves and the nature that they inhabit. Without their presence, no action, good or bad, can be thought or realized. These preconditions of conduct must thus be accounted for prior to the conception of justice.

For our purposes it will suffice to point to the need for such a preliminary investigation of nature and all that is entailed in the constitution of a willing individual. It must be recognized, however, that these preconditions of justice are not in any way determining conditions that prescribe how conduct and institutions ought to be structured. On the contrary, precisely because nature and the existence of willing individuals are prerequisites of any action whatsoever, they provide no basis for distinguishing between what makes conduct right or wrong. Accordingly, when justice is the theme, the problem concerns not how individuals can act in relation to one another, but how their relations, involving all that nature and selfhood imply, can achieve the added self-grounded character granting them the unconditioned universality that normative validity requires.

Keeping in mind how the theory of justice has prerequisites, but not prior determining principles, it bears repeating that what allows justice to be distinguished from mere convention is very much akin to what permits knowledge to be distinguished from opinion. Since justice, like philosophy, can have no foundations, but must be its own ground, the relations of justice must be determined entirely through themselves. Because no independently given factor can prescribe their character, the relations of justice must thus be wholly self-determined. This means that the one and only constituent of justice are self-ordered relations of freedom among individuals. As the theory of determinacy has already indicated, freedom can alone provide normative validity, for what is self-determined has self-grounded unconditioned universality precisely by being determined through itself rather than through any given condition.

Justice must therefore comprise the reality of freedom, rather than a domain of conduct that embodies given norms or stands determined by an antecedent privileged determiner. Accordingly, the theory of justice is properly the philosophy of right. What makes it *philosophy* are two salient points. The independence of justice from given circumstances leaves it beyond the grasp of the positive sciences, which investigate only what is given to them. Further, only philosophical concepts, with their systematic immanence, can exhibit the same self-determined character as justice and provide valid knowledge of valid action.

Secondly, the theory of justice must be the philosophy of *right*, and not a philosophy of goodness and prescribed virtues, to the degree that the reality of self-determination is none other than the objectively respected exercise of freedom in which rights consist. This identification of right and self-determination might appear suspect, given the common confusion of freedom with the reign of arbitrariness and anarchy. Yet the identification holds because the self-determination of the will necessarily involves the reciprocal bonds of right and duty that unite justice and freedom.

This unity of self-determination with the entitlement and obligation of justice need not be defended by making appeal to any wishful assumptions about the sanctity of freedom. The connection of right and freedom is indissoluble due to the interactive structure by which self-determination can alone take place.

8.1.1 Freedom as Interaction: The Deduction of the Concept of Right

The impetus to conceive this connection is already at hand. The theories of liberty and practical reason have demonstrated through their own difficulties how normatively valid freedom cannot be conceived in terms of the natural will or the autonomy of a single agent.

As we have seen, these theories have foundered by, logically speaking, conflating self-determination with the positing of a given determiner. Their problem is straightforward. Because justice must be its own ground, freedom cannot be conceived as a principle out of which the relations of justice are derived. If this is done, the identity of self-determination and justice is broken and both forfeit their validity. Treated as a principle, freedom gets reduced to a determiner of something other than itself, namely the derivative relations of justice. These, on the other hand, lose all self-determined character of their own by being determined by a principle of freedom prior to and separate from them. As a result, the derivative structures of justice lack the self-determination that would grant them legitimacy, whereas the principle of freedom fails to give itself any self-determined character.

The key to these difficulties lies in the failure to determine the entire individual character of the will in virtue of its own volition. There can be no talk of self-determination unless this can be achieved. Liberty is no answer insofar as it bequeaths the will a given form of choice preceding, rather than issuing from its own volition, while leaving the content of choice supplied by independently given alternatives. Practical reason offers no solution either, for an agency that wills the mere lawfulness of its maxims leaves the particular content of action undetermined by freedom. This is well manifest by the fact that the will's lawfulness neither gives it a specific end nor differentiates it from others. Consequently, practical reason remains a given common form of agency that, like liberty, automatically figures as an antecedent principle determining what is secondary to itself.

In order for actual self-determination to occur, the will must instead individuate itself through action whose specific end and concomitant form of agency are both determined by the willing agent. Not only must the content of action be willed independently of inner desire and reason, as well as outer circumstance, but the volition must establish who wills no less than what is willed. If willing is to attain the self-ordered individuality that actual freedom requires, it must give itself a content exclusively its own at the same time that it bestows the form upon its own agency. The resulting form of its autonomy will thus not be a universal nature given prior to its act, but an artificial, conventional agency whose character is a product, rather than a precondition, of its willing. Only then will the form and content of agency be self-imposed, together providing the self-determined individuality that renders action free and just.

By contrast, so long as freedom be conceived either as a natural capacity of choice, in the guise of liberty, or as a non-natural autonomy of the self, in the guise of practical reason, the individuality of self-determination will remain conflated with the logic of positing, separating freedom from justice and depriving both of their common normative validity.

To repeat, the free will cannot be a natural will, for a will whose acts issue from a natural endowment and deal only with nature and given circumstance remains bound to givens that preclude self-determination. Whereas the form of its agency is given to it by nature, its action is defined in reference only to what is neither a will nor a product of willing. On both counts, the will's source of determination lies outside itself, leaving it in external bondage.

Similarly, the free will cannot be a monological structure, that is, a structure of the self, determined independently of the plurality of agents. Monologically defined, the will is something all selves possess as such, which means that it cannot serve to differentiate their agencies or actions from one another. So conceived, the free will is automatically reduced to a solely universal faculty containing no element of particularity that could individuate one will from another through its own freedom instead of through independently given factors. Hence the aspect of particularity, affording freedom the content required for actual self-*determination*, cannot be referred back to the will as a determination of and by its own *self*, but remains a determination of something other. Consequently, no will that relates only to itself, as in an inner application of a categorical imperative, can ever achieve actual self-determination. Since any form of willing specific to the self holds true for all selves without individuating them, a monological agency lacks the freedom to determine either the particular character of the agent or that of its action.

This should come as no surprise, for it is inconceivable that a single will could alone determine both the form and content of its own willing. To do so, the very agency that should be determined through the act of will would already have to be at hand, ready to give itself its form and content. This conundrum shows why the possibility of self-determination seems hopelessly paradoxical when viewed as a problem of the self. So long as the single will be viewed as the parameter of freedom, it is impossible to defuse the question that asks how the will can freely determine its own agency without already being free.

These two lessons, that the free will is neither a natural will nor a monological structure, bring us to the threshold of the identity of freedom and right. They do so by introducing the insight that just as normative validity requires that freedom be the substance of justice, so self-determination requires that freedom be identical to right. This insight arises from the recognition that self-determination can only be achieved when the will acts in reference not to nature or itself, but to other acting wills.

To recognize how self-determination necessarily consists in relations between a plurality of agents involves no denial of the reality of the natural will, whose faculty of choice is indeed an endowment every agent can exercise without any reference to others. What must be observed is that although the choosing will of liberty may be exercised by a solitary individual, the free will transcends the capacity of the single self. Its autonomy cannot be a natural or egological given preceding its activity, but must instead comprise an artificial, conventional agency whose entire character arises in the very action by which it operates. There is only one way the will can determine its own autonomy and escape the dilemma of already having to possess freedom in order to act in a self-determined fashion. This is for the will to interact with other agents so that within their interaction they each exercise an autonomous role that can only be engaged in within the very relationship they thereby establish through their own activity. In that case, the particulars of each will are determined not by externally given factors, but through its own activity in conjunction with that of others whose own agency is therein equally codetermined. Due to this mutuality, where each participant establishes the conditions of its own agency by contributing to that of others, the defining limits of each will are self-mediated at the same time that they are mediated by the freedom of others. This is of key importance, for what eliminates the problem of having to be free in order to determine oneself as free is the simultaneity of both sides of the interaction. By choosing to perform the requisite acts that comprise an interaction in which each participant plays an autonomous role made possible through their action towards one another, individuals are able to enjoy an artificial agency whose character is completely dependent upon the actions in which its exercise consists. Therefore, they need not have antecedent possession of such agency before engaging in its practice. On the contrary, all they need is the body and mind to enter into relations that carry with themselves a specific mode of freedom that exists nowhere else, prior or posterior, but in those relations themselves.

The logic of this solution becomes apparent once its structure is laid bare. As we have seen, the will is free only by actually giving itself a particular content and particular form that both derive from its volition. This means that the free will must will itself, for to be self-determined is to determine oneself as self-determined. Such willing of one's own autonomy cannot, however, comprise an empty solipsism of non-contradiction, where the will simply reiterates its given form, as in the inner application of a categorical imperative. To be self-determined, the will must will new particular character for itself, whereby its act and agency stand individuated in contrast to the acts and agencies of other individuals.

However, as the aporias of social contract have indicated, the free will cannot remain in any immediate, given relation to other free wills.

If it did, their particular differentiation from one another would not be determined by their own volition. Any situation where the relation between agents is antecedently imposed upon their willing is incompatible with freedom, since the particular content of each will would not be self-determined, but delimited through contrastive relations that they have not willed into being. Consequently, for the will to be free, it must will its relation to other free wills as part of its own self-determination.

Furthermore, the free will must do so such that the relations it enters into with others are voluntarily willed by them as well. Otherwise, they would stand in a predicament where the particulars of their agency are not self-determined. In that case, they would not figure as free wills themselves and fail to provide the contrast term the first agent needs to give its autonomy a boundary entirely determined through freedom. For this reason, the free will can will its relation to other free wills only if they concomitantly will that same relation to one another as their own self-determination.

Freedom thus entails a self-relation that is equally a relation to other.[1] In order for agents to exercise self-determination and not merely the negative liberty of choice, each must will a particular act that simultaneously determines its own conventional autonomy and its relation to others while no less cointending their autonomy. This interaction thus defines and establishes the agency of each participant through freedom to the extent that the relationship they enact is one in which they all interact on a self-determined basis.

The conclusion is unequivocal: free willing is not the action of a single will alone, but rather a self-determination of one agent that is inextricably bound up with the self-determination of others. In order to will its agency and action in a particular manner, the free will must engage in a reciprocal relation to other wills, where each codetermines the structure of interaction that consists in their respective exercise of an autonomy that exists only within that framework. Accordingly, freedom is not a natural endowment or a monological capacity, but an actual structure of interaction consisting in the interconnected and mutually concordant actions of a plurality of agents.

Because each agent can only act freely by willing in conformity with the concomitant free action of others, their interaction is a process that further involves what Hegel has termed "reciprocal recognition."[2] Although reciprocal recognition may enter in in other contexts, here it involves the specific process of mutually coordinated actions that generates a non-natural agency whose acts constitute the framework through which its role is defined. Since each agent exercises its artificial autonomy solely by acting in conscious consort with the similar self-determinations of others, there is at play a recognition of other agents and their acts that is both theoretical and practical. Containing the very agency it makes possible, this recognition consists in each participant perceiving how others are willing and conformably choosing to will in a recognizable way that does not conflict with their respective self-determinations. Thus, the participating agents must already possess a natural corporeal being and subjective capacities of mind and choice, even though their interaction involves the exercise of a conventional freedom whose form and content is a product of its own agency. The prior endowments of body and mind are indispensable, for without them, agents can neither recognize how others have willed, nor choose a particular end to will in conformity with those of others, nor finally give their self-determination a recognizable reality in a perceivable act.

Nevertheless, the actions that follow on the basis of these preconditions are by no means determined by them. On the contrary, it is precisely the added, non-natural, intersubjective dimension of the enacted agency that permits the interacting individuals to act with what neither their body nor their self can provide: genuinely self-determined freedom and the normative validity it commands.

These two further qualities go hand in hand. Their conjunction is not due simply to how self-determination alone possesses the self-grounded unconditioned universality required by justice. It is equally rooted in how the interaction of freedom involves mutual respect for the concomitant self-determinations contained within it. That mutual respect renders each self-determination an exercise of right, obliged for its own being to concord with the autonomy of others whose own self-determination rests on carrying out the duty of corroborating the former's freedom. Accordingly, freedom is irreducibly a relation of right, whose very exercise of self-determination is necessarily accompanied by the recognition affording it an honored reality.

This identity of freedom and right does more than testify in the field of practice to the logical identity of self-determination and normative validity. It further frees justice of all foundations by revealing that freedom is not a principle of justice, distinguishable from the legitimate laws and institutions it grounds, but rather an actual structure of justice itself, whose essence is inseparable from its own self-determined existence. The identity of freedom and justice is thus no idle phrase, but rather a structural truth of the will's self-determination. It is this truth that renders the theory of justice the philosophy of right.

8.1.2 The Dilemma of Foundational Theories of Interaction

The interaction inherent in self-determination adds decisive weight to the corollary propositions that freedom is itself an existing relation of right, and that justice is the very reality of self-determination. Nevertheless, it must not be forgotten that although self-determination may be conceived as a category in general within the theory of determinacy,[3] it would be wrong to conceive the self-determination of the will in the abstract. To do so is tantamount to ignoring the specific actuality of the interaction of freedom and reducing it to a regulative principle standing apart from the concrete reality of practice.

In this respect it is not enough to discard liberty and practical reason as candidates for freedom. The temptation to treat interaction as a general principle of justice must also be averted. This temptation has, however, cast its spell over a wide audience following Alexandre Kojève,[4] Hannah Arendt,[5] Jürgen Habermas,[6] and Karl-Otto Apel,[7] who have all taken the reciprocal recognition of interacting individuals as a non-institutionalized ideal that serves to determine and legitimate the concrete structures of justice. The moment this view is adopted, interaction is rendered a general form underlying the separate types of valid conduct and valid institutions, but contributing nothing to determining the differences that make them what they are. Hence the identity of freedom and justice is once more forsaken, reinstating the foundational dilemmas of liberal theory in a new guise.

To avoid this outcome and maintain the unity of justice and self-determination, the conception of the interaction of freedom must fulfill two requirements. First, the most elementary specification of freedom must consist in a real particular relation of justice rather than in a universal form awaiting embodiment. Only then will the basic concept of interaction figure not as a foundation, but as a rudimentary mode of freedom that functions as a structural component rather than a determining principle of whatever more complex interactions may be contained in the reality of self-determination. Second, freedom must be conceived as something concrete, consisting not in a single interaction standing beside other normative structures, but in a self-determined system of interactions constituting the totality of justice. Otherwise freedom and justice will once again remain separated, depriving both of the self-grounding character needed for normative validity.

8.1.3 The Minimal Structure of Right

The first of these requirements is met by considering what the interaction of freedom minimally is, given the actual conditions of its process. These conditions consist in nothing more than a world of nature inhabited by a plurality of individuals endowed with a bodily organism and the cognitive and practical faculties of knowing and choosing selves. Conceptually speaking, it is a matter of indifference whether the individuals in question have the additional natural features that distinguish them as homo sapiens. Those features may be at hand, but they may also be possessed by beings who lack the functioning mind and consciously controlled body required for normative conduct. Infants, brain-damaged persons, psychotics, or comatose individuals may be human beings, but that does not mean that they are currently endowed with sufficient capacities for doing right and wrong. Furthermore, although we may not have encountered or at least recognized the existence of any other species capable of good and evil, the imaginative deeds of science fiction have shown how it is hardly inconceivable that agents could exist in natural forms other than our own. Tying the conditions of freedom to the species being of homo sapiens thus involves the same category mistake involved in restricting rights according to race and sex when racial and sexual differences have no bearing upon the ability to exercise the rights in question.

Taking due note of the generality of the conditions for action, one need only remark that once they are at hand, it is simply a matter of concomitant choice whether given agents enter into and enact relations of justice. All the interaction of freedom requires is that some individuals choose to act in such a way that they relate to one another through reciprocal recognition, establishing a mode of autonomy that operates in and only in the relationship it comprises.

General as this situation may appear, it leaves the minimal reality of freedom with a most definite, unequivocal structure. As the dilemmas of liberty and practical reason have indicated, freedom without any further qualification consists in an interaction of agents where each gives its will a particular objective determination whose limits accord with those that others give their own wills as participants in the same relation. In that way the particulars of their agency are entirely determined through their respective acts of will. This occurs provided that each participant establishes a particular reality for his self-determination that can be recognized by others as the objective embodiment of his willing. However, since the recognition in question is not just theoretical, but realized in action, an objectively respected self-determination is only possible if the other participants simultaneously engage in establishing specific recognizable objectifications of their own wills that do not conflict with the reality the former agent has chosen.

Furthermore, if every participant's willing is to be a self-determination, then its objectification must have no other constitutive character than that of being the particular determination of that agent, respected by other individuals in virtue of their willing corroborating, nonconflicting domains of their own. Although their respective objectifications all have natural, independently given qualities simply by being a reality of some sort, they must figure within the interaction solely as a medium for each agent's recognized self-determination. It may be true that no one can achieve self-determination without establishing some specific reality as the recognized embodiment of his or her will. Nevertheless, to be self-determined, an individual must will nothing other than the objectification of his or her agency in that reality. If instead, the agent chooses that embodiment for the specific natural features that otherwise characterize it, his or her will is not self-determined, but determined by those givens. Accordingly, the natural qualities of the objectification of willing must figure as subordinate accidents of self-determination, rather than as objects of desire that draw the will from without. Only when they count as mere receptacles of the will's embodiment can they provide a particular domain in which the freedom of the individual has existence for others.

By the same token, what the agent wills in interaction with others must be solely the realization of his or her freedom. Nothing other than this, free action for its own sake, could qualify as the self-determination of a free agent.

These parameters define the ensuing relationship. Within it, the will of each participant has no individuating features other than the particular embodiment it gives itself. It is thereby what it has determined itself to be: the will of that particular domain, a domain that no other wills can claim as their own. These are all excluded from it not by external compulsion, but by an internal necessity to the extent that their respective objectifications have respected reality only by being delimited through the domains of other agents. In the entailed interaction, each agent acts and is acted towards exclusively in terms of his own self-determination. As a consequence, each enjoys the status of a free person, signifying an agent whose self-determination has an objective domain through which other free agents relate in virtue of the respective domains they have given their own wills.

On these terms, the minimal reality of self-determination resolves itself into a reciprocal acquisition of property by a plurality of agents. Through their interaction they establish for themselves the artificial agency of individual property owners. This agency is a conventional autonomy no more given by nature than derivative of the single self. To be an owner is to engage in an artificial role that can only operate within the mutually enacted framework where agents give their wills respected concordant domains that determine their reality as owner for one another. As such, it comprises a mode of genuine self-determination since each individual determines his particular identity as owner entirely by his own acts of ownership.

Freedom can have no more elementary structure than this relation of property. At the very least, self-determination involves willing into being some particular entity that stands objectively recognized as the exclusive reality of an individual free will. Property is precisely that entity whose character consists in none other than being the recognized exclusive domain of a free will. On the other hand, the property owner, or the "person" to use Hegel's terminology, is precisely the non-natural, artificial agency that freely individuates itself through nothing more than the particular domain in which it invests its will. To be an owner, an agent must have property, which it can only acquire by an act of its own will. In other words, an agent becomes an owner by determining the very form of its new autonomy as entitled possessor of property. Conversely what distinguishes owners from another are the respective properties they possess, properties that thus define the objective content of their property owning wills. Since what they own is determined by their own decision, the particular content of their agency is just as self-determined as its common form qua owner.

Nevertheless, it must not be forgotten that both these aspects of the form and content of ownership are mediated by the self-determinations of other property owners. Only when each agent acquires property in respect of the property acquisitions of others, do their possessions enjoy an objectively respected entitlement, which makes them more than physically held objects, exhibiting but the accidents of force rather than the embodiment of a free will. Although any individual with a choosing will may be at liberty to appropriate whatever object he or she has the power to take, that individual does not thereby determine his or her agency. The individual's action remains that of a choosing will, whose form of choice is present antecedently to every act of appropriation. Only when the actions of other agents contribute in codetermining a framework of recognition in which entitlement operates, is each participant able to determine a non-natural, novel autonomy for him or herself, the self-determined agency of property owner. Since the freedom that that agency enjoys involves no more than the right to give one's will an external embodiment, it well warrants the name of "abstract right" that Hegel assigns to it.[8] It is the most abstract of all possible rights, for what it involves is the least that freedom can comprise. This becomes especially evident when the basic establishment of property ownership is examined.

8.1.4 The Original Appropriation of Property

The theme of the establishment of property ownership is something that cannot be ignored in attempting to determine the minimal structure of freedom. In fact, properly speaking, the minimal structure of freedom is equivalent to the interaction comprising the original acquisition of property. The reason for this is that no relation of property ownership can qualify as the minimal structure of freedom if it already presupposes the existence of owners and their property. What comes first, in theory as well as in reality, must be the actions whereby ownership and property are generated in the first place. This presents a unique situation where the mode of taking ownership and the object of its appropriation have very particular characters.

If the appropriation of property is to be a strictly original establishment of ownership, fit to comprise the minimal reality of freedom, it must be undertaken by individuals who are as yet merely choosing selves and be directed at entities that neither have a recognizable will of their own nor are already owned by anyone. If the appropriation involved individuals already enjoying the status of property owner or objects already commanding recognition as property, it would obviously not be an original establishment of ownership. If, on the other hand, it involved appropriation of entities with a recognizable will, what would be established would be relations of bondage rather than freedom. At stake is instead the initial enactment of entitled possession, the logically prior acquisition of property that makes possible all subsequent property relations including contractual transfer of preexisting property, as well as acts of crime against the recognized person and property of individuals.

In order for this primary property interaction to proceed, nature must be despiritualized as far as the participants are concerned.

Unless there is some given domain stripped of all mind and will of its own, there can be nothing to be originally taken into ownership in affirmation of freedom.[9] In like manner, the participants must not regard one another as objects of appropriation, or they would annul the plurality on which their own prospective personhood as owners depends.

Provided these conditions are met, an individual can then take original ownership by acting upon an appropriate given entity in such a way as to make manifest to other similarly engaged individuals that he or she is establishing it as the domain of his or her self-determination. For an entity to serve this role, it is not enough that it be neither one of the other prospective owners nor something invested by a will. It must further be of a character allowing it to be acted upon in a recognizable way. The air common to all or some distant galaxy, for example, could not figure as appropriable objects to the extent that neither can be affected so as to reveal its embodiment of someone's will.

When, however, an entity meets this last requirement, it can be appropriated through the options available to a knowing and choosing agent confronted with the task of acting in a fashion manifest to others. These options consist in physically grasping, forming or marking the chosen entity so that others are made aware of the intended significance of these acts and respond by limiting their own respective grasping, forming, and marking to different unclaimed objects.[10] Only when these concomitant aspects of recognition take place will a possession be established that commands the respect making it entitled ownership. The entitlement in question rests on no prior divine or natural laws, nor on any positive commands of some prevailing authority. It resides instead in two coordinate features: that the appropriation is an act of self-determination whereby an agent determines his or her agency as owner, and that it proceeds in harmony with the similar self-determinations of the other participants. As such, it commands the normative validity of freedom, while being an exercise of recognized right that no less involves performing the duty to respect the like right of others.

All these features are indispensable to the interaction giving self-determination its minimal reality. Nevertheless, they are only able to figure as elements of the original appropriation of property due to the particular character of the entity whose ownership they make possible. If any property at all is to be appropriated, a special kind of property must first be acquired, and acquired not by just one person, but by all who are engaged in the ensuing interaction. This property is the body of each individual, which must be recognized as the object of that individual's own will if agents are to be able to manifest their own free volition in any objective manner. If instead their bodies stand unclaimed or subsumed under the will of another, nothing they do, not grasping, forming, marking, or any other act will exhibit the free will of the self inhabiting each body by nature. So long as the physical being of an individual is not recognized by others as an inviolable object of his or her own free will, nothing that individual says or does can represent an exercise of freedom. Without ownership of one's own body, an individual is a virtual slave of nature, the unrecognized arbitrariness of the self, or the will of others. In each case, the individual stands deprived of the basis for engaging in any further self-determination. Since every action would be that of a body failing to reveal the reality of the free will of the self inhabiting it, the individual simply could not engage in any relations of right. Not only would all free participation in the family, society, or politics be excluded, but all exercise of moral agency would be rendered impossible. Without one's actions counting as one's own, one's intentions would have no deed to inform and there would be nothing for which one could be held morally responsible.

Taking ownership of one's own body is therefore the precondition for all further relations of right, including most immediately the entitled appropriation of other unclaimed entities, their subsequent transfer through contract, and the acts of non-malicious wrong, fraud, crime, and punishment that may follow upon them. Since the ownership of one's body cannot be relinquished without losing the capacity for free action, this original property not only presupposes no other, but has the unique characteristic of being inalienable.[11] Although one may contract to let another have use of the activity of one's body for a restricted period of time, the body's activity cannot be alienated as a whole. If it were completely alienated, one would rob oneself of the ability to be self-determined, canceling one's own personhood, which no one has a *right* to do.[12]

This is a point not understood by the young Marx, who argued in the *Paris Manuscripts* that the relation between labor and capital rests on a total self-alienation of the laborer consisting in the selling of his or herself to the capitalist.[13] Contrary to the avatars of wage labor alienation, it makes no sense for an individual to sell his or herself, for, as Locke pointed out in the chapter on property of his *Second Treatise On Government*, no one can enjoy the autonomy of being party to a contract and at the same time forfeit that autonomy by entering into slavery as an object of contract. To give Marx his due, it should be noted that in *Capital* he did finally correct the error of his youthful conception by distinguishing between labor power and labor, and recognizing that the transaction between worker and capitalist consists in the former's sale of his or her labor power for a restricted period of time, rather than in a wage slavery where the worker hands his or herself over in exchange for the means of subsistence reproducing his or her servitude.

8.1.5 *The Solution to the Vicious Circularity of Original Appropriation*

For all its obvious primacy, the process of obtaining ownership of one's body seems to suffer from a hopeless circularity, casting in doubt the entire reality of freedom, and with it, the quest for justice. The difficulty is painfully simple. Whereas ownership of one's body is a prerequisite for engaging in any recognized free action, taking entitled possession of it requires acting upon oneself in a manner that others can recognize as an act of self-appropriation. To accomplish this the body must act explicitly upon itself. For this purpose, the mode of forming and marking would appear more suitable than a grasping that would here be indistinguishable from what it grasps. The problem is how can one form or mark one's physical reality to designate it for others as the object of one's will if the body with which one acts is not already recognized as the vehicle and property of one's will? The original establishment of right seems compelled to presuppose itself, which is just what it must not do if it is to represent the minimal structure of self-determination.

What makes possible a solution to this dilemma is the distinction between the choosing will, with which the self is endowed independently of its relations to other individuals, and the free will, which an individual can actually exercise only within an existing interaction of right. Prospective owners engaged in appropriating their own bodies do, and indeed, must have minds and choosing wills prior to entering into any rightful relation with one another. If they did not, they could not possibly perform or understand any deliberative actions whatsoever. In that case, slavery would be equally unthinkable, for a slave, as opposed to a domestic animal, is precisely an individual who has a mind and a will, but no acknowledged rights. Just as concentration camp victims may suffer total bondage without losing their capacity to judge and choose, so citizens of a republic may enjoy conventional political freedom without deriving from them their ability to deliberate and decide. Relations of justice may be unworkable without individuals with functioning minds and wills, but possession of a functioning mind and will does not depend upon any institutional conditions. Consequently, before individuals establish any relations of right, they can act in an understandably voluntary way, just as they can distinguish between the voluntary and involuntary actions of others and comprehend what their actions mean if proper explanations are given. Voluntary action whose meaning is explained is not, however, rightful action of a self-determining agent unless it figures within a reciprocal relation between individuals where what one freely does enjoys the respect of others and corroborates what they freely do.

Therefore individuals can succeed in taking entitled possession of their bodies so long as the actions with which they designate their bodies as their own are recognized by and proceed in recognition of other correlatively occupied individuals. Provided that this reciprocal interaction ensues, their choosing wills attain the additional status of free wills of persons lording over the inalienable property of their own bodies. Then and only then does their freedom gain an existence allowing them to engage in other acts of self-determination.

In this fashion the minimal structure of freedom builds a real relation of right that all others must presuppose and preserve within their own interactions as an irreducible structural component. No further institutions of self-determination can fail to incorporate the entitled appropriation of the individual's own body, for otherwise, no agent could rightfully perform any act as his or her own. This means that the reciprocal establishment of personhood, the conventional autonomy of property owners, is not a principle of justice from which other institutions are derived. Although it does comprise an indispensable relation of right that must be incorporated within all other structures of justice, it does not provide a principle for determining what they should be in their own separate right. Consequently, the minimal structure of freedom does not raise the problem of foundationalism any more than does indeterminacy in its role as the starting point of the development of categories.

8.2 The Move beyond the Minimal Structure of Justice

The original establishment of property, where individuals become owners of their own bodies, may provide the rudimentary structural component needed for any other relations of freedom, but it does not itself determine their character, nor how many further institutions of justice are necessary, nor what connection they should have to one another. Due to its constitutive elementarity, the minimal relation of right offers no more direction to the theory of justice than indeterminacy provided for the development of categories. How then can the theory of the reality of freedom, the philosophy of right, have any further systematic development?

Only two aids are available to provide any guide: rational reconstruction and the negative prescriptions entailed by the normative validity of self-determination.

Rational reconstruction offers the strategy of advancing to those relations that bring something new to justice without requiring any resources beyond what has already been established. In the present case, two basic factors are at hand, the natural reality of choosing selves inhabiting a common world and the minimal relation of right in which they have appropriated their own bodies as the inalienable property of their wills and thereby assumed the status of entitled owners, obligated to respect each other's property. Rational reconstruction must therefore be employed to determine what further relations of right can be constructed from these terms, and these terms alone.

The immediate answer is familiarly straightforward, and provides a succession of relations that logically follow upon one another. Hegel has developed these relations in detail in his discussion of "Abstract Right" in the *Philosophy of Right*. Although he tends to obscure the role of interaction in the property relations that precede contract, his argument generally follows the proper sequence. It is the basic outline of this development, rather than Hegel's particular presentation of it, which is our concern here.

Once agents have taken ownership of their own bodies, the first order of right consists in the way in which they, as owners, are now entitled to use their property. This is a simple matter. Since ownership of one's body is an inalienable right, the use of one's body is exclusively and totally one's own prerogative.

Given the enjoyment of this right to be one's own master of the living organism one inhabits, the next option for a person's self-determination consists in appropriating other objects. No added resources are required for this to occur, since now that agents have gained ownership of their bodies, to the exclusion of slavery, they can readily grasp, form or mark other appropriable objects in ways explicitly representing to others the embodiment of their wills. Furthermore, individuals can here join together and take common ownership of objects, establishing a type of owner who no longer comprises a natural individual, but a wholly artificial self constituted by the wills of those owners combining to establish its reality as owner.[14] Either way, the property established through these recognized actions can be freely alienated by its owners without canceling their freedom, unlike the inalienable property of their bodies, Thus, even though an individual requires property to enjoy the conventional autonomy of property owner, one can dispose of all one's other objects of property and remain a free owner, since one will still retain entitled ownership of that unique inalienable property, one's body.

This presents an opportunity for further types of self-determination. Once individuals have taken ownership of objects in addition to their own bodies, the resources are at hand for the additional property relations consisting in their free disposal of their alienable possessions. Since the appropriation of alienable property can be undertaken by an owner who is a single natural individual or an artificial self in which a plurality of natural individuals have combined their ownership, every relation that follows can involve these two types of owners in all possible permutations.

Because ownership entails the right to use one's property, the disposal of property can involve either relinquishing the use of the property or alienating its ownership entirely. Insofar as the unrestricted use of property is tantamount to owning it, the distinction between alienating the use and alienating the ownership of property only has meaning when the former consists in alienating the use of the object in a limited way.

In the first instance, the disposal of property can consist simply in complete abandonment where one withdraws one's will from the object in a fashion duly recognized by others. The object then becomes an unclaimed thing ready for appropriation and use by someone else.

Secondly, the property can be alienated by transferring its ownership or restricted use to someone else. Naturally, since ownership or entitled use of property are both modes of self-determination, one cannot transfer them to another party unless that party agrees to appropriate or so use it. Consequently, all transfer of property involves reciprocal acts of will by both parties involved. This is true even when the transfer is a gift, where no property is received in return. The transfer of the ownership or restricted use of property thus comprises a relation of contract, where two or more parties concur in willing the transfer and thereby assume the obligation to respect the change in ownership or use that their actions have consummated. Since the transfer can be onesided, as in presenting a gift, or an exchange of properties or of the restricted use of properties, contract takes two basic forms, that of gift and that of exchange. Each may involve either appropriation of the entire property of the object involved, or merely its use for a limited period of time, or both together in any variety of combinations. It should be evident that all these contractual relations rely for their operation on nothing more than the presence of choosing individuals who already have inalienable ownership of their own bodies, including some who have appropriated alienable property of one sort or other, which might consist simply in ownership of restricted use of their own capacities.

The progression from original appropriation to the ownership of alienable property and the disposal of the latter would not be complete either conceptually or in actuality if due note were not taken of the parallel relations of wrong that they make possible. The moment individuals have determined themselves as owners of their own bodies, the abiding presence of their choosing wills allows for each and any agent to commit wrong upon another, either with intent to violate the established right of ownership of others or non-maliciously out of ignorance or a conflicting interpretation of where their respective rights and obligations extend. In the former case, the perpetrator consciously violates the property right of an owner and thereby commits a crime. In the latter case, the perpetrator commits a non-malicious wrong, infringing on the self-determination of another without intending to do so. Crime and non-malicious wrong both refer to the preexisting self-determination of owners, without which they can no more occur than be conceived. Furthermore, the performance of criminal and non-malicious wrong requires no more than the contribution of the arbitrariness of choice, which enables each owner to violate the very obligations which provide for his or her own rights. Since their prerequisites are thereby entirely accounted for, these two types of wrong can be systematically introduced as part of the development of property relations in strict observance of the demands of theoretical self-responsibility.

Nevertheless, it could be objected that wrong has no place in the theory of justice since the doing of wrong is not itself a form of self-determination, but only an exercise of arbitrariness running counter to the existing reality of the freedom of owners. Certainly, the performance of wrong does not give the free will a new respected objectivity. It instead places the perpetrator in a position of self-contradiction, committing an act contrary to the very relations of right on which rests every individual's autonomy. However, for just this reason wrong belongs as a topic of property relations, comprising as it does a form of activity defined exclusively in reference to those relations and building an endemic part of their reality.

The development of the forms of wrong naturally follows the development of the forms of property. Once alienable property is at hand, the range of crime and non-malicious wrong expands beyond infringement of the individuals' exclusive rule over his body to include the ways in which alienable property relations can be violated. With contract, their range extends yet further to include the possibility of committing fraud, the crime consisting in using the form of contract to misrepresent the transfer of property for the express harm of an owner.

In this fashion, the minimal reality of right spawns a whole system of property relations, exhausting the possibilities of self-determination available to agents in their capacity as owners. Just as the acquisition of alienable property presupposes and incorporates the ownership of inalienable property, and relations of contract presuppose and incorporate both of these, so crime and non-malicious wrong presuppose the entire slew of obligation and entitlement in violation of which their acts proceed. Finally, only with the doing of wrong, resting upon and referring to the prior relations, can there be conceived or actualized the process of righting wrong where, given the resources of interacting property owners, the injuries of victims are compensated and violators of right receive their due.

8.2.1 The Limits of Property

Through rational reconstruction, the theory of justice is able to move from its necessary starting point, the minimal reality of freedom, to conceive the entire domain of property relations consisting in the self-determination of owners who, as yet, confront one another in no further right-bearing capacity. Having come this far, it is necessary to step back and ask whether there is any need to go farther, and if so, towards what destination. The answer to the first part of this query is not provided through rational reconstruction, which would have to take up forms of conduct given in reality or theory and then reconceive them as relations of freedom constituted out of what property relations make available. Instead, the impetus for extending the theory of justice beyond property relations comes from examining these relations in light of the terms of normative validity provided by the concept of self-determination. As we have seen, justice must consist in the self-ordered reality of freedom, not in relationships incapable of sustaining themselves through their own means. The problem with property relations is that although they consist in self-determinations, they cannot maintain the freedom they involve without relying on factors beyond themselves.

What makes this evident is the predicament of owners in the face of wrong. Although the mere plurality of choosing selves provides all that is necessary for establishing and exercising the freedoms of ownership, property relations by themselves cannot prevent the incidence of non-malicious wrong, fraud, and crime from putting the rights of owners in jeopardy. Because property relations involve concomitant personal decisions determining which entities are recognized as property and who is acknowledged as their owners, it is always possible for individuals to dispute what has been taken into entitled possession and by whom, to defraud others by misrepresenting an object of contract, or to openly violate the person and property of someone else. Property relations provide no adequate means to adjudicate such disputes, punish offenders or provide victims the retribution they are due. All property rights involve are persons interacting on an equal footing, with none enjoying any recognized privilege to mandate what is just. As a consequence, cases of nonmalicious wrong remain unresolvable so long as the disputing parties refuse to come to a common interpretation of what are their respective properties and/or contractual obligations.[15] Similarly, criminal acts can receive neither an objectively binding judgment nor any objectively valid punishment. Without a universally recognized authority with an entitled prerogative to right wrong, anyone who attempts to punish another risks committing a further wrong of revenge if others do not recognize the act as appropriate.[16]

These problems signify that the freedom of property owners cannot secure its own reality. This leaves two alternatives. Property relations are sustained thanks either to the support of conduct and institutions that are not relations of freedom or to the aid of other structures of self-determination. In the former case, justice would be subverted, since property rights would have as their condition relations that lack the self-determined character required for normative validity. Justice therefore dictates the second alternative, that property relations be realized through the activity of some further structures of freedom.

This requirement, mandated by the terms of normative validity, ordains a further provision in light of the prescriptions of rational reconstruction. Namely, whatever structure of freedom comes to the aid of property rights must be constituted solely out of the material supplied by the relations between owners.

Provided such a mode of freedom can be conceived, an additional prescription must be served. Since the unity of different institutions of freedom cannot be imposed upon them by something outside the order of justice, the form of self-determination insuring that wrong be righted must either unite itself with property relations or else be subject to further institutions of freedom that unify the system of rights to which they belong. Naturally, this proviso need not be answered immediately by the structure of freedom that follows upon property relations.

Taking heed of all these points, the theory of justice can advance beyond the domain of property and owners to address its next theme.

8.3 Morality and the Realization of Right

It must not be forgotten that the required move beyond property relations cannot consist in making their interaction a first principle of justice from which additional institutions are derived. To avoid reinstating the dilemmas of liberty, one must rather take the self-determination of owners as the most elementary component of the reality of freedom, incorporated in all further relations of justice without, however, being their determining ground. If individuals do not have recognized ownership of their own bodies, that most basic property presupposed by all other property relations, they certainly cannot engage in any further independent activity and exercise the rights that might be at stake in morality, the family, society, or the state. Nevertheless, disposing over property does not determine what are the other freedoms individuals ought to enjoy.

Hegel's *Philosophy of Right* is instructive in suggesting what follows from the internal problems of property relations. There he proposes that the unresolved wrong endemic in abstract right calls for neither household, social, nor political institutions, but for morality, understood as the interaction in which individuals seek to bring right into existence through their autonomous action towards others, recognizing that only in so doing will their own conduct be just.

Two complementary factors make Hegel's suggestion plausible. First, in contrast to the institutions of family, society, and state, moral activity refers to personhood without depending upon any additional relations of right. Indeed, the generic occasion for moral intervention is the perceived inability of the existing order to resolve all problems of right through its own workings. In acting as moral subjects, individuals treat the doing of justice as something depending on an individual initiative and responsibility transcending the roles pursued through given institutions. This can occur in any situation provided that individuals direct their actions at doing right towards one another on the basis of what their own consciences dictate to be good. Since moral action leaves it the responsibility of the subject to determine how right should be realized, it effectively proceeds in indifference to the authority of prevailing institutions. Consequently, it presumes no other elements of justice than the presence of property relations. These are required to the extent that individuals must have recognized ownership of at least their own bodies if they are to be held responsible for their actions. If, on the contrary, they lack the status of owner, they are no better than slaves, whose actions are the responsibility of the masters to whom they belong. Therefore, as much as moral autonomy leaves righting wrong the responsibility of the individual, the right that moral action seeks to realize at least involves the entitlements of property owners.

On the other hand, although moral action incorporates the duties of property owning persons, morality is not reducible to the self-determination of owners. Moral subjects interact not just as persons, embodying their wills in property, but as individuals responsible for realizing right through their own actions. Morality can thus stand as a discrete mode of self-determination. In contrast to the relations of property by which owners relate, morality consists in the interaction where individuals exercise the right and duty of relating to one another through self-determined actions recognizably prefigured in a conscious purpose aimed at each other's right and welfare.

What makes moral action a mode of self-determination, rather than an exercise of arbitrary choice, are the constitutive features that make it a structure of interaction and not a monological relation. Moral agency necessarily involves relations among a plurality of moral subjects insofar as acting morally consists in doing right to other moral subjects. These other individuals count as moral subjects to whom right should be done only to the extent that they act in a morally accountable way as well. This is something they can do only in reference to other moral subjects fulfilling the very same requirement. As a consequence, one not only chooses to perform a specific deed in acting morally; one first establishes for oneself the artificial persona of moral subject by interacting with others who determine their own new form of agency in the same fashion. In acting morally, individuals therefore fulfill the obligation to do right to others by exercising the correlative right to be recognized as moral agents, duly responsible for their own deeds. Events in this century have given horrendous testimony to what can occur when individuals are robbed of this right and judged and condemned for factors independent of their actions, such as their race, religion, or class background. The concentration camps of the Holocaust and GULAG should dispel any doubts that moral action is a structure of interaction, and not just a monological endeavor.

If these brief remarks suggest how morality can appropriately follow property relations as a second form of self-determination, it is worth examining Hegel's suggestion that moral action has its own endemic limits that leave it anything but the culminating structure of justice.[17] The problem that Hegel identifies lies at the very core of moral interaction. Whereas the subject exercises moral autonomy by acting to realize the good encompassing right and welfare, this moral good has no intrinsic particular content. The reason it has none is that it is constitutively an ought requiring action by the moral subject to determine and bring it into being. Even though the rights of owners have an objective form that moral action should heed, the entitlements of particular individuals are no more unequivocally determined than who has violated property rights or what must be done to right their wrongs. Thus, the universal rights of property relations still leave room for the moral situation where it is up to each individual to take the realization of right into their own hands as a matter of conscience. The dilemma afflicting the moral predicament is that the putatively objective good that the moral subject ought to intend and realize can only obtain its actual content through the subjective determination of individual conscience. Conscience, however, has nothing but its own subjective arbitrariness to rely on in deciding what is good. Consequently, it cannot come to any unquestionably valid moral determinations. Yet, conscience has no lesser task than guiding the moral subject to perform what is unconditionally right. The resulting discrepancy leaves every moral action a moral problem, both for its author, as well as for the others who interact with him or her in view of one's responsibility for one's deed.

Despite this difficulty, morality retains as much legitimacy as property relations, for moral action still comprises a mode of mutually respected self-determination, carrying with it its own right and duty. Even if it remains always debatable whether a particular moral act has succeeded in achieving the good its author intends, that author has assumed a self-imposed role of moral accountability by taking that deed. Be this as it may, the correlative abstractness of the good and the inability of conscience to determine it objectively do indicate that moral interaction cannot be the crowning form of freedom with which the theory of justice can safely conclude. Although morality does provide a new form of autonomy commanding its own authority, morality fails to resolve the wrongs endemic to property relations. Accordingly, the need remains for further institutions of justice to attend to this abiding problem. In addition, morality introduces a problem of its own that conscience addresses but cannot unambiguously solve, namely the problem of establishing an existing structure of freedom in which the recognized reality of right and welfare is objectively at hand in the self-determination of interacting individuals.

Taken together with the limitations of property relations, those of morality indicate how freedom cannot be restricted to personhood and moral autonomy, as traditional liberal theory and Kantian practical philosophy tended to do in presenting their own naturally determined versions of these relationships. By themselves, the actions of owners and moral subjects cannot enforce the very rights of which they are the exercise. Once again, there are two alternatives: property relations and morality are sustained either by institutions that are not institutions of freedom, leaving the rights of property owners and moral subjects grounded on injustice, or by further relations of self-determination that ultimately give all spheres of right a unity grounded in freedom. For the theory of justice, there is little choice — the second option must be conceived as the next order of business.

In light of the demands of normativity, the structures of property relations and morality provide two guidelines for what should follow. First, the next structure of freedom must be irreducible to them, yet require no other relations of right in order to be constituted. Second, this further structure of freedom must either by itself, or in conjunction with additional structures, attend to realizing the rights to which owners and moral subjects are entitled. Ultimately, this means that justice requires an existing institutional framework embodying the reality of the rights of the individuals belonging to it. As an institution of freedom in its own right, such a framework will consist in an exercise of self-determination by agents who thereby constitute the regime securing their other freedoms as well. In such a domain, the good its participants realize through their actions will be the very order making those actions possible.

These requirements might suggest that political institutions of freedom are next on the agenda. The path of rational reconstruction indicates, however, the presence of two other pre-political spheres that can be reconstructed as institutions of freedom incorporated by the state without themselves presupposing political relations. These are the domains of family and society, which can be drawn into the theory of justice provided they can take a form consisting entirely in relations of self-determination.

Hegel is perhaps the first thinker to suggest that household and society can both be conceived as normatively valid institutions of freedom. Although his account provides a basis for conceiving them in this fashion, it is also burdened by frequent introductions of extraneous relations that owe their content not to self-determination, but to either natural differences or the given institutional forms of his day. In the discussion that follows, an attempt will be made to outline how family and society can be ordered as valid institutions of justice, free of the extraneous elements that mar Hegel's own presentation.

Chapter 9

The Family As An Institution of Freedom

If the family is to have an integral place in the realm of justice, it must be reconstructed as an institution comprising a new mode of autonomy transcending property and morality without implicating society or the state. This might appear to be beyond the limits of the household for the reason that membership in the family has traditionally been rooted as much in the natural necessity of birth and gender as in any contribution of freedom. If indeed individuals are born into families, to which they are tied by blood rather than will, and then form families of their own by entering a bond based on gender differences, how can the household provide a mode of self-determination worthy of normative validity?

9.1 The Basic Structure of the Free Household

An answer to this problem begins to take form when one considers an idea of family unity present in Hegel's discussion of the household.[1] This idea consists in understanding the just family as an association established by individuals through mutual consent wherein they freely unite into a joint person with a common property and welfare, sustained by their reciprocally recognized desire to make that bond the end of their action towards one another. In forming such a household, each party assumes rights and duties specific to being a family member. These rights and duties consist not in following natural inclination or any other extraneous end, but in acting freely so

185

as to promote the autonomy of the family itself. Only as a family member can an individual exercise that particular type of freedom, just as only as a family member is one obliged to contribute to the household good in which the like autonomy of the other members is rooted.

If this scheme is examined in light of the previously established rights, the structure of household freedom takes on a more concrete character. As we have seen, property relations provide all the necessary resources for establishing common ownership. Morality, on the other hand, provides a framework of mutual accountability where individuals are obliged to act for the sake of one another's right and welfare. As an institution of freedom, the family incorporates both of these dimensions into the common household it establishes.

Like any other form of ownership, the joint person and property of the family achieves rightful existence through respect for and recognition of other persons. Consequently, the enactment of the family bond must be made in a publicly recognizable and recognized form. In other words, the act of mutual consent whereby individuals join together as family members must take the form of a marriage respected by others. By the same token, any subsequent agreement by spouses to dissolve their bond must take shape as a publicly recognized divorce.

This role of recognition signifies that the just family is situated from the start within a context of other persons, bearing the same rights of ownership and moral accountability that qualify one to enter marriage. As a consequence, being a family member involves playing a role with two dimensions. Besides acting towards other household members according to the rights and duties they share, every family member is in the position of acting towards individuals outside the family. In this capacity, each family member relates to outsiders not merely as a person and moral subject, but as a representative of the family, responsible for promoting its right and welfare.

On these terms, the family comprises a household of freedom, erected through the recognized agreement of its founders. They need no other qualification than that of sharing what can aptly be called, following Hegel, an ethical love.[2] This consists not in a psychological feeling, but in the desired commitment to treat one another as moral members of a common person and property, with both the right and duty to act for that end. Romantic feelings and physical passion may wax and wane, but neither comprise necessary nor sufficient conditions for entering or sustaining the bond between spouses. That bond has its rights and obligations not through the compulsion of body, feeling, or external authority, but solely through free will as expressed in the reciprocal pledge to form a common home. United on these terms, the household enjoys normative validity because it is an institution of self-determination. Arising out of mutual choice, it has no other purpose than to provide an association entirely determined by the wills of its members who therein give themselves a form of autonomy whose reality and end is their association itself.

9.2 Natural Difference and Household Rights

Reconstructing the family as an institution of freedom presents a challenge to many of the household forms that have dominated world culture. Marriages arranged without the consent of the parties involved are incompatible with its concept, as are marriages that cannot be dissolved by the will of the marriage partners. So too are any requirements that tie the validity of marriage to the performance of the natural function of procreation. Whether or not family members give birth to children is a matter of both involuntary circumstance and choice on which the unity of the free family does not depend. In this regard, the relation of parent and child is an optional one whose absence in no way compromises the validity of the household.

9.2.1 Gender, Sexual Orientation, and the Rights of Spouses

This point is relevant to a further issue of considerable current interest. If the just family is to be an association of freedom, given differences of gender and sexual orientation cannot mandate household roles. Although historically both marriage and child rearing have been limited to couples of the opposite sex, this restriction violates justice by allowing a natural distinction to determine the family rights of individuals. Since gender and sexual preference have nothing to do with an individual's capacity to accept the rights and duties of family membership, it makes no difference as far as justice is concerned whether spouses and parents are of the same or different gender and sexual orientation.

Similarly, although the generic family relations to those within and without the household have been historically divided between woman and man as distinct feminine and masculine roles, the just household cannot be bound by these customs. No matter what their gender, household members have as much right and obligation to attend to internal domestic matters as to represent the family in dealings outside the home. Although spouses may decide to divide duties along traditional lines, this has validity only if it is done with mutual consent. Of course, when the family consists of members of the same gender, the traditional identification of masculinity and femininity with male and female gender reveals its utter arbitrariness.

This makes it all the more evident that Hegel doubly violates the spirit of his own ethics of freedom by limiting marriage to a heterosexual relation where man and woman have different roles based on their gender, the man taking charge of the household and representing its affairs in the outside world, the woman restricting her activity to child rearing and domestic chores.[3]

9.2.2 Monogamy and the Nuclear Family

It might appear that the modern monogamous nuclear family is particularly suited to comply with all the requisite prohibitions of natural discrimination and stand, aptly reconstructed, as the model of the free household. Hegel, for one, is quite ready to canonize its form as paradigmatic for the just family. Yet, it is worth considering whether the rights and duties of the free household are automatically incompatible with either a polygamous[4] arrangement or a nonnuclear, extended family.

Hegel rejects polygamy on the grounds that it involves a nonreciprocal relation contradicting the equality and exclusive tie between spouses that is constitutive of a household born of mutual consent.[5] Certainly, many cultures have had polygamous families in which spouses are not on an equal footing. Nevertheless, a family with more than two spouses can have totally reciprocal rights and duties, so long as each spouse has the same prerogatives and responsibilities as every other. Of course, it might be argued that such an arrangement is psychologically impossible, and cannot help but lead to violations of freedom rooted in emotional and sexual domination. Hegel makes no such argument, although his objection to polygamy would require something of that order if it were to be sustained.

It is worth noting in this connection that Hegel's attempt to justify the traditional incest taboo suffers from similar problems.[6] He suggests that members of the same family cannot be married, since marriage can only occur between individuals who have distinct personalities, something they do not have if they belong to the same household. With regard to freedom, the only "personalities" that could here be of relevance are the psychological identity whose health could be considered a precondition for autonomy or the personhood of the individual, something that is joined together in the common property and welfare of the household. Due to the latter unification, parents and children, and brothers and sisters who are still part of the same home certainly cannot face one another as distinct persons in the sense in which prospective spouses would have to. Yet, once children have reached maturity and established homes of their own, the unity of personality would no longer be a factor, nor ever be a factor if one were to take a case as extreme as that of Oedipus. Other reasons are needed to justify the incest taboo, but Hegel fails to deliver them.

As for the extended family, it might appear at odds with the strictures of freedom to the extent that not only its children but its adult members seem to belong to their household due to blood relations rather than mutual consent. However, the fact that several generations of relatives live together in a common household does not necessarily mean that their family bond has been imposed by nature rather than by their respective wills. Certain cultures may indeed be characterized by extended families based on consanguinity rather than freedom, but that does not eliminate the possibility that an extended family could be reconstructed along lines in accord with self-determination. However, in a case where the members of the extended family form a common household through mutual agreement, the question would arise as to whether the adult members all bear the rights and obligations of spouses to one another, raising all the issues germane to polygamy. If, on the other hand, those rights and duties did not apply indiscriminately, one could question whether the extended household were really a united family, or rather an arrangement in which separate families have banded together without completely submerging their discrete character. Any claim that the nuclear family has an exclusive validity depends on resolving these questions.

9.2.3 Natural versus Ethical Parenthood

Whether a family be nuclear or extended, the exclusion of natural discrimination has particular significance for the relation of parent and child. Just as being a spouse and parent should not be tied to natural factors that are irrelevant to exercising freedom, so too the ethical duties and rights of parent and child have no direct connection to the natural relation between biological parents and offspring. They cannot, for if freedom is the substance of justice, no rights and duties can simply issue from biological givens. If the young are to figure as children in the family, with household rights of their own, it must not be in virtue of blood, but by the publicly accepted commitment of their parents to give them the shelter and care needed to enable them to develop into autonomous persons, moral subjects, and family members. Thus, the rightful children of parents need not be their off-spring, but can legitimately be adopted by individuals who have no natural tie to them. What counts is that the bond between child and parent be sustained in the parent's acceptance of the obligations of child rearing and the recognition of that acceptance on the part of others. When this acceptance is withdrawn or ignored, right requires that new individuals assume the duties of parent.

9.3 The Place of Children in the Family

Of course, all talk of parental rights and obligations rests on the legitimacy of child rearing within the family. This is a principal conceptual problem for any discussion of the household, for it refers to the natural process of maturation that might appear to have no place in the system of freedom. Nevertheless, justice must grapple with the fact that individuals are born into the world as helpless infants who not only must undergo natural growth before they are able to attain the understanding and will to exercise rights and perform duties, but must be cared for in order to reach their maturity.

Because freedom is for its own sake, children have an unconditional right to be brought up to the stage at which they are in a position to gain their autonomy. At that point, they cease, from a juridical point of view, to be mere children, and become instead fullfledged agents, entitled to all the rights and obliged by all the duties that freedom involves. The exact moment at which maturity is reached can vary according to the individual as well as according to the culture in which the child is raised. It is not something that can be conceptually specified. What is conceptually mandated is that whenever maturity is reached, one is entitled to dispose freely over property, be treated as a morally accountable subject, and leave the place of one's upbringing to establish a home of one's own. Before that time, however, the child must endure the special predicament of being an individual who is not actually free, but has the recognized potential for autonomy. As such, the child is entitled to be subject to the authority of others provided they act so as to promote the child's maturation to autonomy.

These strictures enable the home to be an institution of freedom even though one can be member of a family by birth or adoption and be subject to its authority without willing to be. So long as one does not have a recognizably competent mind and will of one's own, that is, as long as one remains a child, one's family membership is not an infringement of autonomy, but rather a precondition for its realization. When, however, one ceases to be a child one has a right to cast off parental authority and form a family of one's choice. Consequently, the family membership of an autonomous individual can always be determined through freedom. The presence of child rearing in the home thus does not prevent it from being an institution of justice.

One can still ask, of course, whether the upbringing of children is something that ought to occur in the family or under some other aegis. That children can be brought up in accord with freedom itself testifies to the legitimacy of rearing children in the home. However, it does not automatically establish the home as the exclusive place for raising children. As we have seen, the natural parents of children have no unconditioned right to rear them. If the household is to be a place where the right of children to mature is observed, then parents are obliged to provide the needed upbringing, and if they fail that obligation, they relinquish their right to parental authority, no matter whether their children are their offspring or adopted. Although another family may then step in and take charge of the abandoned or illtreated children, it is not inconceivable that no families be available to take on parental responsibility as needed. This possibility suggests of itself that securing the child's right to a proper upbringing may be beyond the powers of the family and require at least the supplement of some other institution.

9.4 The Limits of Family Freedom

As an institution of freedom, existing for the sake of the rights and duties proper to its own form of self-determination, the family provides a type of justice beyond the ken of what its members enjoy as mere owners and moral subjects. Unlike property relations, which leave each owner determined in terms of external objects, and unlike moral action, which always seeks to realize a right not yet at hand, the freedom specific to the family member reproduces the same freely established association that already comprises the framework in which such action occurs. In this way, the free household embodies the existing unity of autonomy and realized right for which morality always strives without ever unequivocally achieving.

Nevertheless, the freedom of the family is still burdened by deficiencies that call for further institutions of justice. These deficiencies are of two kinds, each defined entirely by the limits of household right and each providing a mandate for extending the reality of freedom.

First, it is no secret that by themselves, family relations have no means to insure that household members abide by the rights and duties of spouses and of parents and children. Although spouses unite to form a common person with a common property and common welfare, this does not prevent disagreements from arising between them concerning how to serve the good of the household. The problem is that when conflicts do break out over management of the home or the raising of children, there is no third party available within the family to adjudicate the dispute. Recourse to other individuals and families outside the stricken home can be of no avail. The mere plurality of persons and families offers no one possessing the binding authority to establish objectively when a marriage has been duly convened or annulled, or to compel spouses to respect each other's equal stake in household affairs, and to act responsibly for the welfare of their children and home. On the contrary, every other family and outside individual stands in the same predicament of bearing family rights and obligations that households cannot enforce either alone or in their plurality.

As a result, the family leaves the respect for its own right at the mercy of the arbitrariness of its members. There is no need to appeal to any outside criteria to realize that something must be done. The justice of the family itself requires some further institution to secure its own exercise of freedom.

This requirement, however, is not the only prescription that emerges from the concept of the normative household to guide the theory of justice in its further development. Besides the household's inability to realize its own freedom, there is the problem of the limited content of that freedom. Family freedom is limited to the extent that the autonomy realized in the existing bonds of the home has its sole legitimate end in the common weal of the household. Although this common weal depends for its rightful status on the recognition of others outside the home, it is still merely particular, being the right and welfare of a single family. Furthermore, this common weal is contingent since it rests on a shared feeling of ethical love, which may dissipate whenever spouses agree to dismember their family. True, they may still be obliged to fulfill their duties to their children, but the common good they shared together as spouses no longer survives.

An additional problem is that the common personhood and welfare of the household leaves no room for its members to interact on the basis of different particular ends of their own separate choosing. As members of the same family, all they have a right to will are actions that promote and maintain its common bond. The moment spouses begin to perform their household roles as individuals with divergent welfares and private domains, the home loses its constitutive unity. Admittedly, this is only a deficiency if the pursuit of private interests can be reconstructed as an interaction of freedom with rights and duties of its own. In that case, it would not be enough to secure the freedom of the family with an institution also realizing the rights of owners and moral subjects. Such an institution might satisfy the normative requirement of uniting property relations, morality and family right in an order of justice determined by a free activity of ruling, but if it did so in neglect of another mode of freedom, it would fail to complete its duty.

As we shall see, a community of interest can be reconstructed as an institution of freedom attending to the mandate of family justice without introducing political relations. In light of the limits of household freedom, this community will comprise a civil society whose members act towards one another in pursuit of their particular interests, as participants in an association that is universal in scope, yet consists in nothing but the reality of their self-determination. Given the abiding tasks of securing the rights of owners and the freedoms of the family, this society must also insure the property and household welfare of its members.

If such a society is to be introduced as the next institution of justice, it must incorporate property relations, morality and free households without requiring any further resources to compose its own normative community of interest. Our task is thus to consider how there can be a civil society consisting in the institutional order whose members enjoy the recognized freedom to pursue particular ends of their own choosing in public, so far as their action forwards the similar pursuit of interest on the part of others. Without such a society, individuals may dispose over property, act with moral accountability, and participate in the common weal of their family, but they cannot interact in pursuit of their chosen interests. This may not be the most sovereign freedom, but if it is lacking, the institutions of justice are left at odds with the interests of individuals. How wrong that would be can be demonstrated in only one way: by showing how the pursuit of interest can comprise a form of self-determination and so achieve normative validity.

Chapter 10

Economic Freedom and the Just Society

10.1 Justice and the Just Society

In modern times the quest for justice has been increasingly identified with the quest for a just society. Part and parcel of this identification has been the widespread conviction that the key to the just society lies in the order of its economy. Although little agreement has been reached over what that order should be, it has everywhere become a public issue of crucial importance. In this one respect, all sides seem to concur. Whether the economic order be promoted under the banner of bourgeois independence from serfdom, civilizing industry for the non-Western world, free enterprise to counter totalitarianism, or the free association of producers to end all exploitation and class division, the design of the economy has almost universally been granted a prime role in the making of the just society.

The pervasiveness of the current attention to society and economy cannot, however, mask the controversial nature of all this concern.

The identification of justice with the just society must first be called into question. This identification takes its most radical form in the vision of a communist utopia, where property has been abolished, the family has been disbanded, the state has withered away, and the only institution left is the society of associated producers. Obviously, every theory of justice that grants normative validity to non-social associations such as the household and the state presents a challenge to such a view. What must decide the issue is the structure of freedom. If the reality of self-determination is exclusively social in character,

194

then indeed, justice is one and the same as the just society. If, however, freedom can be shown to have non-social institutions, then the exclusive right of society is refuted.

The conception of property relations, morality and the household as modes of self-determination has already provided just such a refutation. It has demonstrated that a purely social order cannot possibly be the paradigm of justice for the simple reason that such a society would automatically exclude aspects of the reality of freedom, aspects that have been shown to be prerequisites for any further self-determination.[1] In addition, the normative requirement that the unity of justice be determined by an exercise of freedom already suggests that no order lacking institutions of political self-determination can possibly be a just order.

If the problem of a just society cannot be equated with the problem of justice, it can well be asked whether society and its economy deserve any place in the realm of the good life. Certainly Aristotle questioned their normative character by relegating village society and its market affairs to the secondary role of a precondition for politics, lying outside its exclusive domain of praxis. Although Aristotle's calling into question of such a thing as "social justice" may appear extreme to modern ears, it is striking to observe how pervasively modern thinkers have conceived economic affairs so that they lack all normative content.

10.1.1 The Problem of a Just Economy

Instead of conceiving the economy as part of a sphere of social justice with its own rights and duties, theorists of every ideological stripe have tended to purge economic activity of all normative dimension by construing it either as a natural function or as a monological working of a single self.

The natural conception of economic relations portrays them as a metabolism between man and nature endemic to the human condition. Its point of departure is the undeniable truism that man, as a living creature, has biological needs that must be satisfied through dealings with nature if human survival is to be assured. What the natural conception does that is not undeniable is presume that economic relations are essentially extensions of this law of survival. The result is that the economy gets reduced to a sphere of necessity, removed from all considerations of right and wrong. With its relations given by nature rather than determined by the free will of its participants, the economic order becomes a domain of necessary functions that make all action possible, but for whose design no actions are responsible. On these terms, the economy is a realm in which questions of justice can no more arise than in horticulture or physiology. If it has any laws of its own, these can only be the object of an economic science that is descriptive and not prescriptive in character. When classical political economy conceives need to be naturally determined by human physical requirements, derives exchange from a natural inclination to barter, and defines capital as the stock of goods required to sustain the laborer's life during production,[2] when neoclassical economics defines the factors of production as naturally scarce resources,[3] and when Marx[4] and Arendt[5] characterize production as an anthropological fact of man's species being, the natural conception is at work, whether or not all its consequences be recognized.

By contrast, the monological conception arrives at a like exclusion of normative considerations by determining economic relations through some function of the self. Once again, the point of departure is an undeniable feature of economic reality. The monological conception begins by observing that the agents in any economy have psychologically determined needs and engage in technical activity where an individual acts upon some material, impressing it with form. All this may be true, but it is another matter to assert that economic relations not only contain such aspects, but are defined by them. The monological account makes this reduction, which can take a variety of forms. It can consist in the adoption of a governing psychological principle, as in marginal utility theory, which determines the values of commodities by estimates of psychological desire. Alternately, it can involve conceiving economic activity as a technical process, following the paradigm in which a single agency acts upon objects according to causal laws. This technical model can be limited to production, rendering it a process where a laboring agent employs an instrument to impose new form upon a given material, or equally extended to distribution, making it a unilateral assignment of goods to consumers who get thereby treated as ordered objects as well. Either way, economic activity is left bereft of any normative content, for all it involves are functions of a single agency and objects, rather than relations between individuals wherein rights and duties can enter. This exclusion of justice from economics is the common outcome whether the monological approach take the form it does when marginal utility theorists draw their demand curves, when Heidegger[6] and Habermas[7] reduce production to technique and instrumental action, or when econometricians and socialist planners attempt to guide economies with schemes for technically allocating given resources.

Although the classical representatives of metaphysical and transcendental philosophy have largely followed the natural or monological conceptions of economic reality, they have not been blind to those conceptions' common implications for the theory of justice. Aristotle, for one, clearly recognized that if economic activity consisted entirely of *techne* and *poiesis*, that is, in instrumental action and making, then it would not be performed for its own sake, but for resultant products and satisfactions predicated upon purely particular needs rooted in either nature or arbitrary appetite. In that case, economic activity could not comprise the valid conduct of *praxis*, but would warrant exclusion from the affairs of justice, as an occupation unfit for citizens in their privileged capacity as political animals.[8] Kant, on his part, observed that if economic activity consisted in a technical working upon nature in response to psychologically determined needs, then it did not involve normative relations between autonomous selves. As a consequence, the economy would not be a proper province of the kingdom of ends, and economics would have to be excluded from practical philosophy, relegated instead to a positive science applying causal rules of the understanding to an empirical subject matter. This might lead to hypothetical imperatives indicating how certain results could be obtained by following a particular economic policy, but not to any categorical imperatives prescribing what economic ends are valid in themselves.

These conclusions underline that if economic reality can only be conceived in natural or monological terms, then the problem of a just economy is a false problem, ascribing normative significance to a type of activity that has none. If further, society incorporates the economy and is largely defined by it, then the whole question of social justice takes on a very doubtful cast. Society might provide a field in which other normative concerns make themselves felt, such as property entitlements, moral duties, household rights, and political prerogatives, but whether society involves entitlements of its own would appear debatable at the very least.

There is only one way to determine whether the concepts of a just economy and a just society are empty slogans or valid sections of the theory of justice. An attempt must be made to reconstruct economic relations as irreducible structures of freedom. If this can be achieved relying on no further resources than those provided by property relations, morality and free households, then the possibility of a just economy will be demonstrated together with the structures it must possess in order to have validity. This will require conceiving economic relations that are defined neither by natural necessity, psychological desire, or technical mastery, nor by other structures of freedom such as property or household relations. If the economy is to be a discrete domain with a justice of its own, it must be determined exclusively in terms of self-determinations whose form and content are specific to the economic interactions in which they consist. Provided an economic order of freedom can be so reconstructed, it will then be possible to investigate what further institutions can join with it in forming a just society, a society whose rights and duties are not political in character, but still irreducible to those of property, morality, and family.

10.2 The Critique of Political Economy

Despite the prevalence of natural and monological economic theories, the project of conceiving the economy as a sphere of justice has not gone unattended. Political economy, classically represented by Adam Smith, took up this task early on by seeking to conceive the wealth of nations as an economic system distinguishing proper civilized society from the forsaken life of savages.[9] In so doing, political economy portrays an economic order liberated from the confines of the household and free of direct political control. This economy occupies its own integral place within a civil society, operating according to laws of its own, worthy of treatment by a separate science of economics.

10.2.1 The Dilemma of Political Economy

Despite the normative claims that should have restricted political economists to using reason to conceive what order the economy should have, their new theory can well be understood as a descriptive account of the lawful motion they observed in the rising industrial economy of their age. Of course, the fact that a prescriptive theory has descriptive power does not disqualify its normative claims. It may just be that the described reality does correspond with what that reality ought to be. In the case of political economy, however, there is a problem at hand, reflecting a basic ambiguity underlying its approach. Although political economy seeks to conceive the just economic order as an independent social sphere of justice, it does not develop economic relations exclusively as interactions of self-determining agents. Instead, political economy situates its economic order within a civil society of such a nature that the economic relations within it are equally natural, monological and political in character.

This problem results from political economy's adoption of the framework of liberal theory. As we have seen, liberal theory conceives justice to lie in a civil order whose society and government have the common goal of realizing a liberty defined by the individual's natural capacity to choose freely among given alternatives. Accordingly, society is civil provided it builds a sphere where individuals can enjoy their naturally grounded liberty to dispose over property and pursue their particular interests. This is made possible thanks to the regulation and protection provided by a government exclusively devoted to securing the harmonious exercise of the liberty of each civilian. Political economy embraces this natural right construction of society and its concomitant reduction of politics to civil government by conceiving the economy as part of a society whose pursuit of particular interest is equally the end to which government is subordinated. Consequently, the economic order can well be called a "political economy," given that in the civil society to which it belongs, politics consists in nothing more than protecting the same liberty at work in the market.

If this blurs the independent character of economic justice, what undermines the political economy's claim to normative validity is the form its own activity takes as part of liberal civil society. Because individuals participate in their political economy by exercising the natural liberty to pursue particular ends of their own choosing, their economic activity is defined in the same natural and monological terms that characterize liberal civil society.

This is well exhibited in Adam Smith's classic account. Despite his intention to uncover the economic order by which the just society is defined, Smith continually reduces relations that might be construed as interactions of freedom to relations of human metabolism and technical function. From the very outset, *The Wealth of Nations* characterizes economic needs and the goods satisfying them in terms of human physical requirement and correspondingly reduces labor to a technical process where an individual works directly upon objects of nature.[10] As a result, the division of labor is conceived to develop not from any social process involving rights and duties, but from a propensity in human nature to truck and barter.[11] So construed, it arises as a division between individual private producers who first work technically upon nature and only afterwards exchange the part of their product that they do not directly consume for their own sustenance.[12] Although this division leads to exchange relations that would seem to involve a mutual exercise of freedom, they are left governed by a labor theory of value that determines the prices at which commodities are bought and sold not by the wills of their owners, but by the labor embodied in their production. What makes this regulation completely external to freedom is that the labor in question consists in a technically defined labor process mandated by the anthropological necessity of human metabolism with nature.[13] Finally, capital itself, the ultimate form of wealth, gets introduced via the normatively neutral scheme of private producers. Despite capital's attested social power and indifference to any natural limits upon the magnitude of wealth, Smith baptizes it as the stock of subsistence goods needed to tide over the private producers while they await the sale of their respective wares.[14]

Although it is certainly true that political economy does not limit itself to these natural and monological terms in attempting to conceive how a normatively valid market society operates, all its efforts remain undercut by their abiding presence. By introducing the problem of the just economy in this ambiguous fashion, political economy calls for critique.

10.2.2 The Failure of Marx's Critique of Political Economy

A critique of political economy, committed to purging all natural and technical reductions from its theory, can serve as a means for reconstructing a proper concept of the just economy. Marx undertakes his critique of political economy with this goal in mind. In executing this goal, he resolves the critique of political economy into a theory of capital that conceives an economic order that is presumably social in character. Marx's theory of capital, however, does not pretend to be a theory of the just economy. It rather conceives of the economy of a specific historical formation, modern capitalist society, a society that Marx considers to be anything but just. Nevertheless, Marx suggests that his descriptive theory of the capitalist economy has prescriptive consequences that can serve as guidelines for a revolutionary politics.

Although an attempt to draw normative lessons from a descriptive theory might seem to be a nonsensical endeavor, Marx and his followers have sought the key to justice in the descriptive concept of modern capitalism. Marx's theory of capital presumes to offer normative conclusions on two accounts. First, it purports to show that a capitalist economy violates the principles of freedom and equality that are internal to it. Second, it claims to reveal how capitalism is victim of a dynamic that pushes towards the overthrow of its own relations of production and the establishment of a new economic order, an order in which justice is supposed to lie.

Even if Marx's claims be granted, they provide no basis at all for conceiving the just economy. That a capitalist economy violates its own values does not make it unjust unless its internal values are normatively valid and worthy of realization. It might be that those values are invalid, and that the internal inconsistency of capitalism is a mark in its favor. No descriptive theory of capital can decide the issue, for all it offers is a conceptualization of what the economic order is at a particular stage in history, and not what it ought to be. What is needed is a theory evaluating what principles should be observed by an economy. This is something Marx's theory of capital does not provide, even according to its own self-understanding.

By the same token, no dynamic of capitalist development can provide criteria for passing judgment on the justice of capitalism or the society that is to emerge from its ruins. Although the fascination of history has instilled a faith in progress leading many to identify what is progressive with what is just, mere succession in time is no guarantee that what follows is normatively superior to what precedes. Perhaps capitalism does necessarily give way to a socialist society. That fact does not make socialism any more desirable, nor cast aspersion on the justice of capital. What comes after may be a millenium of misery, whereas what history casts aside may be a vulnerable, unstable regime, but just all the same. Even if the theory of capital did demonstrate that capitalism engenders its own supersession by a communist society consistently embodying all its bourgeois ideals, the consistency of communism would be no mark of honor unless an independent theory of justice can certify that those ideals are the measure of the just society.

It is a notorious fact that Marx provides little in the way of the ethical theory needed to pass judgment on the legitimacy of capitalism. Although his theory of capital remains burdened by many of the natural reductions of political economy,[15] it does provide insights into commodity relations that have bearing on conceiving the just economy.[16] Nonetheless, when Marx turns his attention beyond capitalism and attempts to depict communist society, his sparse portrayals only bring the natural reductions of political economy to an empty extreme.

It is worth tracing Marx's line of thought to see how he reduces the problem of justice to a problem of the just society, only then to limit society to an economic order where normative considerations can have absolutely no role.

To begin with, Marx accepts the liberal assumption that politics is not a self-determined sphere, with sovereign goals of its own, but a domain determined by pre-political factors. He diverges from liberal theory by identifying the determining factor as class interest rather than natural right, and by then considering this foundation of politics to be the source of not its legitimation but the tainted particularity that robs it of all validity. For this reason, when Marx criticizes the modern republic for being a bourgeois state, imposing class rule under the guise of democratic equality, he does not call for a new body politic that will finally provide a universal self-government rising above all particular interest. He instead advocates seizure of political power by the proletariat so that it can impose its own class rule in order to abolish government and politics altogether. In this way, the dictatorship of the proletariat will carry out to its ultimate extreme the reduction of politics to society already expressed in the doctrine that the state is but an instrument of class interest. The proletarian dictatorship will presumably effect this collapse of political into social life by eliminating class differences in society, thereby annulling its own class rule and permitting the state to wither away leaving nothing in its wake but a communist society of free associated producers.

This sacrifice of political justice at the altar of class interest has its parallel in the treatment that Marx affords society. At the same time that he relegates the state to an instrument of class interest, he leaves society determined by an economic base. Although this might at least leave room for economic justice, Marx undermines that possibility as well by conceiving the economic base as a sphere of natural necessity endemic to the human condition and thus underlying, rather than emerging within, history.

Certainly, it is true that Marx makes efforts, particularly in his mature theory of capital, to conceive economic relations in social rather than natural terms. Nevertheless, in his theory of communist society the natural conception he adopts from political economy comes to the fore with fateful results for Marxist theory and practice.

Marx's famous sketch of his communist ideal in the third volume of *Capital*[17] is especially telling in the directness with which it exposes the natural reduction underlying the whole theory of communism. Undercutting any way of coherently conceiving the just economy, Marx here commences by declaring that economic relations comprise a realm of natural necessity only beyond which the realm of freedom can first begin. On these terms the economy is not a historically emergent social structure in which justice is at play, but a suprahistorical base, an inescapable natural feature of the human condition that can only limit, rather than realize, freedom and the rights and duties it involves. Therefore, if mankind is to create for itself a realm of freedom, it must restrict as much as possible the hold of economic concerns upon its activity. This is not an insoluble problem that people are fated to bear. Because economic relations are but matters of natural necessity, they can be managed with the same purely technical domination by which mankind puts nature under its control.

The exclusive task of communist society is here mandated and defined. Communism is to free mankind from natural necessity by replacing the multilateral society of the market with a planned administration of the economy reducing the working day to a minimum through an unrestricted automation of production and an automatic distribution of its products. The "society" of communism thus gives justice its fulfillment by transforming the economy into an econometrician's dream: a sphere in which technique reigns supreme, supplanting all social relations of commodity exchange, wage labor, and capital with a collective "administration of things," as Engels aptly remarks.[18]

Since communist society consummates its new order through the annulment of civil institutions and the withering away of the state, it can come as no surprise that Marx describes the realm of freedom it establishes in terms of purely private activity, of hunting in the morning, fishing in the afternoon, being the critic in the evening, and so on.[19] Reduced to this hobby existence, communist man may have lost his chains and won a world, but he has not gained the institutional order of freedom in which justice consists. Marx can well be commended for observing that communist man has reappropriated his species being, for without any society or state in which to interact, what else is left but the natural liberty of one's anthropological existence? If, however, the just economy is to be conceived, the natural utopia consummating Marx's critique of political economy must be left behind.

10.2.3 The Promise of Hegel's Critique of Political Economy

The inconsistencies of political economy and Marx's failure to overcome them are not all that past theory offers for the reconstruction of the just economy and the society to which it belongs. In the section entitled "The System of Needs" in the *Philosophy of Right* Hegel attempts to carry out the critique of political economy by casting aside the natural and monological paradigms of economic activity and reconceiving economic relations as structures of freedom. In so doing, Hegel draws the economy into the realm of right as a proper theme of the normative economics whose task is to determine what economy the just society should have. Hegel's efforts are incomplete and often marred by the introductions of estate relations that may have been current in his day, but have no place in the structures of economic freedom. Nevertheless, Hegel's account provides a workable outline with which to begin.

10.3 Economic Freedom as the Minimal Structure of Social Justice

In undertaking to conceive the just society, the first task consists in establishing the minimal structure of social freedom. Rational reconstruction requires that this be done by employing no other resources than what property, moral, and household freedoms make available. Naturally, if economic relations are elements of the just society, they can properly be treated only after all their social prerequisites have been conceived. However, if economic relations are the most elementary structures of social freedom, then the theory of the just society will begin by conceiving the just economy. Hegel's conception of the System of Needs as the first sphere of civil society suggests that this is indeed the case.

As we have seen, the mandate for a just society consists in providing an institution of freedom offering a new mode of self-determination for owners, moral agents and family members that does not involve political freedom, yet is incorporated by the free state. For social justice to have legitimacy, it must involve an exercise of right presupposed by politics but supplied neither by property, moral, nor household relations.

What satisfies this requirement is a social order giving individuals the entitled freedom to realize particular ends of their own choosing in reciprocity with one another. This right can qualify as the content of social freedom first because it meets the test of irreducibility to the other non-political freedoms. Even though it can only be exercised by individuals bearing the rights of persons, moral subjects and adult family members, it is still something lacking in property relations, morality, and the household. Being an owner is a prerequisite for social as well as any other freedom, since without ownership of one's own body, none of one's actions can be recognized as rightfully one's own. Nevertheless, disposing over property does not by itself realize any particular interest of the owner in reciprocity with others. Strictly speaking, the property holding will of an owner first acquires determination by embodying itself in some external entity. Consequently, it has no particular end lying within itself that is even available for realization.[20] This is not to deny that an individual owner can choose to pursue any variety of particular ends. It only signifies that disposing over property does not involve such pursuits unless some further type of willing be adjoined to it whereby the will does more than determine itself as owner of a particular property. In that case, where an owner does determine his agency in terms of a particular end realizable through the like pursuit of others, that owner enters a relation in which the agency he exercises involves more than his role as property owner.

Similarly, it can be granted that morality underlies social institutions to the extent that it renders individuals responsible for realizing justice through their own actions. Yet, the aim of moral action is not the mutual realization of particular interests, but doing whatever conscience determines to be good for others. This might involve pursuing the freedom of interest, but it equally might not.

Finally, the household may provide its members with a private realm in pursuit of whose rights and duties they are free to enter society. However, the unity of the family is destroyed the moment its members interact at home as bearers of completely independent interests. Only outside the household in a separate institutional sphere can individuals pursue their private interests without forsaking their obligations and violating each others' rights.

All this indicates how a social order providing for the freedom of interests is not redundant with the achievements of these other spheres of right. Further, whatever be its actual institutional form, the pursuit of particular interests is radically distinct from the universal concerns of political freedom, where individuals exercise their right to determine the totality of justice. Although political power may be wielded to promote a particular interest, such political activity still involves a ruling agency whose governing of the entire order of the state is qualitatively different from the activity that simply satisfies particular interests in reciprocity with those of others. This distinction between political activity and the individual pursuit of particular ends is testimony enough that the social freedom of interests cannot be dispensed with if the state is to unite under its rule all forms of freedom and achieve normative validity. In both respects, as irreducible to property, moral, and household relations, and as presupposed by just politics, the social freedom of interests would seem to warrant respect.

Of course, the tentative legitimacy of such freedom does not tell us what the just society actually is, nor how economic relations figure within it. Instead, it first poses the question of what institutions can realize interest as a right and make the just society more than a wishful slogan. On these terms, the great challenge confronting the rational reconstruction of the just society lies in conceiving the institu-

tional order where the pursuit of independent interests builds a
normatively valid freedom instead of an exercise of natural liberty
where all do as they please irrespective of any mutual recognition of
rights and duties.

10.3.1 Social Freedom and Commodity Relations

If the just society is to save the pursuit of interest from a war of
all against all, it must provide the institution through which that pursuit is so determined that each individual can achieve his freely
chosen ends only by realizing and respecting the similar pursuit of
others. Only in that case will action towards others for particular ends
of one's own choosing rise beyond selfish arbitrariness and become a
relation of justice. Then it can qualify as just conduct, for it will be
undertaken as part of a mutual observance of right and duty where
each interacting participant determines himself in view of his own
interest with the consent and cooperation of others while simultaneously honoring and enabling their concordant exercise of that same
freedom. If such an interaction can be worked out, it will allow for a
normative community of interest in which the free realization of each
member's particular ends figures as a right that all are obligated to
respect not just for the sake of others, but for their very own freedom
of interest. This is because within that interaction the only way one
could pursue one's interest would be by promoting the same pursuit
of others.

Exercising social freedom accordingly consists in willing particular
ends of one's own choosing that are attainable only by action towards
others through which these individuals concomitantly fulfil their own
chosen ends. For this to be so, these ends must be independently
selected interests that their bearer cannot realize with what nature
directly provides. If nature did supply whatever realized the interests,
then action in their pursuit would not involve a relation to other independent individuals within which justice could come into play. The
same would be true if the ends in question could be fulfilled with
what lies within their bearer's private property and household. In that
case, the realization of interest would involve no social interaction, but
simply a use of property adding nothing to the individual's autonomy
as an owner. By the same token, a normative interest cannot be such
that what satisfies it is something others can furnish without thereby
realizing an interest of their own. Although an interest realized
through another does introduce a relation between individuals in
which rights and duties could be at stake, the absence of reciprocity
would render the act a unilateral volition lacking all connection to the

wills of others. Without that interplay, the pursuit of interest is nothing more than a one-sided exercise of choice, whose form and content are given rather than determined by willing.

Consequently, if the pursuit of interest is to have normative validity as an activity of social freedom, the interests at play must not only be realizable solely through what other individuals can supply, but these individuals must be able to offer the needed means solely by voluntarily obtaining in return what satisfies their own chosen ends. What allows the just economy to provide the minimal institution of social freedom is the identity of the particular ends meeting these requirements. They are none other than needs whose content is entirely determined by personal preference, yet which can only be satisfied by what someone else is willing to offer under the condition that the bearer of the first need own and agree to trade something satisfying the similarly advanced need of the latter. Such normatively valid need can be defined neither naturally, as a physical want for what the body requires, nor monologically, as a psychological yearning for what the self may desire. It may be true that every person has a right to satisfy his subsistence needs, for the reason that the maintenance of life is a precondition for any exercise of freedom.[21] By the same token, it can well be granted that each individual is entitled to have those psychological needs satisfied whose satisfaction is a precondition for the sanity enabling one to exercise rights and respect those of others. Nevertheless, the maintenance of life and sanity is not what comprises the new justice specific to the civil freedom of the just society. Property relations already entail the right of individuals to own what they need to live sanely, since otherwise, all disposal over property would be canceled together with every other opportunity for self-determination. What the just society now affords above and beyond this right is legitimacy to the pursuit of reciprocally realizable interests whose content is free of any natural limit. What can figure as a need in the civil interaction of the just society can be prescribed not by natural or psychological requirement, but only by the exercise of social freedom itself.

Accordingly, what characterizes normatively valid civil need is simply that it is directed upon means of satisfaction that can only be obtained from other needy individuals in conjunction with the satisfaction of their respective need. Although the particular content of such need is a matter of personal preference, and may well coincide with physical or psychological wants, what makes it a civil entitled need is that it is pursued in reciprocity with the needs of others as a vehicle of social freedom. In complete consonance with the exclusive validity of relations of freedom, it is only the complementary self-determination of the parties to the interaction that can mandate what figures as a need in the just society. If conditions are such that individuals are able to satisfy certain physical or psychological needs without interacting as proprietors of what the other seeks, those needs play no role in the society of interest. One may need air, water, or for that matter affection, but if these are available independently of entering into a reciprocal satisfaction of interest, the needs for them do not figure within the exercise of social freedom as civil wants. On the other hand, a need serving no natural or psychological want can nevertheless be justifiably realized so long as the individual who seeks to satisfy it does so in reciprocity with the satisfaction of some need of another.

These features of civil need entail that what figures as an object of it must be alienable property. Yet, being alienable property is not enough, for involvement in social interaction requires the additional feature of being property that is needed by other property owners who have alienable property of their own bearing the same reference to the needs of others. This means that the exclusive objects satisfying civil need are not just objects of will, but property that are objects of socially legitimate need. Such objects are none other than *commodities*, goods owned by individuals who are willing to exchange them to satisfy their wants by acquiring commodities from others on the same terms.

Only within the social community of a plurality of commodity owners can need attain the legitimacy of being the particular end pursued within the reciprocal self-determination of civil freedom. Conversely, only within a society of individuals who need what others have and have what others need, can property function as a commodity, related not only to the will of its owner, but to the civil need of others bearing commodities of their own. Finally, only by interacting as owners of commodities that others need and as bearers of needs for commodities that others own can individuals determine themselves as members of a community of interest, exercising a mode of autonomy whose form and content are products of the willing in which that very society consists. What this signifies is that the minimal structure of freedom satisfying the mandate for the just society is an economy in which needs have the normatively economic character of being needs for commodities, needs that as such can only be satisfied in reciprocity with the like needs of others.

The just society therefore has as its most elementary structure a market where individuals interact at one and the same time as bearers of needs for the commodities of others and as owners of some commodity that others need. Through this web of commodity relations, a strictly social economy comprises itself, providing the freedom of interest with its basic reality and giving prescriptive economics its generic subject matter. In order to participate in its society, an individual must both choose to need a commodity owned by someone else and own a needed good. Through these acts of will, individuals can effect the reciprocal satisfaction of their needs and thereby realize particular ends of their own choice in relations of justice involving the mutual recognition of each other's right to make their need the factor of their self-determination.

Chapter 11

Capital and the Legitimacy of Commodity Relations

That social freedom has for its minimal structure a market of commodity owners does not of itself indicate the ultimate structure of the just economy, nor does it remove all doubt of the validity of commodity relations. The contrast between the economic theories of Hegel and Marx is instructive in this regard.

11.1 The Questions Raised by the Conflicting Theories of Hegel and Marx

Certainly Hegel does view commodity relations to be legitimate interactions of freedom proper to civil society. Significantly, when he conceives the entire commodity economy he does not subsume it under a system of capitals whose profit derives from wage labor commodity production. Furthermore, he conceives classes as necessary elements of the just economy. Yet, while granting legitimacy to commodity relations, Hegel still argues that they cannot secure for every member of society the opportunity to exercise the right they alone can realize, namely, the respected freedom to satisfy needs of one's choosing in reciprocity with others.

By contrast, Marx rejects the legitimacy of commodity relations together with the civil society that incorporates them. He questions

210

their validity because he views them to be inextricably bound up with capitalism. For Marx the capitalist economy is hardly a normative ideal, but rather an unjust historical formation insofar as it rests on the exploitation of labor and subjects society and state to rule by the bourgeoisie in the interest of capital. Consequently, Marx analyzes commodity relations not in a prescriptive economics belonging to the theory of justice, but in a descriptive theory of capital contributing to a science of historical development. In that theory of capital, Marx conceives commodity relations to be swallowed up within the accumulation process of capital, such that the system of capitals encompasses the entire commodity economy. On these terms, the capitalist economy comprises not the elementary structure of a just civil society, but the determining base of a historically given bourgeois society that must be overthrown to bring into being the genuine just society: communism.

Significantly, Marx's critique of commodity relations does not deny that the market is an institution of freedom. What Marx argues is that the very workings of freedom and equality in the marketplace spawn social relations of inequality and domination that subvert social freedom by subsuming commodity relations under the rule of capitalist production.

If the just society is to involve a commodity economy, then Marx's critique of commodity relations must be countered by showing that the commodity economy is indeed a structure of freedom not only irreducible to capital, but containing none of the bonds of domination that Marx ascribes to it. Accomplishing this will equally demonstrate that the civil society containing the commodity economy cannot be the bourgeois society that Marx condemns.

Freeing the commodity economy from the taint of capitalist exploitation will not, however, exonerate the unbridled free enterprise of the market if Hegel's account is vindicated. His argument that commodity relations cannot automatically guarantee for all the freedom in whose exercise they consist contradicts the classic view of political economy that the market orders itself with an invisible hand insuring the welfare of everyone. If Hegel's position is correct, then the just society will have to remedy the limits of commodity freedom with further institutions addressing the problem of social justice that the market introduces but cannot solve.

Needless to say, the adjudication of these issues is of fundamental importance for evaluating the competing claims of laissez-faire capitalism, social democracy, and communism. By now, it should be clear that the sole way to decide the matter is by turning to the minimal structure of social freedom and examining how the just economy can develop on its basis. Only by considering to what extent the economic structures of freedom coincide with commodity relations can judgment be made on the role of the market in the just society.

11.2 Justice and Commodity Exchange

The theory of the just economy properly begins with the most elementary relationship of need and the means of its satisfaction by which individuals can reciprocally realize their self-interests. This consists in nothing other than a market whose participants interact simultaneously as bearers of personally chosen needs for the commodities of others and as owners of some commodity that others similarly need. This dual relationship forms the starting point of all further just market activity because the only way an individual can participate in this society of interest is by both choosing to need a commodity belonging to someone else and owning a good that that other individual needs. Clearly, being a property owner, a moral subject, and a family member furnishes one with all that is necessary to participate in the market save for the concordant choices by which commodity owners actually satisfy each others' needs. Equally clearly, every facet of commodity production, the total wealth of the market and class relations incorporates and presupposes the basic relation of reciprocally needy commodity owners, and hence must be treated subsequently.

11.2.1 Needs and Commodities as Factors of Freedom

It is here with the minimal relation of market participants that prescriptive economics must begin to develop the structure of economic freedom. The first point to be observed is that both the needs and commodities by which individuals interact in the market have an artificial multitude and diversity in keeping with the freedom they realize.[1] They may include naturally given wants and objects as well as conform to the possibilities of material reality. Yet their content cannot be prescribed by any natural principles. Although political economists and Marx have tended to view economic need and use value as anthropological factors of the human condition,[2] within the just society, the utility sought by civil need is as social as the want it addresses. Both have their specific character determined through the freedom of the reciprocal realization of particular ends. Utility enters into this just convention only by being borne by commodities satis-fying not the given wants of human nature, but the specifically social need of individuals who own a commodity they are willing to exchange. Within the enacted context of this market interaction, the variety and plenitude of utilities is no more restricted by the natural requirements of life than that of the needs individuals choose to have and realize in reciprocity with one another. In the market, need and its object are matters of preference limited only by what others concomitantly choose to need and own.

For this reason, the possible differentiation and duplication of needs and commodities is as measureless as it is capricious. What needs should be satisfied and what should be the means of their satisfaction therefore cannot be preordained, as has been done by those who would discriminate between rational and irrational needs, or truly human wants and superfluous needs for items of luxury. Given the previously established strictures prescribing what can and cannot be alienable property, an individual's civil need can have any content so long as what satisfies it is alienable property owned by someone else, just as a commodity can be anything so long as it is alienable property needed by someone else other than its owner.[3]

Inherent in the self-determination of the participants in the market, this multiplication and differentiation of needs and com-modities has fundamental importance for social justice and the legitimacy of commodity relations. By liberating need from the set bounds of natural subsistence and socializing it as a civil need as unlimited in magnitude and variety as the commodities required to satisfy it, market interaction establishes a whole new domain of right in which need is transformed from a burden of necessity to a matter of entitled preference. Here the content of need is determined entirely by how commodity owners freely interact instead of by the physical requirements of individuals and the natural scarcity of those things that satisfy their bodily wants. As a result, the need for commodities attains the dignity of a medium of self-determination, which each market participant has the right to enjoy and the duty to respect in regard to others. This right and duty go hand in hand, for only by allowing others to satisfy their need through one's own goods, can one legitimately satisfy one's own need for commodities. Commodity relations thus comprise a structure of freedom through which the right of need to be satisfied is no longer restricted to the physical and psychological necessities a person requires to exist and act towards others. Because the market activity satisfying the need for com-modities realizes the freedom of interest in a reciprocal exercise of right and duty, the justice of that freedom extends to whatever needs figure within it, no matter how artificially kaleidoscopic and multitudinous they may be.

This presents the just society with a challenge much more far-reaching than that of securing everyone's person and property. Due to market freedom's willful multiplication and refinement of needs and commodities, the economic right of each member of society applies to the reciprocal satisfaction of an endlessly diversified and discriminating need whose means of satisfaction are all already owned by others in an equally unnatural wealth and variety. Although this gives each market participant the opportunity to choose from a mass of luxury beyond all natural use, it also leaves each in a dependent poverty without end. Not only is every individual's need without limit, extending however far personal preference may elect, but it can only be satisfied by what others own and willingly relinquish for those goods satisfying their equally capricious needs. Consequently, satisfying civil need is not a problem of overcoming the obstacle of nature's parsimony, which technical activity can master. It rather involves contending with the barrier of entitled commodity ownership, which may be violated by theft, but which can only be removed in conformity with civil justice through the free consent of the owner.[4]

The unsatisfied need for commodities thus does not comprise a want of the means of subsistence. Individuals can have all their survival needs provided for and still stand before the market deprived of the goods addressed by its conventional needs. As a participant in the market, an individual faces the problem not of balancing natural necessity with natural scarcity, but of resolving the socially specific poverty of a boundless want for an artificial wealth of goods, none of which can be justly attained without a commodity of one's own that others want in return.

11.2.2 Commodity Exchange and Exchange Value

If this civil predicament makes the continuance of such poverty a social wrong, comprising the failed exercise of the poor's economic freedom, it also prescribes how it should be righted. As members of a market, the only way needy commodity owners can obtain what they need through self-determination is by entering into commodity exchange with one another. Through the reciprocal deed of exchange, each participant establishes his identity as the entitled bearer of a recognized need determined by his own will, satisfying it through a voluntary action dutifully respecting the concordant exercise of freedom by his partner in exchange. In this freely entered relation of commodity exchange, where individuals acquire a good they need from someone else by voluntarily giving in return a commodity of their own needed by the other, the community of interest of the just society has its most basic realization.

Having determined the character of need and commodities from which exchange proceeds, the theory of the just economy must next turn to the exchange process itself and consider what is entailed in its operation. The first point to be observed is that although commodity exchange requires that there be owners of alienable goods that are needed by one another, when they enter exchange, the goods they trade take on a new quality determined by the acts of will effecting their transfer. This added feature is the entirely non-natural, social quality consisting in the equivalence in exchangeability of one good for the other that is determined in their actual exchange. This quality is exchange value, the equivalent exchangeability of two traded commodities, resting on the meeting of wills of their complementarily needy owners.[5]

Although a commodity can have exchange value only if it also possesses the social utility or use value consisting in being the object of a certain civil need, its exchange value is not derivative of its use value, but dependent upon the exchange relations in which it actually figures. Because commodity exchange occurs as a mutual agreement, exchange value is something neither intrinsic to the natural qualities of the exchange commodities, nor rooted in a psychological estimation of their worth, nor determined by anything preceding the exchange act setting them in their actual relation of equivalence. No natural or monological factors can prescribe exchange value due to the voluntary bilateral character of the exchange act. It is that act of concurring wills, with all the arbitrariness its very structure allows, that finally decides which goods will be traded as equivalents of one another. The natural scarcity of a good cannot dictate what individuals agree to exchange for it, no more than the psychological worth of a good to an individual can mandate the terms on which others will choose to trade it. In every case, no matter what other factors come into play, what finally makes two commodities exchangeable are the concurring decisions of their respective owners. Because they are independent participants in the market, free to need what they choose and to dispose of their property as they will, they need not be swayed by any particular external factors, nor conform to any model of "economic rationality." It may be that certain exchange decisions have consequences prejudicial to the wealth of the party involved. Nevertheless, the participants in the

market are constitutively free to trade however they will even if the
resulting transactions do not abet what others judge to be "the self-
interests of capital" or cost-efficiency. The only constraint market
participants face is the necessity of reaching agreement with other
commodity owners, who face the same predicament of having to
accommodate the needs of others in order to satisfy their own. If this
free interactive character is forgotten, and market participants are
conceived to obey some principle of optimal performance, the reality
of commodity relations is falsified.

Any market situation where goods are traded at proportions fixed
independently of the choices of the parties to exchange would
therefore violate the constitutive freedom of commodity relations.
Such constraint upon economic self-determination would comprise a
social injustice unless it were dictated by matters of right, such as
political sovereignty or public welfare, having priority over particular
exercises of market freedom but not entailing their complete
annulment.

11.2.3 The Labor Theory of Value and the Justice of Exchange

It follows that any labor theory of value that determines the
exchange values of commodities by the conditions of their production
misconceives commodity relations. By rooting the setting of exchange
value in a process preceding exchange, such theories completely
ignore the ubiquitous truth that every commodity exchange is determined by the free mutual agreement of the exchange partners. This
holds even if the conditions of the market, themselves resulting from
prior exchanges, leave sellers with certain price levels below which
they cannot go without losing wealth. That buyers contend with such
limits does not alter the fact that they are free to refuse the going
market price, leaving even the most monopolistic of sellers with the
option of either sitting on their goods or selling them at a loss.
Regardless of the pressures and limited choices of a given market,
when an exchange is finally made, it is still always entered into voluntarily by both parties.

What makes it possible for non-produced items, such as labor
power and land, to be exchanged and bear exchange value as much
as any product is precisely the reciprocal freedom in which every commodity exchange consists. No matter what origin a good may have, be
it the fruit of nature or of manufacture, so long as some individual
agrees to trade another commodity for it, that good acquires exchange
value set by the transaction in which it figures. Once this is recog-

nized, the exchange value of non-produced goods is no longer the puzzle it remains for advocates of a labor theory of value.[6]

Consequently, when exchange value is considered as it arises in commodity exchange, what is addressed is a relation of commodities in general, rather than something specific to the particular class of commodities comprising products. For this reason, commodity exchange is properly analyzed prior to and independently of commodity production.

By contrast, a labor theory of value puts itself in the unhappy predicament of having to discuss production prior to the exchange of commodities, insofar as it derives exchange value from the labor process. In that case, none of the elements of production can coherently be conceived as commodities without falling into the vicious circularity of having production presuppose independently given commodities at the same time that all commodities are supposed to be products. As a result, no labor theory of value can handle a capitalist production process involving previously purchased factors without falling into self-contradiction.

This does not mean that it is wrong to speak of labor impressing its product with value. The trap of the labor theory of value can be avoided provided no claim is concurrently made that labor's act sets the exchange value at which its products are bought and sold, or, for that matter, furnishes surplus value that surfaces through subsequent sale in transformed form as profit. Labor's production of value properly signifies none of this, but merely that when a commodity is produced, the labor expended in its manufacture gives the material on which it works a new form and corresponding utility. Labor's creation of a new use-value in the product may indeed allow it to have an exchangeability different from that of the factors entering its production, but what the product's new exchange value will actually be is something finally determined not in the labor process but in the interaction of the marketplace where the product is subsequently sold.

These points are of crucial significance for the justice of the market because they effectively rule out the principal objections that Marx has directed against commodity relations.

In *Capital* Marx opens his assault on the legitimacy of commodity relations by arguing that market exchange entails a fetishism of commodities where the social relations between individuals operate as relations between things ordering their actions.[7] The previous analysis has revealed, however, that commodity exchange consists in a bilateral exercise of freedom entirely the reverse of what Marx laments. The goods exchanged in the market are not things of merely natural character but commodities bearing the socially specific qualities of use and exchange values in function of the interdependent willing of their owners. What allows these goods to be exchanged rather than unilaterally appropriated is not their power over individuals, but the free agreement of their owners to treat one another both as self-determined persons, with ownership of their respective commodities, and as independent bearers of interest entitled to satisfy needs of their own choosing in reciprocity with others. As a consequence, when individuals enter into commodity exchange, they do not interact as subjects of things that rule their lives. Instead, they therein enjoy their civil right as masters of commodities, utilizing them as subordinate means to satisfy their civil needs. Far from losing their autonomy, the parties to exchange actually realize their honored freedom to achieve those particular ends of their own that advance the interests of others.

Nevertheless, even if commodity exchange does operate with a freedom and equality granting it the justice of a civil right, its justice would be purely formal if, as Marx further argues, exchange value derives from expended labor and commodity production involves the exploitation of labor by capital. The core of Marx's critique of commodity relations lies in these two claims. Celebrated as they may be, these claims fare no better than the doctrine of "commodity fetishism" when judged against the concept of exchange.

Following the political economists, from whom he never succeeds in parting ways, Marx introduces his labor theory of value in *Capital* in answer to the quandary that exchange presents when the determining role of interaction is ignored. Caught in the natural and monological perspective of his British predecessors, Marx argues that commodities could not be exchanged if they did not share some prior factor giving them all a commensurable exchange value. Since marketable goods have different physical properties and utilities, these cannot provide the common feature that supposedly allows for their exchangeability. Oblivious to the contribution of the concordant decisions of the parties to exchange, Marx concludes that the commensurable basis of commodities' equivalence in exchange must lie in the labor embodied in them once it is reduced to its quantitative character as expended abstract labor time.[8]

In arriving at this conclusion, Marx's argument falls into the trap of all labor theories of value by not only assuming that every commodity is produced, but by contradicting the voluntary character of commodity exchange. As we have seen, the reduction of all commodities to products leaves incomprehensible the production of commodities by means of commodities, as well as the exchange value of non-produced commodities, including the labor power so central to Marx's theory. For its part, the determination of exchange value through expended abstract labor time runs completely counter to the bilateral freedom with which every exchange occurs. Because exchange occurs solely through the free agreement of the owners of the traded commodities, their equivalent exchange value is actually determined by the common resolve of these individuals to exchange them on the terms to which they have agreed. Since the parties to exchange are free to trade any alienable properties that are objects of their respective needs, the commodities they exchange need not be produced. Further, since every buyer is free to refuse the price at which a seller offers his wares, the production process of traded products can have no binding effect on the proportions at which they are bought and sold. What the factors of production can alone determine is the minimum price the product must command if its sale is not to result in a loss in relation to the costs of its manufacture. In doing so, however, these factors determine the minimum break-even price of the product not through the function they play in the production process, but through the aggregate price at which they were previously purchased by the producer. Naturally, their purchase price no more derives from production than that of any other commodity.

For these reasons exchange relations involving money and the earning of profit are properly conceived prior and without reference to commodity production and expended labor.[9] All that is needed for a commodity to function as money is for commodity owners to recognize and employ it in their commerce as the universal equivalent and standard of measure of the exchange value of every other commodity. Once individuals interact in this fashion, a variety of forms of monetary exchange become possible, all incorporating the fundamental bilateral freedom of every market transaction. Granted the enabling interdependent decisions of commodity owners, money can operate as a means of exchange, traded directly for another commodity, or as a means of commodity circulation, facilitating the trade of particular goods according to the schema, C-M-C. On the other hand, commodity owners can equally spend money so as to receive more in return simply by finding someone willing to sell them a commodity that they can then resell at a higher price to some other willing party. The reciprocal freedom of exchange makes all this possible, which is why profit can be made through speculative buying and selling without any engagement in production.

Ignoring this capacity of interaction, Marx bases his whole theory of the exploitation of labor on the idea that profit cannot arise out of exchange alone, but must be accounted for by a creation of new exchange value occurring within the process of commodity production. When he analyzes the sequence of commodity exchanges, represented by the schema M-C-M', where one individual buys the commodity of another (M-C), and then sells it for more money than what he paid (C-M'), Marx treats the traded exchange values as if they were invariable givens independent of the wills of the parties to exchange. As a consequence, he reasons that the added exchange value received at the end of the second transaction would contradict the constitutive equivalence of commodity exchange and be utterly inexplicable if it had no other origin. For an individual to advance money and receive more in return, he must obtain his increment, Marx concludes, by engaging in an intervening production of commodities where he pays the hired laborer less for his labor power than the exchange value his labor produces.[10] This discrepancy between payment received and value produced comprises the notorious "exploitation" of labor so crucial for Marx's critique of capitalism. Significantly, Marx does admit that labor's exploitation involves no juridical wrong since the laborer is paid the equivalent exchange value of his labor power and does not own his labor, which is not a commodity with exchange value, but only the form in which the labor power already purchased by his employer is consumed.[11] Nevertheless, because Marx conceives the rate of this exploitation to determine the rate of surplus value upon which profit and capital investment ultimately depend, his argument leaves commodity relations ruled by a factor relatively independent of the wills of commodity owners, condemning the principle of economic freedom to an empty formality.

The fatal flaw in Marx's theory of the exploitation of labor is its total dependence upon the claim that commodities have their exchange values determined by the quantity of abstract labor time embodied in them. When, however, account is taken of the constitutive role of interaction in commodity relations whereby exchange value is finally determined by the mutual agreement of the parties to exchange, it becomes evident not only that profit can arise through an M-C-M' exchange sequence without any intervening commodity production, but that there can be no exploitation of labor in Marx's sense of the term.

What precludes the exploitation of labor is the absence of any necessary relation between the exchange value of any product and the amount of labor expended in its production. A product's exchange value, like that of any commodity, rather depends upon the wills of its prospective buyers. It is their independence as commodity owners, free to refuse any producer's terms of exchange, that entails all the variation in sales volumes and price settings that make capital's realization of profit not an automatic consequence of its internal organization of production, but a contingent achievement of successful competition. Precisely because an owner of capital cannot unilaterally obtain a profit, but must reenter exchange to attempt to sell his products above their costs of production, there is no labor-posited exchange value by which an exploitation of labor could be defined, nor any surplus value determined by what goes on in production.

By the same token, the relation between labor and capital involves no more an unequal exchange than exploitation. Because the purchase of the worker's labor power by the owner of capital is a commodity exchange and not a unilateral appropriation, what determines the actual exchange value of the traded labor power is the free agreement of that transaction. Since this precludes any independent standard from setting that value, there can be nothing unequal about the exchange. For this reason, the market determination of the wage is a purely conventional matter subject to all the bargaining efforts that workers and employers may use in consort or individually to solicit a final agreement to their respective advantage.

Finally it bears repeating that since the labor capital consumes cannot determine the price at which the product is actually sold, it only contributes to producing the new utility that helps make the product a marketable good. There is thus no exchange value of any determinate measure created by labor, let alone one that would exceed the price of the purchased labor power and so seal the exploitation of labor that Marx condemns.

If these basic features of commodity interaction call into question the very core of Marx's theory, they also have central consequences for the character of capital and its place in the just economy.

11.2.4 Capital and the Just Economy

Granted that commodity exchange is a structure of freedom whose legitimacy is not subverted by any labor theory of value, the question still arises as to what role capital plays in commodity relations. Does capital have normative validity as a necessary component of the just economy, consonant with the freedom of interest realized in commodity exchange? Or does capital inject into the market a blind power restricting the self-determination of its members? And if capital does shackle the freedom of interest, is it a distortion of commodity relations that can be purged from them, or is it an inseparable outgrowth that undermines their legitimacy together with the civil society to which they belong?

In order to answer these questions and establish the justice or injustice of capital, it is necessary to focus upon its essential structure rather than particular forms that neither exhaust its reality nor permit distinguishing between capital's intrinsic aspects and the extraneous contingencies that have clothed its historical existence.

To this end, due account must first be taken of capital's constitutive M-C-M' circuit of exchange, which comprises its most elementary reality and is incorporated in all its further forms. As we have seen, the M-C-M' exchange sequence is not only completely accountable in terms of commodity exchange, but the commodity relations in which it consists proscribe any other factors from necessarily determining its interaction. All that is required for someone to purchase a commodity and then sell it for a profit is that some other commodity owner be willing to sell him that commodity and that then someone agree to purchase it at a higher price. As in any commodity exchange, both sequences of M-C-M' proceed in terms of equivalencies that are established on no other basis than that the exchangers agree to trade their commodities. Since this can occur regardless of whether the commodities are products, the capital relation need not involve a production process at all, but can merely consist in a speculative purchase and resale of goods.

By the same token, the bilateral freedom of exchange leaves nothing automatic about the sequence of transactions comprising the capital circuit. Each of its commodity exchanges, M-C and C-M', depends upon the concurring choices of the participating commodity owners to decide at what price their goods will be traded. The prospective owner of capital may thus utterly fail to sell the commodity resulting from his first advance of money in the M-C exchange, or he may only be able to sell it at a loss or a break-even price. No preceding production process nor any other factor independent of the arbitrariness of the other commodity owners in the market can mandate that a profit be achieved or that it have a certain magnitude. To suggest any such external mandate is really nonsensical, for it would violate the mutual voluntary agreement constitutive of every commodity exchange and eliminate the M-C-M' exchange sequence on which capital's very identity rests. The concrete dynamic of capital's accumulation is instead based upon the non-automatic character of profit realization rooted in the market freedom of other consumers and suppliers to refuse the price offerings of the owner of capital, as well as upon the freedom of the owner of capital to make market decisions that need not obey any strictures of what "rationally" serves the interests of profit. It is precisely these constitutive freedoms that entail the inherent contingency and variability in the sale of commodities. That is what makes competition both possible and compelling, for it confronts the owners of capital with the necessity of dealing with the independent wills of the commodity owners who form their market. Winning them as customers may require altering the price, the publicity, or the character of the marketed commodity, but whatever be involved, the mutual decision to exchange still remains the ultimate arbiter of realized exchange value.

For this reason, capital always faces a realization problem, contrary to the rote calculations of the labor theory of value. Although the profits and losses of an owner of capital do determine what wealth that owner has to reenter the market and seek further profit, the results of that reentry remain bound to the same contingencies confronting all its prior entries.

In this regard, it is worth noting that the market conditions of capital accumulation contradict the notion of a perfect competition according to which capital freely moves from one type of investment to another in search of the highest return, resulting in the approximation of an average rate of profit in all branches of capital. This conception falsifies the reality of capital by assuming both the unrestricted mobility of capital from one investment to another and the automatic realization of profit in function of the cost advantages of different enterprises. These assumptions ignore the barriers to entry inherent in the arbitrariness of capital investment and consumer choice, as well as the fixed elements of investment that cannot be moved from one field to another without loss. Due to such barriers, competition is inherently imperfect in character, allowing for monopolizations that counter the averagings of profit rates between different branches of commerce. Those who suggest that capitalism necessarily goes through a development from a stage of perfect competition to a stage of monopoly capital fail to understand that free competition involves monopolization as part and parcel of its basic structure.

As for the identity of the bearer of capital, the M-C-M' relation offers no restriction other than that this bearer be a commodity owner needing commodities of others to earn a profit. Like any other member of the market, the capitalist is obligated to honor the property and civil need of the other commodity owners to whom that capitalist must relate. To be an owner of capital, a commodity owner need meet no other qualification than that of entering exchange so as to achieve the increase in wealth realized through the M-C-M' circuit. For this reason, the bearer of capital can be a single individual, a family, a corporation, a public enterprise, or even a worker's cooperative, provided that agent engages in the M-C-M' sequence of exchanges.

This latitude in the identity of the bearer of capital is of key importance, particularly when viewed in conjunction with how capital involves neither any exploitation of labor, nor any necessary engagement in commodity production. It makes markedly clear that conceiving capital in its proper universality requires rejecting Marx's all too influential reduction of capital to a social structure based upon the capital-labor relation specific to privately owned industrial capital employing wage laborers. Although capital may certainly take that particular form, as history can testify, capital is misconceived if its reality is conflated with this one shape, to the neglect of the various other forms that capital can assume. Marx's own account of the emergence of modern capitalism provides ample evidence that the predominance of privately owned industrial capital employing wage labor in modern England was not the result of some dynamic arising from commodity relations alone, but the product of a sustained political intervention that separated the peasants from their land, concentrated wealth in the hands of private individuals, and compelled the pauperized masses to enter the employ of a rising bourgeoisie.[12] The subsequent history of communist revolutions has demonstrated the contingency of that predominance by showing how political upheaval can enable publicly owned capital to supplant private enterprise as the dominant force in the economy.

No verdict on the justice of capital can properly be drawn if one confuses particular economic conditions that are the product of non-economic factors with what is inherent in capital per se. To uncover what is entailed in capital's universal structure one must not ignore how capital can as easily involve no commodity production as produce commodities and sell them at a gain without employing wage labor.

As we have seen, capital need not produce commodities, for although capital cannot be capital without involving an M-C-M' exchange sequence, it can complete that circuit and make a profit entirely within the sphere of exchange through a speculative buying and selling of commodities.

On the other hand, if capital does involve commodity production, it can only do so on terms compatible with the M-C-M' relation. Since these terms preclude any labor theory of value, as well as the exploitation of labor decried by Marx, they free capital's production of commodities from any exclusive limitation to the private employment of wage labor. Because the realization of capital's profit through the sale of its product is not independently determined by what occurs in production, but depends instead upon what exchange agreement is actually reached between capital and its prospective consumers, how production is internally organized is a matter of indifference to the identity of productive capital. Just as the bearer of capital in general can be a private individual as well as the state, so commodity producing capital can permissibly take any of the possible forms the market makes available, including everything from publicly owned enterprises employing wage labor to worker cooperatives paying dividends instead of wages to its members.

Of course, the production of commodities for a profit can take place under public or private ownership with slave labor and other forms of servitude, as has been demonstrated by the experience of the antebellum South and the Nazi and Soviet forced labor camps. Such arrangements, however, are not inherent in the structure of capital, and it would be wrong to place the blame on capital for their specific evils. By itself, capital necessitates no abrogation of the legitimate freedom of commodity relations, either in its market realization of its profit, or in its internal organization. Although a unit of capital can have an unjust existence, just as property, family, and political relations can be distorted in ways that violate the rights of individuals, its defining structure presents no obstacle to organizing production through the same social freedom in which market activity consists. The free reciprocal satisfaction of freely chosen interests can be the basis of relation just as well among the workers of a self-managed profitable cooperative as among the employees of a publicly owned enterprise or between a private owner of capital and his or her wage laborers. Far from undermining the legitimacy of commodity relations, commodity-producing capital rather shares their justice inasmuch as it requires nothing more than them for its own operation.

In any event, whether capital produce commodities with or without wage labor under public, cooperative, corporate, family, or individual ownership, it will always face the same realization problem on which competitive pressures are based. The bearer of capital may wish to sell a product at a price above the aggregate sum paid for the factors consumed in its production, and, as a good Marxist, may measure it against the expended labor. Nevertheless, he or she will succeed in doing so only if buyers are willing to pay that price. If not, the product will only be saleable at a different price, which will then represent the realizable exchange value of the product. No form of capital can escape this realization problem for the simple reason that its relation as a producer to its consumers is one of exchange, issuing from mutual agreement rather than from any unilateral command. Consequently, it is a universal principle of the production of commodities by capital that neither the expended labor nor any other factor in the production of the commodities can determine the price at which they are sold and the profit that may result. Whether a factory be worker self-managed, state owned, or privately run, all its factors of production can determine is the price above which the product must be sold for a profit to be gained, and this they provide not in virtue of their role in production, but by the price at which they themselves were purchased.

For these reasons, the M-C-M' exchange sequence incorporating commodity production does not subordinate the determination of exchange value to powers lying beyond the wills of the parties to its two exchanges, the purchase of the factors of production, and the subsequent sale of the product. At each step, what limits the options of each participant are not violations of social freedom, but the necessity of acting in conjunction with the market freedom of others.

These universal features of capital have consequences that have gone widely unobserved by its critics and apologists alike. Contrary to those socialists and advocates of private enterprise who have equated state ownership of the means of production with the abolition of capital, capital can just as well be publicly as privately owned without in any way altering its interaction in the market in pursuit of profit. No matter whether a unit of capital engage in commodity production, pay wages, or be owned by an individual, a corporation, the state, or a workers' cooperative, it will still face the same market predicament of fulfilling its M-C-M' circuit of exchanges by which the logic of its accumulation is defined.

For this reason, those who advocate worker self-management or state ownership of industry as an automatic remedy to the "evils" of capitalist accumulation are caught in a double bind. If their economic revolutions eliminate all commodity relations by unilaterally determining production and distribution according to plans laid down by either the codetermination of workers or state edict, they commit the injustice of depriving individuals of their civil freedoms to choose what they need and what actions they will undertake to satisfy their wants in reciprocity with others. This is the case even in a radical kibbutz whose members all vote on what jobs each will perform and what goods each will receive. Although every member here has an equal voice in determining the economy of the community, none has the freedom of independently choosing a vocation or the needs one wishes satisfied. On both counts members must subordinate their interests to the will of the majority, whose will is no substitute for the freedom of interest it eliminates.

If, on the other hand, worker self-management or state ownership involves maintenance of the market and the production of commodities that need be sold, their solutions remain subject to the same dynamic of accumulation they seek to escape. If worker self-managed enterprises face one another as autonomous market agents, as they must to have independent control of their own economic activities instead of being ruled by some central plan, they cannot help confronting the same competitive pressures facing any private firms that produce for a market whose members are free to refuse what is offered for sale. The same holds true for any state enterprises that seek to sell their wares for profit.

These daily confirmed realities bring home once more how everything essential to capital is thoroughly determined through the same type of self-determinations generic to commodity relations. As a consequence, capital shares the same exercise of right at work in every other market activity. Rather than being the object of special opprobrium, capital rather stands as an essential form of commodity relations, enjoying in common their validity and their limits.

This signifies that the theory of capital does not just describe a historical mode of production with no bearing on the conception of justice. Instead, the concept of capital falls within prescriptive economics as the conception of a structural element of the just economy. Like the other institutions of justice, it can certainly have a distorted existence that obstructs rather than realizes self-determination. Further, it may well be incapable of extending the freedoms in which it consists to all members of society without being supplemented by further institutions of justice. Nevertheless, that capital can operate entirely in terms of market freedom is indication enough that its elimination would involve a significant infringement on the self-determination of civilians.

What accentuates the indispensability of capital, be it private, worker self-managed, or public, is the unlimited character of civil need. The self-determined want for a conventional standard of living calls for economic institutions capable of promoting the expansion of wealth so as to permit the freely chosen interests of individuals to be satisfied in reciprocity. If on the contrary, capital's self-expanding exchange value were prohibited as an economic evil in favor of an economic order in which the diversity and multitude of commodities and employments were frozen, the interests of individuals would be hemmed in by a boundary their interaction could not extend.

11.2.5 The Subordinate Role of Capital in the Commodity Economy

Although capital's unlimited pursuit of wealth plays a key role in making possible the realization of freely chosen needs, capital is still a subordinate element of the commodity economy, rather than its encompassing subject. This must be understood if commodity relations are to be properly conceived. Just as capital must be grasped in its full universality without being reduced to the particular shape of privately owned industrial capital employing wage labor, so the market must not be reduced to a function of the accumulation of capital.

Marx misconceived the commodity economy to be entirely absorbed into the system of competing capitals because he derived exchange value from labor embodied in capital's production process. On this basis, the circuit of capital cannot help but be the all-encompassing master of the market. With labor employed by capital creating the very exchangeability of goods, commodities would all have to issue from capital and then enter circulation entirely through sales and purchases by the owners and employees of capital, who buy and sell thanks to earnings resulting from the capital relations in which they participate.

Since, however, exchange value does not derive from embodied labor of any sort, let alone from labor exploited by capital, exchange relations do not resolve themselves into the accumulation process of capital. Commodity relations instead involve produced and non-produced commodities whose exchange may, but need not, form part of any M-C-M' circuit of capital. Conversely, since there is nothing about commodity exchange that precludes transactions in which profit is neither sought nor realized, capital's M-C-M' circuit represents but one possible form that commodity exchange may take.

Similarly, although the accumulation of capital may very well tend towards an ever-widening circuit of wealth, that does not guarantee that the circulation of capital becomes the dominant factor in the circulation of commodities. The collateral decisions of commodity owners may just as well lead to a predominantly non-profitable circulation of goods, and even the disaccumulation of capital. Admittedly, the latter would pose potential restraints upon the satisfaction of freely multiplied and refined needs, but it is still conceivable that market freedom could conform of itself to such limits for a greater or lesser period.

Naturally, if commodity exchange is irreducible to the accumulation of capital, so is commodity production. Since goods can bear exchange value as commodities without issuing from capital, commodity production can occur with or without profit as well as with or without wage labor. The theory of the just economy must therefore conceive commodity production so as to allow for all these options. This requires conceiving in their full generality the three varieties of production: the elementary labor process where the act of laboring produces a whole new commodity, manufacturing where mass production is achieved by both a simple duplication of laboring acts and a division of labor where each act completes only one step in the product's formation, and finally mechanization where machines step in to replace the rote work of detail labor under the supervision of technicians. Although these three manners of production have often been treated as historical forms that successively displace one another, their coexistence in the commodity economy cannot be excluded. This is true also with regard to justice, for all three of these forms of production can figure as normative relations of the just economy so long as they produce commodites for the market such that those engaged in their production thereby satisfy their own needs in free reciprocity with others. Every one of these forms can accomplish this as much on a non-profit basis as for profit, with or without the payment of wages, and under private, cooperative, or public ownership.

The freedom of the market permits all these arrangements. Their diversity testifies anew to how commodity exchange and commodity production are irreducible to relations of capital, just as exchange value is not determined by the latter's production process. Instead of making the accumulation of capital the all-determining principle of the market, the theory of the just economy must accordingly conceive capital accumulation as a subordinate process within commodity relations, subject to the influence of market factors exogenous to capital, but endogenous to the commodity economy of which capitals are part.

This is of key importance for the problem of social welfare. If it were the case that the accumulation of capital had exclusive reign over commodity relations and that the accumulation process left certain members of society unable to realize their freedom of interest, then righting that wrong would be impossible. It would require curtailing commodity relations, even though the right to be realized consists in participating in them. The inherent latitude of commodity relations, however, removes this dilemma. Although the right to a personally determined conventional livelihood does encourage the accumulation of wealth, commodity relations are not incompatible with private and public non-profit undertakings. Consequently, it is possible to assist the needy without having to eliminate the market and the freedom of interest realized in its commodity relations. As will be shown, this is a problem that refers to the market, but brings to bear further social institutions. For this reason, it can only be systematically treated after conceiving the full structure of the commodity economy. To this end, an outline of the just economy cannot conclude without turning to the formation of classes endemic to commodity relations and finally to whatever problems of social freedom remain unresolved and unresolvable by commodity relations alone.

11.3 Class and Economic Justice

If the interaction of commodity relations does not result in the automatic hegemony of any particular form of capital, it does entail the formation of economic classes. Although Marx would exclude class divisions from the just economy, their essential place in commodity relations warrants consideration as a necessary feature of social freedom.

The delineated process of commodity relations already reveals how the reciprocal satisfaction of need involves a variety of engagements in exchange and production, where different types of earning are linked to different types of commodity ownership and need. Whoever undertakes the M-C-M' circuit of exchange needs capital to advance in the market in order to earn a profit. By contrast, a laborer needs a marketable labor power to be hired and earn a wage, whereas someone interacting as a landlord needs landed property or some other rentable commodity in order to obtain income in the form of rent. As these basic options show, whenever an individual participates in commodity relations, he or she exercises at least one and possibly several different modes of earning shared by whatever other commodity owners have chosen to satisfy their needs in a similar way. This means that commodity relations necessarily entail classes containing those different groups of individuals who have chosen to engage in a common type of earning with its associated needs and goods.

Because commodity relations involve no exploitation of their own, the economic relation between classes is not one of domination, where one group unilaterally lords over another. Classes instead interact through the same mutual exercise of freedom characterizing all activity in the commodity economy. The owners of capital, be they private individuals, self-managing workers, or public authority, earn their profit only by participating in the market exchanges of the M-C-M' circuit, where the members of other classes enter in only through the voluntary satisfaction of their own chosen needs. If these capitals engage in production and employ wage labor, both of which are optional for capital accumulation, their owners' relation to their employees is once again mediated through exchange, rather than one-sided mastery. The same is true for the earners of rent, who receive their common form of revenue only through freely entered exchanges with those who rent their goods.

Moreover, since each class carries on its distinctive mode of earning in a voluntarily entered interdependence with the others, in a market subject to all the contingencies and vicissitudes endemic to commodity interaction, no class has any automatic command over a privileged amount of earnings. This is particularly true given the great latitude in the forms of capital and the subordinate place of capital within the market. Even though capital may be driven to accumulate wealth without limit, there is no guarantee that profits will outdistance wages and rents, especially when commodity exchange and commodity production can be undertaken on a non-profit basis. Competition certainly can make the continual reinvestment of profit a condition of a firm's viability, leading more and more production to be undertaken for profit. Yet the freedoms of the market equally permit consumers to be indifferent to the cost economies, product revolutions, and marketing improvements such reinvestment can allow and retain sufficient loyalty to non-profit enterprises to enable them to hold their own or even expand.

In addition, even if one class were to garner more earnings than the others, that would not guarantee that its members also enjoy a greater individual affluence. This holds especially for the owners of capital, who may well outnumber the members of other classes depending on whether individual, cooperative or public ownership of capital predominates.

What further prevents any necessary inequality due to class divisions is the non-exclusivity of class membership. Although most theorists, Hegel and Marx included, have taken for granted that an individual belongs to only one class, the freedom of commodity relations allows individuals to belong to more than one, provided they choose to satisfy their needs by engaging in several different types of economic activity. In terms of economic function, which alone has relevance in determining class, an individual can belong at once to all three classes of wage earners, owners of capital, and landlords simply by working for hire, while earning interest from holding shares in capital, and renting out property. An individual can even hold dual class membership by participating in the same unit of capital, as would be the case of employees in a worker self-managed firm who draw wages for their work, as well as dividends from their joint ownership.

Only when all these varieties of commodity relations are duly taken into account, is it possible to diagnose the actual causes of social injustice, and to avoid promoting easy cures that never touch the real problem. Then it becomes apparent that class membership does not automatically condemn an individual to rags or riches, any more than class divisions comprise the root cause of disparities in wealth.

For all these reasons, belonging to a class is in all respects an act of social freedom. Individuals belong to one or several classes not by birth or some other factor independent of their wills, but through exercising their civil right to satisfy freely selected needs in reciprocity with others through action of their own choice. Although market conditions and the commodites an individual owns may limit the type of economic activities in which a person can participate, whatever activity is undertaken is still mediated by the will of that individual in conjunction with the wills of others. This is not a matter of form, masking a material domination, but part and parcel of the content of commodity relations. Due to the interdependence of classes, realized through commodity exchange, each individual's freely entered class affiliation equally involves relating to members of other classes in recognition and respect of their exercise of that same freedom. The class division issuing from commodity relations is thus nothing but a realization of social freedom. This means that the just society is a class society, even if commodity relations require further institutions of freedom to secure the economic rights of all.

By contrast, the Marxist ideal of a classless society is unjust in principle because it requires entirely canceling the social freedom to choose one's needs as well as how one will satisfy them in reciprocity with others. These freedoms would have to be curtailed insofar as their exercise comprises the commodity relations that create class differences in the first place. Consequently, a classless society could only be established by supplanting the market with a social regime forcing individuals to restrict their needs to the same type and to limit correspondingly the type of exchange and earning in which they engage. Instead of permitting individuals to need whatever commodity they desire, needs could be limited, for example, to consumer goods rather than capital or rentable commodities, just as the activities undertaken to satisfy these needs could be restricted to wage labor. In this manner, class society would give way to a universal proletarization in violation of every individual's freedom of interest. Since such a social transformation is entirely possible, a classless society is not some wistful utopia lying beyond reach at the end of history, but a real threat to the institutions of freedom in which social justice consists.[13]

Chapter 12

The Realization of Social Justice

12.1 The Limits of Economic Freedom

Although the system of commodity relations provides an economy of freedom whose members enjoy the right of satisfying personally selected needs through activity of their own choosing in reciprocity with others, its market institutions are tainted with a problem that they cannot resolve. This endemic limit to the justice of economic freedom consists in the inability of commodity relations to realize for all the exercise of right in which they consist. The problem has two sides, each rooted in the very structure of commodity relations and each calling for remedies falling beyond the power of economic action.

First, although all commodity relations operate in terms of mutual respect for the ownership of exchanged goods, commodity transactions provide nothing to prevent violations of the property entitlements they presuppose and incorporate. Just as property interaction is subject to conflicts of non-malicious wrong, fraud, and outright crime that owners cannot themselves remedy in an objectively binding manner and just as the family is liable to domestic disputes over household property that its members cannot resolve, so the just economy cannot secure the contracts and commodity ownership of its participants through its own market relations. Since commodity exchange can only take place so long as the property rights of each party are not violated, market activity is incapable of guaranteeing either the entitled possessions forming the preconditions of every transaction or the altered commodity ownership in which each results. Thus, whenever an individual does manage to acquire the commodity he needs, no economic relation can prevent another individual from taking it away through fraud or theft, nor punish the malefactor and retribute the victim.

Second, precisely because the just economy consists in commodity relations proceeding through freely engaged exchange agreements, its members can never be assured of finding other commodity owners who not only have needs and commodities correlating with their own, but the will to enter into a mutually agreeable transaction.[1] It makes no difference whether the commodities involved be produced or non-produced, whether their exchange be part of a circuit of capital or whether that capital be advanced by an individual, a private corporation, a worker cooperative or a state enterprise. In every commodity relation whatsoever, each participant's ability to satisfy his particular commodity needs still depends upon the free and therefore arbitrary decision of others to market the needed goods in return for what that participant offers, be it money, labor power, capital, or some other commodity. Although this leaves open the possibility of mutual satisfaction, it equally means that no member of the market can count on meeting consumers or producers able and willing to conclude any sought exchange. As long as commodity relations have free sway, this precarious predicament is the common fate of every member of society.

What compounds this contingency in entering exchange is commodity relations' irrepressible formation of disparities in wealth that create barriers hindering the less wealthy from satisfying their needs in the market. Even though the constitutive freedom of commodity relations offers every commodity owner an opportunity to participate in trade, this same freedom always allows for some economic agents to amass commodities of such great value as to enhance their opportunities for further exchange while prejudicing the respective opportunity of others. Since the exchange value of goods is rooted in agreement, rather than in any intrinsic quality or antecedent production process, any commodity can be a vehicle of relative enrichment, so long as other commodity owners are available to purchase it on favorable terms. Consequently, not just products, but non-produced goods such as labor power or land can equally provide the means for obtaining wealth of disproportionate advantage.

Because such specifically social inequality requires nothing more than commodity exchange to develop, its existence is not limited to any particular type of commodity ownership. No matter what form happens to predominate, so long as economic agents interact through commodities, there can be no precluding the relative enrichment of some and the impoverishment of others. This may take the form of inequalities in individiaul wealth as well as in differentiations between advantaged and disadvantaged enterprises of every category. Even in a market dominated by worker self-managed or state-owned firms, the dynamic of ongoing exchange will allow for certain enterprises to achieve a commanding position enabling them to prosper at the expense of others. Since nothing in the internal structure of a market participant can free it from engaging in commodity exchange with other independent participants, every type of enterprise is subject to all the pressures of imperfect competition through which the contingencies of market freedom produce unequal fortunes. As a consequence, neither non-profit nor profit making businesses, private nor public enterprises, corporate nor worker self-managed firms can prevent differences in wealth from arising that give some competitive advantages undermining the equal opportunity of individuals to satisfy their chosen needs in reciprocity.

For these reasons, there can be no invisible hand with which the market orders itself so as to guarantee the economic welfare of all, as political economists would like to believe. Although commodity relations always do involve normatively valid reciprocal satisfactions of need, they are endemically unable to insure that all members of society actually succeed in satisfying their freely chosen needs by spending money, finding work, or trading goods. This is of fundamental importance for social justice. Because the entitled opportunity to participate in the just economy is left unsecured by the very commodity relations comprising the exercise of that right, no principle of organization endogenous to the economy can resolve the problem of satisfying need as a normative relation of freedom.

Consequently, any "free enterprise" system leaving the market to its own fate necessarily entails social injustice and must be repudiated. This applies not only to a system of unregulated private capitals, but to any social order that seeks to resolve the problem of economic opportunity through a principle of solely economic organization. In this regard, worker self-management is no more of an answer than public ownership of individual enterprises. Either way, the logic of the market remains in force, despite the altered ownership of capital.

These problems might suggest that social justice can be achieved by replacing the market with a totally planned economy where either a centralized state authority or decentralized communes determine the occupation and goods that each individual receives. Since, however, the problem of economic injustice is not a matter of unilaterally furnishing jobs and commodities, but of insuring that each member of society can exercise their economic freedom to secure an autonomously chosen livelihood, the suppression of commodity relations only exacerbates the infringement of equal opportunity. It bears repeating that this is true even if the ordering of employment and distribution is accomplished through democratic procedures, as in a radical kibbutz. Although each participant would exercise an equal voice in collectively determining the economic plan of their community, they would still lack the freedom of particularity that requires commodity relations in order to enable individuals to choose independently both what they need and how they will earn a corresponding living in conjunction with others. Precisely because the social wrong that should be righted is the inability of some to exercise this freedom of interest, the "democratization" of the economy offers no cure for the abiding problem of economic disadvantge. It is worth noting that such schemes do not contribute to political freedom either, since they limit their collective decision-making to questions of economic policy rather than extending it to the specifically political affairs of government. For these reasons, worker self-management can be seen as a system that neither eliminates social disadvantage nor achieves political democracy.

What must not be forgotten is that the problem of economic disadvantage, like all problems of justice, concerns the realization of a particular mode of self-determination, and not the collective imposition of fixed goals. Accordingly, the remedy to social inequality does not consist in eliminating commodity relations, the very vehicle of economic freedom, but in providing all the unprejudiced opportunity to participate in their reciprocal satisfaction of freely chosen needs. If any solution is to be achieved, it must lie not in the overthrow of the market, but outside the economy altogether in additional institutions of social freedom. They will have to contend with the special normative character granted the need for commodities by the very market relations that make possible their satisfaction, without securing it for all.

In order to comprehend the full scope of the social wrong of economic disadvantage and poverty, it must be remembered that the needs whose satisfaction has become a matter of right do not have a natural limit given by the physical and psychological requirements of individuals and the natural scarcity of those things ensuring survival. As we have seen, the need for commodities can have anything as its object, so long as a commodity owner chooses to want it and it is the alienable property of someone else. Consequently, the needy commodity owner must overcome the barrier of entitled ownership to obtain the object of satisfaction, a task that can only be accomplished through the free consent of its owner to offer it in exchange. Because of these socially specific features, the poverty endemic to commodity relations comprises the unsatisfied need of a limitless want facing an artificial wealth of goods attainable only in exchange for a commodity of one's own.

On these terms, what makes poverty a social problem is not its unrestricted magnitude, but rather the rightful status that commodity relations accord to the satisfaction of an individual's need for commodities through action of one's own choice. Independent of commodity relations, the satisfaction of physical or emotional need is not an issue of justice except in view of maintaining the bodily and psychological preconditions of freedom, which enable a person to enter relations of right and duty. By contrast, the satisfaction of the need for commodities is just for its own sake because it consists of an interaction of self-determining commodity owners involving mutually respected realizations of freely chosen particular interests. Therefore, it is an unconditioned economic right that members of society be guaranteed the opportunity to satisfy their need for commodities by entering into an exchange of their choice, in which they obtain what they need in return for their money, their labor power, or any other commodity they are willing to relinquish. Poverty and economic disadvantage are social wrongs because they represent a condition that leaves it victims unable to exercise this right of economic freedom to which all members of society are entitled. The just society must right these wrongs, as well as protect the property and family rights of every commodity owner.

12.2 *The Social Enforcement of Property and Household Rights*

If the just society is to realize the social freedom of its own members, it must provide a remedy to the market's inability to enforce the property and household rights of commodity owners, on whose basis they are first free to enter society. This calls for some social authority empowered to stand over commodity owners as the recognized arbiter and enforcer of their rights as owners and family members. Since these rights are universal, applying equally to every property owner and family member, they warrant application as laws binding every individual in society.

The social authority enforcing these laws faces the task of applying their general rules to the concrete context of the commodity economy. This involves both judging how individual cases fall under these laws and carrying out whatever punishments and restitutions are due. Although the rights over which such authority has jurisdiction derive their content from the prior interactions of owners and family members, their implementation within the context of the market by a recognized social authority entails specific formalities of its own that give these rights a socially specific stamp as publicly realized civil laws. These include all the specifications that must be fulfilled for acquisitions and assignments of property, convenings and dissolutions of marriage, or adoptions and relinquishments of parental duties to have a recognized and guaranteed civil form.

As a result, the social enforcement of property and household rights engenders an irreducible civil right of its own. It consists, broadly speaking, in the right of all members of society to enjoy their property and household freedoms under the protection and arbitration of a recognized civil authority. By the same token, the exercise of this right entails an institutional practice of its own, consisting in the implementation of civil law by police, civil courts, and penal institutions.

Although their workings may well enforce the rights and duties of domestic freedom and secure what individuals own before, during, and after engaging in economic activity, they cannot themselves remedy the social wrong of unsatisfied need for commodities. Although these social institutions realize a valid civil right by publicly protecting owners and households, they do so by preserving the given distribution of wealth. Their activity as authoritative enforcers of property and family rights therefore cannot breach the problem of altering commodity ownership so that all members of society have the actual opportunity to satisfy their needs through action of their own choosing.

For this reason, the just society must supplement the public enforcement of property and household rights with social bodies that specifically attend to the unsatisfied needs continually generated by commodity relations. Since their aim should be guaranteeing all members of society the freedom to satisfy their chosen needs through freely entered exchanges, these institutions cannot annul commodity relations. After all, commodity relations comprise the very exercise of freedom to which the economically disadvantaged should be given equal access. Instead of tearing down the market, these social bodies must somehow intervene upon its commodity relations so that their reciprocal satisfaction of need is not suspended, but made available to all.

The framework of social freedom allows for two types of institutions to address this task: economic interest groups and a public welfare administration.

12.3 *Economic Interest Groups and The Just Society*

In extension of the freedom of interest given basic expression in commodity relations, the just society offers its members the right to join together into economic interest groups to promote their common needs so long as they do so in conformity with the market and civil law. On this basis, these groups can issue from any sector of society.[2] What gives them social legitimacy is that they have voluntary membership, advance particular interests that can only be realized in reciprocity with those of others and accordingly pursue their common cause solely by participating in, rather than supplanting, civil institutions. By meeting these requirements, economic interest groups integrate themselves entirely within the bounds of social freedom. Although this renders them instruments of justice, it also mandates that their proper field of action lies in the market and institutions of civil law. Their arena defines the limit of economic interest groups' ability to right the social wrongs endemic to the just economy.

What underlies the formation of economic interest groups are the different shared interests that arise from the common forms of earning by which classes are distinguished. However, due to the limitless variegation of need and commodities within the market, the interests motivating such groups need not extend to those of every member of a single class, but may be focused on any civil need, however narrow or broad, that its members have chosen to pursue in common. Accordingly, economic interest groups can just as well include labor unions, leagues of worker cooperatives, professional associations, cartels of private firms, federations of state enterprises, and other organizations with members from the same class, as consumer groups, environmentalists, and other social bodies whose members belong to different classes. Further, since the basis for an economic interest group lies in some jointly held need enjoying the normative validity of commodity relations, group memberships cannot legitimately be restricted with regard to any extraneous factors. So long as an individual shares the particular interest championed by the group as well as the resolve to join in its common advocacy, membership should be extended.

Whatever their membership, because economic interest groups legitimately aim at realizing the freedom of their members to satisfy their particular needs in reciprocity with others, they must participate in social institutions and use the market and civil law to their members' best advantage.

Before the law, the members of economic interest groups can take collective legal action to secure their commodity ownership with greater effect than through individual litigation. However, even if this results in more successful legal advocacy, economic interest groups still face the same limits that leave individual civilians unable to secure the satisfaction of their needs through law alone. Although an economic interest group may make common suit in the courts with more legal resources and public impact than a single individual, it cannot overcome the fact that the civil enforcement of property and household rights in no way alters the distribution of wealth resulting from legal market activity. Consequently, joint action by an interest group may expedite the protection of its members' property, but not resolve the problem of their unsatisfied need. To attend to the latter, some action must be taken in the market.

Within its limits, the members of economic interest groups have the opportunity to decide collectively under what terms to enter into exchange so as to facilitate transactions in their joint interest through the pressure of their common front. The options available for pursuing this strategy naturally reflect the variety of exchange forms and economic agents that commodity relations can involve. The freedom of the market equally permits labor unions and professional groups to withhold the services of their members until their employers or clients agree to an acceptable payment; consumer groups to withhold their purchasing power until their demands for product quality and price be met; and for associations of worker self-managed concerns, private corporations, or public enterprises to control their production and marketing in consort to advance their common ends in the market. All such activities entirely conform to the reciprocity of economic freedom, for they involve no unilateral appropriation of what others own, but instead comprise concerted acts of persuasion whereby one group in society aims at reaching a desired *agreement* with some other parties to exchange.

Although this respect for the social autonomy of others grants legitimacy to the market interventions of economic interest groups, it also leaves them burdened with the same problem of contingent satisfaction that calls for their common action in the first place. No matter what an economic interest group does with the commodities of its members, be they their money, their labor power or their products, it cannot overcome the dependence of its members' welfare upon the arbitrary exchange decisions of others. Although an economic interest group may succeed in arranging the exchange its members seek, the very fact that it is but a particular group in the market that can only satisfy its members' needs with the agreement of other independent commodity owners leaves it unable to ever guarantee the abiding welfare of its members. Consumer groups, business associations, labor unions, federations of worker cooperatives, and even public enterprises all bear this limit simply because they must work through the bilateral freedom of commodity relations.

For this same reason, one economic group's success in promoting the welfare of its members need not benefit members of other groups, nor that of unaffiliated individuals beyond what they may receive as opposite parties to an exchange. Although an economic group can advance its interest in the market only by reciprocally satisfying the needs of others, the terms of exchange it secures may well leave the latter at a disadvantage for their next entry into the market, while leaving uninvolved individuals no better off. Just as commodity relations among individuals cannot preclude growing disparities in wealth or failures to enter into desired exchanges, so the market interventions of economic interest groups cannot prevent the development of poverty and social inequalities that prejudice the opportunity of all to satisfy their needs. Despite the best of intentions, labor unions, business associations, consumer groups, leagues of communes, or federations of public enterprises may each just as well worsen as alleviate the maldistribution of wealth.

Furthermore, economic interest groups cannot be relied upon to monitor and enforce the rectitude of their own activities. Discriminatory membership policies, internal corruption, and violations of the freedom of other members of society can well occur, despite the opposition of individuals within or without the offending group. As much as the proper activities of economic interest groups do comprise a further mode of social freedom, they cannot be counted on to remove social injustice.

Therefore the just society requires more for its realization than commodity relations, public enforcement of property and family rights, and economic interest group activity. The plight of economic interest groups reveals that if social justice is to be achieved, these institutions must be supplemented in a dual fashion. On the one hand, civil law must extend its reach to lawfully regulate the activities of economic interest groups in conformity with social freedom. On the other hand, the commodity economy must be subject to an additional enforcement of welfare that is neither directed upon the members of a certain sector of society, nor administered by particular social groups whose efforts are constrained by the arbitrariness of others. The very rights founded in commodity relations instead require that economic interest group activity be supplemented by a *public* welfare administration, extending its assistance to all members of society and emanating from a universally respected civil authority empowered to guarantee them the equal opportunity to satisfy their freely selected commodity needs through economic activity of their own choice.

12.4 Social Freedom and the Public Administration of Welfare

The mandate for a public welfare administration derives from none other than the structure of social freedom. What lies at stake in combating economic disadvantage is securing for all the same freedom of interest whose realization comprises market activity. Consequently, the public enforcement of welfare cannot consist in eliminating commodity relations and the economic interest activity predicated upon them, nor in curtailing the property and household rights upon which they rest. Because the right to satisfy one's freely selected needs in reciprocity with others can only be exercised through these institutions, the public welfare administration cannot supplant, but only intervene upon them.

Marx's ideal of communism falls far short of what must be accomplished. Since social justice involves realizing everyone's equal opportunity to participate in the legitimate freedom of commodity relations, it extends beyond the imperatives of man's species being and the normative neutrality of monological action. Securing the conditions of human existence and human choice do fall within the jurisdiction of civil law to the extent that it must guarantee the prerequisites of self-determination as part and parcel of its enforcement of property rights. However, securing the survival needs of individuals, so as to enable them to dispose over property and enter further relations of right, is a far more meager task than guaranteeing the economic freedom by which one earns a conventional livelihood. The public administration of welfare cannot limit its goals in accord with the motto, "From each according to his ability, to each according to his needs." That would leave both work and need restricted to an exercise of natural liberty, lacking the mutuality of right and duty that first grants them normative validity. Instead, the just society must aim at the much more ambitious goal of guaranteeing the reciprocal satisfaction of freely chosen needs for commodities through freely entered exchange relations.

Because individuals can satisfy their needs in the market only if the commodities they need are available and they own commodities needed by the owners of what they seek, public authority must act on two fronts simultaneously in order to secure the welfare of all as an exercise of their economic freedom. At one and the same time, the public welfare administration must ensure that the market offers an adequate and affordable supply of the commodities needed by every member of society and that all have the commodities they require to obtain in exchange what they need.

As simply as this task may be stated, it presents a formidable challenge that might appear so beyond the power of social institutions as to call into question the very possibility of a just society.

First, it must be recalled that what lies at stake is much more than ensuring the physical and psychological subsistence of individuals. Such subsistence is indeed a civil right to which members of society are entitled in their capacity as persons whose preconditions of personhood must be publicly protected together with their property. The public enforcement of welfare, however, extends beyond the mere survival of the members of society to ensure their earning a conventional standard of living in exercise of their economic freedom.

Further, since social welfare consists in participation in structures of freedom, economic disadvantage cannot be removed through a public dole unilaterally allotting individuals goods to consume and jobs to perform. Instead of providing access to commodity relations, that would deprive individuals of their economic right to choose what they need and how they will earn a corresponding livelihood in conjunction with others.[3] Having goods and work may be an improvement on complete deprivation, but it is still a form of oppression if the possession of those goods and the undertaking of that employment are imposed upon individuals without the mediation of their will.

Similarly, the public welfare administration cannot remedy the wrongs of economic disadvantage by imposing an absolute equality of wealth, stipulating either the specific goods or the total exchange value to which each member of society is entitled. If the commodity ownership of individuals were publicly limited to the same collection of particular utilities, this would clearly eliminate, rather than secure, everyone's freedom of need. By contrast, publicly furnishing all with an identical amount of exchange value might appear to avoid that problem and leave individuals with an absolutely equal opportunity to choose and obtain what they need in reciprocity with others. For all its appeal, this solution is not equivalent to enforcing everyone's social right to realize interdependent interests. Since individuals may freely desire both different commodities and different levels of wealth, imposing uniformity on either score restricts the freedoms to be realized. It limits the satisfaction of need by those who may desire more when this does not automatically prejudice the satisfaction of need by others. Further, it sets restraints upon economic activity, effectively prohibiting all those transactions by which market agents use their equal exchange values to obtain very different wealth. That may well result in a decreasing availability of goods in the market and a declining general level of commodity ownership in situations where neither are required to ensure equal opportunity.

For these reasons, civil authority must take a more flexible approach to insure that all individuals can acquire the commodities they need by having at hand what others will accept in return. Instead of doling out goods to be consumed directly, or rigidly leveling personal wealth, public institutions must provide that every member of society has sufficient commodities to exchange, in light of both the needs they have chosen and the availability of goods in the market. These commodities include a marketable labor power, adequately trained to the individual's choice, as well as whatever money or goods are necessary to earn a livelihood through exchange with others. Of course, providing these means of livelihood is of little use unless public authority simultaneously insures that there be jobs available, as well as an adequate supply of affordable commodities.

What necessarily complicates the achievement of these goals are the unrestricted character of civil need and the inequalities of wealth continually produced by the ongoing process of commodity relations. These factors require a public regulation of the economy as persistent as it is radical.

Since the market's limitless multiplication and differentiation of needs and goods permits individuals to choose to need any variety and amount of commodities, the public welfare administration can never entirely eliminate the possibility of discrepancies between the needs of individuals and the available supply of commodities. To cope with this problem, public authority must address both sides of the dilemma. On the one hand, it must regulate the actual resources of the economy to furnish the market with as much of the needed goods on as affordable terms as possible. Intervention is required because there is nothing about commodity relations that guarantees that production will conform to consumer demand. Not only are over- and under-production continual problems, but certain goods may not be produced with acceptable quality or in any fashion at all unless the public takes it on its own to do so. It should be noted that among the commodities that the market may leave in short supply are desired terms of exchange for labor power. Consequently, public authority must step in to create acceptable employment opportunities. As Hegel has pointed out, public work projects may only magnify the problem by creating redundant production that ends up threatening other jobs.[4] Nevertheless, they need not exacerbate overproduction provided the work opportunities and products a public works project supplies do not overlap with existing branches of industry. Since all these considerations issue from the endemic character of commodity relations, it should not be forgotten that they apply no matter what forms of commodity ownership may predominate.

While attending to the supply of needed commodities, the public welfare administration must take account of the actual resources of the economy and accordingly limit the needs whose satisfaction it guarantees. This restriction involves no violation of right any more than do public interventions to regulate the supply of commodities. Both are just insofar as they apply to all commodity owners and enable them to satisfy needs of their own choosing in reciprocity with others. Although the choice of needs whose satisfaction is publicly guaranteed gets restricted, the limit is determined solely so as to allow all to exercise the freedom of earning a livelihood, involving needs that remain matters of personal preference. As in all cases of justice, what here limits self-determination is nothing but the realization of freedom itself.

While dealing with discrepancies between supply and demand, the public welfare administration must intervene in the market to prevent the continually emerging disparities of wealth from fostering economic disadvantage subverting the equal opportunity of commodity owners. Such intervention must not confuse differences in income with the injustice of poverty. In themselves, inequalities in wealth need not involve any infringement of the freedom of interest by which social wrong is measured. Since members of society have the right to determine their own needs, what and how many commodities they will seek to earn, and the type and degree of activity they will undertake in that pursuit, different individuals can fully satisfy all their needs through completely unequal livelihoods.

Indeed, due to the varying preferences of individuals, it would be correct to say that they can *only* satisfy their chosen needs through unequal accumulations of wealth.

Nevertheless, disparities in wealth can reach such a magnitude as to create economic disadvantage, where certain market participants, be they individuals, private corporations, worker cooperatives or state enterprises, accumulate enough resources to give them a distinct advantage in concluding further transactions, leaving others with lesser means unable to enter the commodity exchanges they require. The inability of the latter to conquer their relative poverty is the social wrong that public action must rectify. Because inequality of wealth is not a wrong unless it presents barriers to someone's desired participation in the market, enforcing the welfare of the disadvantaged does not consist in imposing equal incomes across society, but in ensuring that all do have sufficient means to earn the livelihood they wish through economic activity of their choice.

What determines the extent of public intervention are once again the given resources of the economy, which set the de facto upper limit of which needs can be satisfied in reciprocity by all. If possible, any imposition upon the commodity ownership and market activity of individuals should be avoided. Self-financing public works and public loans may provide sufficient assistance. If, however, the economic situation leaves no alternative, then restoring equal opportunity to the disadvantaged may involve an administered redistribution of wealth taken from the privileged. As the concentration of wealth by state enterprises in many a socialist regime has shown, the privileged from whom wealth should be redistributed may just as well be public enterprises as private corporations. No matter what types of commodity ownerships are involved, the freedom of need mandates that the redistribution cannot comprise the dispossession and receipt of specific utilities. That would leave the beneficiaries with as little choice over what commodities to own as their benefactors. Instead, the distribution of wealth should proceed through monetary taxation and reimbursement, whereby exchange value is publicly appropriated and redistributed. This allows each commodity owner to decide what goods to relinquish or acquire.[5] Although equalization of incomes is not an end in itself, redistribution of wealth through taxation has no normative limit provided the freedoms of commodity relations are upheld. Whatever is necessary to eliminate social disadvantage is justified to the extent that commodity owners remain able to satisfy their needs through free participation in the market.

Due to the inherent contingencies of commodity relations, public intervention is a continually recurring endeavor. Whatever measures are taken must constantly be revised in accord with the ever-changing situation of the market. No matter how extensive be public involvement or what forms of commodity ownership prevail, so long as commodity owners maintain their economic autonomy, any publicly planned welfare policy will require constant adjustment. Because the workings of the commodity economy are not determined by any single will, but result from the independent, yet interdependent decisions of the different participants in the market, no public plan to adjust supply and demand or to redistribute income can ever be assured of achieving its ends. There is simply no telling how successfully equal opportunity will be restored or how quickly economic disadvantage will reassert itself.

Although this leaves the occurrence of social wrong a constant danger, it also leaves the removal of economic disadvantage an endeavor whose current success can never be excluded. Just as the administration of civil law can protect person and property without eliminating the possibility of crime, so the public administration of welfare can ensure the economic rights of commodity owners without extirpating the conditions from which economic disadvantage arises. For this reason, the public struggle for equal economic opportunity is not a mark against the just society, but one of its chief occupations.

Since this occupation is directed equally at all members of society, the interventions of the public welfare administration involve an extension of civil law beyond the protection of property and household rights to the legal enforcement of economic well-being. Although the right of interest brought into being by commodity relations entails a constant and continually revised public regulation of the economy in reaction to the positive circumstances of the market, the administration of welfare still falls within the general guidelines prescribed by the concept of economic freedom. This allows for public intervention to follow laws addressing the problem of economic disadvantage, despite the fact that the measures taken to implement them have a specific content that cannot be derived in any *a priori* way.

On these terms, the public welfare administration does not supplant commodity relations, but rather regulates them so that the rights of economic freedom are externally secured for all. Just as the civil enforcement of property and household rights and economic interest group activity refer to the market as the arena upon which they act, so the public enforcement of equal opportunity consists in an intervention upon commodity relations, rather than in their removal. The just economy therefore remains the institutional base of the just society, both presupposed and referred to by all other civil institutions. Nevertheless, because the realization of economic freedom requires public regulation of the market, the commodity economy is the subordinate and not the determining base of the just society. The very logic of commodity relations ordains that only when society's own public institutions free it from subservience to capital or any other economic factor can society be civil and realize the freedom of interest. If, on the contrary, society stands under the sway of the market, be it ruled by private capitalists, worker self-managed cooperatives or government enterprises, there will be an unfree society, lacking the public subordination of the economy that can alone enable all to exercise their civil right to satisfy their need for commodities through freely chosen activity.

12.5 The Limits of Social Freedom

Although the public administrations of civil law and welfare lord over the commodity economy, they remain social institutions confined to the community of interest of the just society. All their activity affords the members of society are the civil rights to enjoy their person, property, and family freedoms under the protection of public law and authority and to have the publicly guaranteed opportunity to satisfy their needs through free participation in the market. No matter how developed be worker's control, communes, or other forms of economic self-management, neither they nor the public administrations of civil law and welfare provide any political rights to participate in self-government. Nor does the public regulation of the market comprise a self-determining government whose rule is for its own sake and thereby politically sovereign. Instead of determining its own aims, the public enforcement of civil law and welfare is strictly limited to realizing the independently determined interests of the members of society, just as are the managements of economic enterprises. Even if these interests are taken together as the public welfare, they still represent an end for which the administration of society is a separate means. In this respect, the activities of social institutions are relative to the particular pursuits of individuals that they serve and not universal ends in themselves.

These features would not cast limits upon social freedom and call for further rights and institutions were it not for how they render the just society unable to provide the necessary conditions for its own community. Even though the public institutions of society enable the members of society to exercise their economic freedom thanks to their enforcement of civil law and welfare, these institutions have power neither to make the laws they enforce nor to legitimate and determine their own authority. If they possessed the legislative power to furnish the laws they apply and obey as well as the source of authority to give their activities obligatory force for all individuals, they would be able to set their own ends and act for their own sake, contradicting their relative, civil character. Lacking these self-grounding capacities, these institutions cannot, however, independently supply themselves with their own rules, nor command recognition as the public administrator of civil right and welfare.

Left to its own resources, the just society stands in a dilemma that jeopardizes the entire edifice of justice. Although the social freedoms of civilians cannot be realized without these civil institutions, the public administrations of civil right and welfare cannot provide themselves with the conditions for their own interventions. Civil authority may rule over the economy and completely realize civil freedom, but it is still not the source of either the law it enforces or the authority it requires to fulfill its office. Consequently, the public administration of society, on which all social freedom depends, has no independence of its own.

This means that the just society cannot be the crowning order of freedom. By themselves, civil institutions leave the whole domain of right they contain without a ground of support issuing from their own freedom. In the absence of any further institutions of freedom, the just society stands either on the brink of collapse or subject to a law and authority extraneous to justice, upsetting the unconditioned universality giving freedom its very validity.

Chapter 13

Democracy and
The Just State

13.1 *The Mandate of Political Freedom*

The just society's own lack of independence calls for a higher sphere of justice that can give civil institutions the law and authority needed to secure social freedom. Because the reality of freedom would be transformed into a subject realm if its order were imposed upon it by something else, the distinct activity of this higher sphere must itself comprise a mode of self-determination with its own corresponding institutions of right. Accordingly, its freedom must be irreducible to no other, for its constitutive mandate is to determine and realize all relations of right, including its very own.

Therefore, the limits of social justice ordain a further structure of public freedom over and above the society it incorporates and grounds. In conformity with the systematic strictures of rational reconstruction, this new institutional realm must have no further prerequisites than what the just society provides, yet comprise an exercise of freedom resolving the abiding problems of justice while uniting the other structures of right into a self-determined, self-sufficient whole.

Two tasks must be fulfilled to meet these requirements. On the one hand, the needed structure of freedom must provide civil authority with all the means necessary to secure social freedom together with the property, moral, and family rights it involves. On the other hand, this higher public order must do so as an institutional sphere wherein individuals exercise the further freedom of determining the totality of justice that now includes this self-ordering activity as its ruling organ. Otherwise, the unity of the different institutions of right would depend on some power lying outside freedom, contrary to the unconditioned self-grounded character justice must have.

The institution that accomplishes both these tasks is the sovereign self-governed state whose regime of political self-determination builds the crowning order of freedom. It has this ultimate character not just by giving all the structures of justice a necessary realization through its own political activity, but by enabling the whole into which it unites them to be self-determined as well. Within its political domain, individuals accordingly enjoy their highest, most concrete freedom, determining as self-governing citizens the totality of justice in which they exercise not only this sovereign political right, but their property, moral, family, and social rights as well.

13.1.1 The Injustice of Instrumental Politics

Any liberal or socialist state that reduces government to an administration of civil law and/or public welfare fails to meet the dual requirements of political justice, as does any fascist state that subordinates political activity to the advancement of ethnic values. Although the just state must insure civil freedom, giving civil institutions the law and power to enforce property and family rights and social welfare does not render its government an instrument of civil society with no political ends of its own. In promoting these prepolitical freedoms, the just state is still acting for its own sake because what it equally does in remedying the dependence of society is determine itself as the self-ordering unifier of the totality of freedom. To the extent that the just society provides the prerequisites for self-government, the state promotes its own autonomy in providing for social freedom. In this respect, the state actually accounts for its own preconditions, ensuring both that they have means for their own existence and that they maintain the structures of pre-political justice in which their validity resides. Precisely because just government secures all the non-political institutions of freedom as politically guaranteed components of the whole it rules, the state only reaffirms the unconditioned character of its own activity by providing for their existence. In this fashion, the political unity of self-government is able to be an end in itself that must be maintained in all its sovereign primacy if society is to have its own law and authority through freedom. By thus comprising the self-grounded foundation of all other institutions of justice, the state can realize self-government without failing to realize the other structures of right, just as it can secure their freedoms without restricting its own.

By contrast, liberal civil government, the welfare state, and all regimes serving class interest commit the wrong of subordinating politics to social ends. This subverts justice by stripping the state of the self-grounding autonomy it needs not only to realize political freedom, but to enable society to realize its own rights and duties. When this occurs, political rule is reduced to administration, limited to implementing non-political aims that the state has not determined for itself. The government that results suffers from the same deficiency afflicting civil institutions: it cannot establish its own law and authority, but must receive them from elsewhere. So long as this condition persists, the entire order of right depends on independently given factors that rob it of the unconditioned character justice requires.

13.1.2 The Sovereignty of Politics

To escape the debilitating limitation of bondage to external conditions, the state must comprise a self-ordering domain radically independent of the society it grounds and sustains. Given the requirements of political justice that already guide its rational reconstruction, such a body politic has the following basic outline.

First, to realize the primacy of political freedom, the state should be an association through whose institutions individuals interact not as civilians advancing their particular interests, but as citizens determining government policy as the aim of their own action. For that policy to be something citizens can will as their own political self-determination, the state in which they act must be none other than the existing structure of their political freedom to govern themselves. In that case, the universal will of state authority coincides with the particular wills of its citizens, for the state to which they are subject is the organ of their self-rule. When individuals can exercise their rights as citizens by determining government policy, the state enjoys its own sovereign independence simply by being the institutional reality of their political freedom. Since the self-determination of its citizens is participation in self-government, the political order has for its end its own activity of self-rule rather than particular interests or public welfare as in the dependent "politics" of civil government, class rule or the welfare state. As a result, politics attains the stature of being an end in itself, subordinating under its own domain all other institutions of justice.

In comprising this sovereign sphere of self-government, the state cannot, however, cancel the social freedom of interest or any other relation of right. If it did so, it would set itself against its own citizens in their roles as property owners, moral subjects, family members, and civilians, engendering an irreconcilable conflict of right against right in which the order of freedom would equally violate the reality of self-determination. Politics would then preside over the annulment rather than the realization of rights. To the extent that the non-political institutions of justice provide the preconditions for self-government, the state would also be undermining the very basis of its own political unity. On all accounts, the state would fail its mandate to provide the culminating institution of freedom, freeing justice of foundations by uniting all institutions of right into a self-determined whole.

To avoid such self-destruction, the just state must accommodate all other freedoms within its realm, and secure their rights through its own rule. What permits this accommodation to impose no external restraints upon the exercise of political freedom is the role non-political freedoms play as prerequisites of self-government. The right of property is required, for without it, one may just as well be a slave whose every act represents the will of another. Moral rights are equally indispensable, since the moment one is deprived of them, one loses all accountability for one's actions, including all political responsibility. Similarly, if one belongs to a family whose bonds are not relations of freedom, one may either be lord or subject of another family member, undercutting the possibility of political autonomy for all. By the same token a society lacking the institutions of social freedom leaves its civilians prey to all variety of dependency that preclude their participation in self-government.

If this suggests that the state's maintenance of non-political institutions of justice is actually part and parcel of the realization of political freedom, it does not mean that government must refrain from all limitations upon them. While enforcing their justice, the state must preserve its own sovereignty by preventing any of its component non-political institutions from subordinating politics to their own ends. If justice is to be determined by freedom, rather than be externally ordered, the state must ensure that its citizens exercise their property, moral, household, and social rights without letting these undermine their political freedom, either by subverting the political rights of others, or by putting the sovereignty of the entire state in jeopardy. Although the state cannot legitimately cancel these freedoms in their entirety, it has the political right and duty to restrict particular aspects of their exercise when such measures are required to preserve the institutions of political freedom that guarantee their general existence.

For this reason, government has the prerogative and obligation to restrain and punish the arbitrariness of conscience when its moral acts violate the laws of the state. So too, the state is entitled not only to tax its citizens to support government endeavors, but to require them to risk their particular lives for the defense of political sovereignty, which alone protects personhood in general.

13.2 The Just Relation between State and Society

These considerations allow for a preliminary conception of the proper relation between the just state and the just society. Although a systematic treatment of this theme requires a prior account of the institutions of government and the political activities of citizens that comprise one side of the relation, a precursory outline is helpful in dispelling key misconceptions of political justice.

First and foremost, it must be recognized that the legitimate relation between state and society is something determined and secured by political activity. Even though the just society provides the prerequisites for political freedom, the dependence of social justice upon a higher order signifies that it is only through the agency of state rule that social institutions secure a guaranteed existence. In this respect, the state accounts for its own preconditions, ensuring both that they have means for their own existence and that they maintain the structures of pre-political justice that make them valid. If, on the contrary, the relation between society and state were instituted by social institutions, politics would not be self-determined. Instead of comprising an order of freedom uniting all structures of justice into a self-ordered, self-grounded whole, the state would then be an instrument of society, ruled by social factors whose own lack of independence would leave the order of justice once more subject to external control. For this reason, the mediation of social groups with the state cannot occur from within their ranks, as Hegel and Marx suggest by finding a civil foundation for politics in the allegedly universal interest of some privileged class, the nobility for Hegel, the proletariat for Marx.[1] The proper integration of classes and political institutions must instead take place from the side of government through a rule over society enforcing social justice in conformity with political freedom.

Accordingly, the relation between state and society resolves itself into a question of how the state rules over society. Given the tasks of political justice, the governing of society by the state has two dimensions.

As we have seen, the state must provide civil institutions with the law and authority they require to enforce social justice. To accomplish this, government must first enact two types of law applying to society. One consists in the administrative law determining the jurisdiction and organization of the public enforcement of civil rights and welfare. The other comprises the body of civil law that civil institutions administer in securing the property, family and economic rights of individuals. Legislating these is not enough, however, for government must further insure that civil institutions obey the law it has imposed upon them and that they have at their disposal the means enabling them to do so. Only under this *political* supervision can it be assured that civil institutions are able and compelled to carry out their *social* regulation of property relations, households, and the economy.

This intervention of the state in society for the sake of social justice may afford every civilian their equal civil opportunities, but it does not automatically prevent class conflicts, economic power and other social factors from overwhelming politics. These may still succeed in subordinating government policy to some social interest and thereby undermine the equal political opportunity of citizens to rule themselves.

This can occur despite the public enforcement of social welfare for a variety of reasons. First, no matter how just society may be, individuals can still engage in political corruption, fraudulently using government office for their own private gain. Second, even if public regulation of the economy continually remedies the incessant ermergence of economic advantage and disadvantage, the social conditions of political action may still give certain citizens a better chance of participating in politics. Since obtaining publicity for political programs, organizing political groups, and mounting political campaigns all require significant financial resources and labor, as well as access to means of communication and transportation, particular individuals may command privileged resources undermining the equal access of citizens to the social provisions needed to engage in politics. This may arise from inequalities in personal wealth that either are awaiting public regulation or have no bearing on economic disadvantage. It may also be based on the respective inequalities of wealth among different social groups, which need not reflect any inequalities in personal prosperity. Given all the possibilities of commodity ownership, private capitalists, public corporations, trade unions, worker cooperatives, or for that matter, public enterprises, may each dispose over sufficient finances to give their members privileged clout in the political arena. Furthermore, certain groups may have special command over the means of political action not in virtue of their wealth, but due to their social position. Workers in the communication and transportation industries can well use their freedom to withhold their services to those opposing their political views, just as the public, cooperative or private proprietors of the media, and other related fields can use their enterprises to political advantage.

In face of these eventualities of political corruption and social domination of political affairs, the state must take whatever measures are necessary to ensure the equal political opportunity of every citizen. Only when society undergoes this regulation for purely political ends can political action be free of social privilege. Then and then alone does politics attain its proper unconditioned universality, where the affairs of state are more than a formal universal, masking the domination of particular interests. By assuring that all its citizens enjoy equal access to the means of political participation, self-government enforces its own reality, countering the threat of social oligarchy with a regime where ruler and subject are not mutually exclusive.

In this sweeping fashion, the state secures the conditions for political freedom by regulating its own relation to society. Through its two modes of intervention, one for social and the other for purely political ends, the state insures that its citizens' freedoms as property owners, moral subjects, family members, and civilians are realized in unity with their political self-determination.

Nevertheless, the interventions of government in society do not determine how the state mediates its own universal rule with the particular political wills of its citizens. Since the free state can only regulate society by employing its own institutions of self-rule, their structure must be established in their own right as the internal basis for any relation between the state and either the non-political institutions within its domain or other nations. Although the political movements of recent times have focused their attention upon the order of society or some other pre-political foundation of the state, the order of justice requires that the question of the state's internal structure have paramount importance. If it be ignored through acceptance of the sanctity of existing constitutions or wholesale rejection of political justice, there can be no deciding whether freedom can attain the self-grounded reality that the just state can alone provide. What lies at stake in determining the institutions of political freedom is thus much more than resolving whether self-government consists in parliamentary democracy, a federal system of participatory assemblies, or some other form. The overriding question rather concerns whether right will exist on its own account, and so achieve the unconditioned universality that justice demands.

13.3 The Justice of Democracy

Conceiving the just state as a regime of political freedom inevitably raises the issue of the legitimacy of democracy. This is not because democracy is so evidently equivalent to self-government, nor because the proper form of democratic government is so obvious that the legitimacy of democracy can be unambiguously examined. What makes debate about democracy immediately relevant is that it puts in focus the principal problems of political justice.[2]

13.3.1 The Apparent Injustice of Political Freedom

Chief among the arguments against democracy are those that challenge the legitimacy of political freedom from the vantage point of the metaphysics of justice. As the originators of praxis theory were well aware, the rule of freedom is incompatible with any normative order involving given ends and functions prescribed by reason independently of the will. Although a sovereign political will may well adopt policies conforming to preestablished norms, the discretionary license of its political freedom leaves any such conformity a nonobligatory matter of choice. So long as the authority and power of government reside in a sovereign will free unto itself, what is and should be done cannot be preordained by reason, but only perceived after the fact of the sovereign's arbitrary decisions. This indifference to set ends and functions is not mitigated by conferring sovereignty to the people's will, as expressed in the democracy of majority rule. With the people at liberty to choose however they will according to majority decision, there is no telling what goals will be mandated or which activities will be undertaken to fulfill them.

For just this reason, it makes no sense objecting to the political equality and lack of expertise of those who rule under such democracy. Since the majority can do as it pleases, there are no given duties for which citizens need special qualifications. Instead of having to execute preordained functions requiring certain skills, the people enjoy the power of first deciding what goals should be addressed, as well as how they shall be implemented. All citizens need to exercise this democratic freedom is the choosing will they each have by nature, provided they are neither severely retarded, insane, comatose, nor too young to choose. Need for special skills would only arise subsequently to administer what has already been politically decided.

Granted the appropriateness of political equality under democracy, the problem remains of how political freedom can be justified in its own right. Since, in the abstract, the exercise of political freedom cannot be counted on to achieve any antecedently prescribed norms, democracy cannot be legitimated as a means to any end distinct from itself. For this reason, the defense of political freedom would appear to require denying that there are any given ends to which politics should be subordinated. Historically, it is just such a denial of the authority of given ends that provides the point of departure for the justification of liberty inaugurated by Hobbes' rejection of any teleological conception of man. Nonetheless, as the dilemmas of liberal theory have themselves revealed, denying that there is a good life of given character may set the will free of external prescription, but this does not of itself vindicate the rule of freedom. Contrary to the instrumental role given civil government by liberal theorists, political freedom must be shown to be an end in itself if democracy is to have legitimacy.

This requires confronting the powerful objections that argue against any normativity for freedom, objections that led Plato to try to exclude liberty from his ideal state. First, although the autonomy of the choosing will may be a necessary precondition of justice, that it permits right as well as wrong action seems to indicate that freedom cannot be an end in itself, but must be subject to limiting norms that guide its exercise. Extended to political freedom, this objection seems to rule out any justification of democracy. Left to its own democratic designs, the will of the majority is oblivious to the distinction of right and wrong, whereas if it be made to follow prescribed ends, it sacrifices its own autonomy, abolishing the democratic freedom in which its exercise consists.

Furthermore, even if political freedom were an end in itself, democratic rule could not guarantee its own perpetuation. As recent history has shown, so long as majority decision has free sway, there is nothing to prevent the majority from supplanting democracy with another form of government.

The impasse could not be more complete. Although the legitimation of democracy seems to rest on the demonstrated illegitimacy of all prescribed restraints upon the will of the majority, the absence of such limits appears to leave democracy beyond good and evil, as well as unable to maintain any commitment to its own form of government. Yet, if fixed standards must be imposed to bring reason to the will of the majority, how can democratic government have any validity?

A satisfactory answer to this problem has not been provided by the traditional defenders of democracy. Nevertheless, an examination of the arguments of such disparate advocates as Jefferson, Rousseau, and Lenin turns attention to the terms on which a solution may be drawn.

13.3.2 The Wrong Defenses of Democracy

13.3.2.1 Jefferson's Appeal to Praxis and Liberty

Jefferson's advocacy of democracy is especially instructive because he draws upon both praxis and liberal theories, inadvertently demonstrating how neither can legitimate democratic government.

In his letter to John Adams.[3] Jefferson embraces the classical ideal of aristocracy, declaring that the just state is governed by those who are most virtuous and talented. As we have seen, such a conclusion can hardly be avoided once the teleological view is accepted that justice consists in the achievement of rationally prescribed ends through conformably set functions. Unlike Plato and Aristotle, however, Jefferson claims that democracy is the best government because the best individuals will most likely be selected to rule by democratic election. Jefferson does admit that the many may be blinded by birth and corrupted by wealth and fail on occasion to choose the best candidates. Nevertheless, he still maintains that for the most part, the electoral victors will not be artificial aristocrats, winning power through caste and riches, but be natural aristocrats, gaining office by being the wisest, most virtuous and ablest of men. Just to be sure, Jefferson calls for a ward system of public education and for the abolition of entails and primogeniture, believing that these measures will prevent social privilege from spawning a pseudo-aristocracy.

The problem with Jefferson's argument is that no matter what be done to instruct the public and eliminate social disadvantage, there can be no guarantee who the majority will elect so long as they retain their liberty to decide. Due to the arbitrariness their prerogative allows, democracy can no more insure rule by the best than the adoption and execution of any given policies. All that majority rule automatically entails is its own momentary exercise. For this reason,

Jefferson's attempt to legitimate democracy as the privileged means to aristocratic rule cannot possibly succeed.

Jefferson fares no better when he leaves behind notions of praxis and rests his advocacy of republicanism upon the liberal principles of social contract. Their uselessness for the legitimation of democracy is revealed no more plainly than in *The Declaration of Independence*. In its famous call, Jefferson reaffirms the liberal credo of Locke, declaring that all men are born free and equal with inalienable rights to life, liberty and the pursuit of happiness, that government is properly instituted to secure these rights, deriving its just powers from the consent of the governed, and lastly, that the people have the right to alter or abolish their government whenever it violates its mandate, and replace it with a new regime that will protect their person and property with the consent of the governed.

Significantly, *The Declaration of Independence* refrains from any mention of democracy and political freedom. Consistent with its liberal roots, it limits its call for independence to the establishment of no more than the civil government prescribed by contractarian theory. Since all that government is charged with is securing the non-political freedoms of property owners with their consent, it need not have democratic institutions. As Locke rightly acknowledges in Chapter X of his *Second Treatise of Government*, civil government can well fulfill all its duties as a monarchy or oligarchy. Its authority may rest in the consent of the governed embodied in the social contract, but this does not entail citizens' participation in self-government. Civil government with the consent of the governed does not guarantee its citizens any political rights, but only the liberty to enjoy their civil rights, together with the pre-political right to select who will rule over them to protect their person and property. In exercising the latter right, they can certainly choose themselves as rulers, but they can just as well select one or several individuals to govern them, and even consent to a dynastic succession. Given this latitude, it should be no surprise that many who took up arms in answer to *The Declaration of Independence* could follow its message by later attending the Constitutional Convention fully expecting to enthrone George Washington as King of the United States of America.

Of course, civil government can be democratic provided its majority rule not only enjoys the consent of the governed, but also secures the non-political rights of individuals that liberal theory locates in a state of nature as adjuncts of the privileged legitimacy granted the natural will. Since this state of nature exists by definition

in any situation where there is no legitimate government, and not
merely in some pre-historic age antedating the rise of civilization, its
natural right cannot possibly involve any exercise of political freedom.
If it did, the state of nature would already contain valid political institutions. Liberal theory, however, maintains that government only has
legitimacy as a product of the convention of social contract, which
puts an end to the state of nature. Accordingly, insofar as civil government is contractually instituted to secure the liberty all men have a
right to by nature, its goal is necessarily restricted to the realization of
non-political rather than political freedoms.

Liberal theory therefore cannot treat democracy as an end in itself,
but can only tolerate it as a means to civil liberty. Since other forms
of government can equally secure non-political freedoms, the instrumental role of civil government leaves democracy at best an optional
alternative. Far from having any exclusive authority, democracy would
be potentially inadmissible given the ever-present possibility of the
majority adopting policies violating the person and property of
individuals.

Jefferson's promotion of the ideal of republican democracy thus
receives no succor from the liberal premises of *The Declaration of Independence*. If anything, they point to the expendability of democratic
rule. By conceiving entitled freedom as the non-institutional natural
liberty of individuals, rather than as the institutional participation of
citizens in self-government, social contract theory leaves democratic
rights beyond the pale of justice, as suspect ornaments to the enforcement of civil rights.

Although Jefferson never fully comprehends the radical distinction between liberty and political freedom, he inadvertently brings it
to a head in his attempt to apply contractarian principles to the constitutionality of his democratic republic. Following liberal theory with
uncompromising consistency, Jefferson writes to James Madison on
September 6, 1789[4] that the liberty of individuals is infringed by any
constitution whose authority rests on ratification by a preceding
generation. In such a situation, liberal theory offers no basis for
citizens of the current generation to be under any obligation to obey
the constitution, nor for that matter, to pay public debts accrued in the
past. This is because neither debts nor constitution have issued from
the consent of the individuals on which they bear, a consent that is
the sole source of all their obligations, granted the legitimacy of
liberty. To remedy the problem, Jefferson proposes that a constitution
be valid only so long as the majority of citizens remain those who

ratified it, whereas once that period elapses, an entirely new constitution should be enacted with the same expiration provisions.

What causes problems is that Jefferson also maintains, albeit without argument, that the just state is not just a government with the consent of the governed, but a democratic republic realizing participatory democracy as much as possible through direct election of all public officials for short terms, complemented by a system of ward assemblies having jurisdiction over local affairs.[5]

Both positions cannot be coherently advocated at once. If Jefferson is to honor the right of each generation to choose its constitution at liberty, then he cannot also restrict legitimacy to any particular form of government in advance of the people's free decision. If alternately, he is to maintain his commitment to democratic government as the mandatory paragon of justice, he cannot also permit the people to determine their constitution however they see fit. This leaves but two consistent options. Either one accepts the contractarian allegiance to non-political liberty and abandons promoting democracy, or one attempts to justify democratic self-government for its own sake without appeal to natural rights. Jefferson follows neither alternative, and falls instead into uncritical self-contradiction.

13.3.2.2 Democracy and Rousseau's General Will

Unlike Jefferson, Rousseau is well aware of the difficulties encountered in employing liberal arguments to redeem democracy. Although Rousseau remains loyal to the social contract view of the primacy of natural rights and the corollary principle that government is legitimate insofar as it protects person and property with the consent of the governed, he equally realizes that democratic government can only be defended as an end in itself. Consequently, when he argues for democracy, he adopts the ingenious strategy of binding social contract to democratic rule by maintaining that democracy is an end in itself precisely because it is the only reliable means for securing non-political liberty.

Rousseau arrives at this novel solution out of recognition of the problems arising from the instrumental character of civil government. He understands that so long as the state is merely a means to an end distinct from its own political activity, the possibility of their divergence cannot be eliminated. Not only can there be no guarantee that government will fulfill its mandate, but there can be no resources sufficient to judge objectively when violations occur, or, for that matter, to counter them. As we have seen, Locke's appeal to the judgment of the people offers no answer since it leaves unresolved how they will be able to convene and judge with authority. Even if the people could assemble in immediate response to transgressions of government, there would be no way for the people to reach a legitimate decision that could be executed effectively. This is not due just to the difficulty of determining what counts as a valid expression of the people's judgment and will. There is no need to dwell on that problem because none of the possible alternatives are capable of redressing abuses of government. If unanimous consent were required for the people to pass its judgment on the conduct of government, then no judgment of censure could be expected for the simple reason that the officials subject to indictment are themselves members of the "people." If instead only majority decision were needed, the door would be open for a tyranny of the majority adding its own violations of civil freedom. If, finally, one were to follow Locke's suggestion that each individual be free to rely upon personal judgment to determine when government has transgressed its mandate and no longer commands obedience,[6] the authority of the state would become subject to the rule of individual arbitrariness, reinstating the condition of all-sided license that civil government was instituted to prevent.

Rousseau concludes that these difficulties can only be solved by eliminating the gulf between the liberty of individuals and government rule. This is accomplished, he reasons, by bringing direct democracy to the legislative power of civil government. In that case, where sovereignty is invested in a general will that acts by making law according to the majority decision of an assembly of all citizens, government will automatically achieve its legitimate end of protecting person and property. Rousseau's fundamental claim is that the general will can do no wrong because it consists in citizens' exercising the genuine freedom of willing law upon themselves. This allegedly precludes injustice on three accounts. First, since no will can injure itself, a government that rules by the general will of those it governs cannot violate their liberty. Second, because all acts of the general will are acts of legislation, they apply equally to all individuals in their capacity as legal subjects. Third, due to its democratic form of legislation, the general will prevents any particular will from subordinating government to its own interests at the expense of others. Both emanating from all and applying equally to all, the general will enjoys an unassailable universality. For Rousseau, this signifies that no matter what the general will makes law cannot help but secure the common good. Even though it serves the liberty of individuals, the democratic legislation of the general will would therefore possess an unconditioned justice making its activity an end in itself.[7]

If the common good were nothing other than the very activity of the general will's democratic lawmaking, Rousseau's argument would succeed in legitimating democratic government. In that case, the general will could not possibly fail to realize justice since justice would consist in the working of the general will itself. Rousseau, however, cannot grant the political freedom of the general will such affirmative weight, for he still ties the common good to the realization of pre-political liberty. By identifying freedom with obedience to law that is not just self-imposed, in the manner of Kantian autonomy, but code-termined by the wills of all other citizens, Rousseau does take one step beyond the contractarian embrace of the natural will as a privileged determiner. Nevertheless, he fails to turn this step into a true break from the liberal approach and instead restricts the general will to fulfilling the familiar aims of social contract: protecting person and property with the consent of the governed. This leaves Rousseau little choice but to qualify the justice of the general will and admit that its democratic legislation does not automatically achieve the common good.[8] Because liberal principles leave the common good with a content determined independently of the activity of the general will, the general will must be guided to legislate in conformity with that content, instead of making laws that serve a particular faction or violate the natural rights of all. However, since Rousseau still retains the sovereignty of the general will, this direction cannot be compulsory. It can only take the form of persuasion, persuasion exercised by a powerless "legislator" who suggests laws for adoption by the general will. Because the will of the majority need not be moved by appeals to reason, Rousseau recognizes that the "legislator" cannot rely on rational argument alone, but must also foster faith in a "civil religion" to lead citizens to will what is rational.[9]

Although Rousseau is perfectly consistent in appealing to these cultivators of the general will, they bring his justification of democracy to its own ruin. The very need for guidance by a legislator and civil religion demonstrates that the justice of the general will does not reside in its democratic structure. It lies instead in the conformity of its legislation to the independently determined rights for whose protection the social contract is convened. Far from being automatic, this conformity is endemically jeopardized by nothing other than the sovereignty of the general will, a sovereignty that gives its democracy license to ignore the guidance of legislator and civil religion and legislate away every other vestige of liberty.

13.3.2.3 The Pitfall of Lenin's Proletarian Democracy

If Rousseau's theory reveals how the defense of democratic government requires a total break from liberal principles, Lenin's argument for a workers' democracy demonstrates that such a break must extend to all ends extraneous to political freedom. In *State and Revolution* Lenin advances the democratic ideal that apologists for "people's democracies" have used ever since to legitimate such regimes. What makes the political injustice of people's democracies relevant to an evaluation of democratic rule is not that they have substituted party dictatorship for proletarian democracy, but that the latter ideal is inherently flawed.

Lenin offers workers' democracy as the proper remedy to parliamentary democracy in view of the genuine problem of preventing social wealth and power from turning into political privilege. Relying more on a bevy of quotations from Marx than on a full-fledged argument, Lenin denounces parliamentary democracy as bourgeois democracy, presuming that parliamentary democracy is rooted in capitalist society and that capitalist society is dominated by privately owned enterprises employing wage labor to the benefit of the bourgeoisie and the misery of the proletariat. On these assumptions, which can well be challenged once the full latitude of capital is understood, Lenin claims that so long as there is a capitalist society, the private owners of the means of production will enjoy such an overwhelming preponderance of wealth as to have privileged access to the instruments of political activity. Even though there be universal suffrage, freedoms of speech and assembly, and the elimination of all political privileges directly tied to class affiliation, the bourgeoisie's disproportionate ability to finance media exposure, lobbying efforts, and campaign organizations turns democracy into bourgeois democracy, where the bourgeoisie operates as a ruling class subordinating government to its own interests under the veil of democratic equality.[10] Although the possibility of such abuse should not be ignored, it certainly can be questioned whether the political advantages of the bourgeoisie could automatically prevent the election of a government representing other interests, a government that might then insure a fair distribution of political resources without eliminating either private capital or parliamentary democracy.

Be this as it may, the problem with Lenin's argument lies not so much in his failure to take account of the full latitude of parliamentary democracy as in the positive alternative he offers to remedy its abuses. This is the dictatorship of the proletariat, which will supplant parliamentary democracy, whose rule by the majority is but a screen for rule by the few, with a regime ruled by the working class through a democracy limited to its own members. Although this violates political equality by excluding citizens of other classes from governing themselves, Lenin maintains that it secures genuine majority rule, believing as he does that the members of socialist as well as capitalist societies are overwhelmingly workers. Even if this were granted, despite the possibility of private and public forms of capital involving no wage labor, it still might be objected that unimpeded majority rule may only result in the hegemony of the particular ends of the majority, ends that may completely lack universal validity. In answer to this problem, Lenin seconds Marx's claim that although the proletariat is but a particular group, its social oppression gives it a uniquely universal interest, directed at no other goal than the elimination of class distinctions, the withering away of the state, and the birth of a classless communist society. The contrast with bourgeois democracy thus could not be any greater. Whereas bourgeois democracy undermines political justice by using the show of universal rule as the tool of a particular social interest, workers' democracy not only realizes genuine majority rule, but subordinates government to a particular social interest that is properly universal.[11] On both counts, the dictatorship of the proletariat would appear to provide a democracy beyond reproach.

What prevents Lenin's argument from succeeding is nothing less than the incompatibility of workers' democracy with the revolutionary goals of communism on which the validity of proletarian rule should rest. The cause of this discrepancy lies in Lenin's basic conception of politics. Following Marx, and anticipating Max Weber and most contemporary social and political scientists, Lenin takes the liberal reduction of politics to civil government one step further by conceiving the state to be a purely instrumental institution, defined by holding the monopoly of coercive power over society. As an instrument of power, government can no more have ends of its own, than politics can be an end in itself. Since power for its own sake is empty and pointless, what gives the state specific meaning are the independently determined ends that it serves, ends that Lenin traces back exclusively to class interest given the economic determinism of his reading of Marx. This renders the state an instrument of class domination, breaking any social deadlock by allowing whichever class that rules the ability to oppress the others thanks to the overwhelming force of political power. On these terms, politics not only has no legitimacy of its own, but government becomes an inherently unjust institution of domination that ought to be dismantled. Accordingly, any talk of a just state is a contradiction in terms that had better give way to concern for the just society. Hence, the goal of the dictatorship of the proletariat is not to found the true republic but to eliminate class divisions in society and thereby eliminate the basis for any state at all.[12]

Workers' democracy therefore cannot be an end in itself. Instead of enjoying any unconditioned validity, it is only justifiable to the degree that it paves the way to communist society by adopting the correct social measures that progressively undermine the economic bases of class divisions. There cannot, however, be any guarantee that workers' democracy will implement such policies so long as the proletariat is at liberty to govern itself. Even if the majority of workers do wish to establish a classless society, this does not ensure that they will choose the proper route or that there will be any workable consensus on how to proceed. Having a common interest is one thing; knowing or willing the means to realize it is another. Furthermore, if Lenin be granted that the goal of revolution is antecedently prescribed by "scientific socialism" independently of any exercise of political freedom, then the rule of revolutionary experts, schooled in the incorrigible truths of Marxism, would surely be more reliable than any workers' parliament.

As much as Lenin wishes to legitimate workers' democracy as the genuine form of majority rule, there is no way he can allow it free reign and also maintain his teleological commitment to the construction of communist society. Lenin has little choice but to fall back upon a "solution" that translates Plato and Rousseau into an all too common contemporary idiom. Just as Plato made philosophers guardians of the polis to instruct their subjects in the good life and Rousseau introduced a legislator and civil religion to bring reason to the general will, so Lenin calls upon the vanguard party and its ideology to guide the proletariat to its true destiny.

To his credit, Lenin does not hesitate to give the workers' vanguard the character and role it must have to fulfill its historical mission. Because the goal of the revolution is not workers' democracy nor any form of government, but a communist society preconceived by Marxist "science," the vanguard cannot be a mass party governed by the rank and file. To counteract their arbitrariness, the vanguard must instead restrict itself to a political elite, whose members qualify to be true guardians of the revolution by being schooled in the wisdom of dialectical materialism and unconditionally devoted to its cause. Their tasks alter with the advance of the revolution. Prior to the seizure of state power, the vanguard party has no choice but to rely upon persuasion to influence the working class. Since the untutored proletariat is more susceptible to ideological faith than the rational apprehension of "scientific socialism," the vanguard can best cajole the proletariat to rebel by addressing it with a mass line employed like a civil religion. After the revolution. however, the conquest of political power puts the vanguard party in a position to discard its mimicry of Rousseau's powerless legislator and play its version of Plato's ruling class. In order to reach the "rationally" ordained goal of communist society, the party must now free itself of subordination to any constituent assemblies, workers' soviets, trade union movements, or other institutions and eliminate all their prerogatives to deviate from a revolutionary course. To guarantee the transition to communism, the vanguard simply has no alternative but to make itself the supreme arbiter of society and state, vigilantly restricting every social and political freedom of the working class whenever necessary to forward the revolution.

The results of Lenin's political vision have made familiar history ever since the Bolsheviks disbanded the constituent assembly, abolished the workers' soviets, liquidated all independent trade unions, and married party and state. Far from providing any justification for the dictatorship of the proletariat, these developments testify to the inexorable conflict between a workers' democracy and communist rule. Whereas liberal principles can be realized with or without political freedom, the road to communism must cast democracy aside. By reducing the state to a disposable tool of preordained social ends, Lenin and his epigones have deprived the dictatorship of the proletariat of all rationale for political freedom.

It is telling that when Lenin provides a rare glimpse of the redeeming goal of communist society, where the working day, the market, classes, and the state have all been swept away, his sole resource for sustaining the new order is the prophecy that habit will insure that individuals take what they need in harmony with one another.[13] Perhaps Aristotle is right that habit is the midwife of virtue. Nevertheless, because individuals must have choosing wills to acquire habits, let alone to do right, it is inconceivable how habit could preclude conflicting choices and guarantee any type of justice without a reintroduction of the ruling agency of political authority. In the social and political void of associated producers, where man has been reduced to his species being by shedding market and state, and where history has ended with the extinction of every institution by whose alterations historical change could occur, Lenin would like to imagine an unthreatened hobby existence of purely private activities, where individuals "realize" themselves free of economic necessity and political responsibility. Whether this could provide a good life is as questionable as whether it could avoid turning into a life nasty, brutish, and short. What is unequivocally clear is that democracy would have no more place in it than any other public endeavor.

13.3.3 The Three Requirements for the Justification of Democracy

Clearly, democracy cannot be legitimated by following the paths of Jefferson, Rousseau, or Lenin. If, however, the common failures of their arguments are considered in view of the validity of self-determination, the terms for vindicating democratic government begin to take shape. What becomes apparent is that democracy can only be justified as the proper form of government if the three following requirements are met.

First, democratic political freedom must qualify as an end in itself, instead of figuring as a means to independently determined ends. Only then can democracy play a necessary and reliable role in realizing its legitimate purpose.

Second, whatever affairs fall under the prerogative of democratic decision must be unsusceptible of any prior prescription by reason. If, on the contrary, these matters were subject to rationally preordained policies whose validity was independent of what the majority might will, then justice would require that they be handled by knowledgeable experts instead of by democratic procedures.

Third, democracy must be bound by non-amendable constitutional statutes obliging government to uphold its own democratic process and secure all legitimate non-political relations. Otherwise, majority rule may just as well vote itself out of existence as trample on every other institution of justice.

In order to understand how these requirements can be met in conformity with the foundation-free character of justice, it is best to begin with the last requirement first and work back to the fulfillments of the other two, upon which the legitimacy of democracy ultimately rests.

13.4 Constitutionality, Positive Law, and Democracy

Constitutionality is necessary to counteract the endemic arbitrariness of majority rule and enable democratic government to operate within limits that insure its normative validity. The need for constitutionality is already apparent in two imperatives arising in the failed attempts to justify democracy. Because majority rule cannot guarantee that the majority will choose to maintain democracy, any commitment to democratic government requires constitutional provisions constraining the majority to observe and preserve democratic freedom. Otherwise, democracy is free to overturn the democratic process. By the same token, since majority rule need not respect any other relations of justice, the constitution must also obligate democratic government to honor and enforce all other freedoms. Although the first of these imperatives refers to political activity whereas the second refers to non-political rights and institutions, they converge to the degree that maintaining non-political freedoms is itself a precondition for the exercise of democratic liberty. To take the most extreme case, if certain individuals are deprived of their right to inalienable ownership of their own bodies, as occurs under slavery, they can no longer act in their own name as participants in democracy, any more than in any other capacity of right. Similarly, if social disadvantage is tolerated so as to leave certain groups with privileged access to the resources for political action, democratic freedom can hardly have more than a formal reality as the public mask of oligarchy.

Whether or not non-political relations of justice are preconditions of democratic freedom and whether or not the protection of democracy may on occasion call for their limitation, does not alter the situation. The enforcement they are due can only be guaranteed under democracy if the will of the majority be bound by prescriptions it can neither alter nor rescind. Just as democratic government can be secured only if its form is not subject to positive law, but the irrevocable framework of all legislation, so democracy can remain strictly consonant with non-political justice only if it is subject to non-amendable constitutional laws spelling out every relation of right that should be unconditionally upheld, including the right of government to restrict non-political activities when necessary to maintain the free state as the bulwark of every right.

In this respect, the United States constitution is doubly at fault. While it fails to guarantee the social freedom of equal opportunity by committing government to remove social disadvantage and unemployment, it allows for constitutional amendment. Although the mandated amendment procedures involve more than acts of Congress, the mere admission of amendment undermines the fundamental distinction between constitutional and positive law by granting citizens the right to alter the constitution in any way they will. So long as this right is retained, the constitution provides no firm commitment to political democracy or any other relation of justice, including the amendment procedures themselves. Constitutional amendment may have become a hallowed tradition due to liberal notions of the consent of the governed, yet Jefferson's inability to apply them in defense of democracy already speaks to what a Pandora's box any amendment procedure represents. With constitutional amendment, anything from prohibitions of budget deficits and abortion to genocide or religious rule can be legally adopted provided enough citizens push such measures through the amendment procedures. The fate of the Weimar Republic should give an inkling of the possibilities.

This is not to deny that constitutional amendment can permit warranted peaceful reform when a given constitution is unjust and worthy of change. Such has been the fortunate experience with the American constitution, which has received needed amendment to eliminate the injustices of slavery and the political disenfranchisement of women. Nevertheless, the only valid purpose of constitutional amendment remains the establishment of the just constitution. Because its provisions can hardly be left a matter of choice, the just constitution must be non-amendable to guarantee that the institutions it prescribes are not dismantled with legal impunity.

The other side of the inadmissibility of constitutional amendment in the just state is the exclusion of constitution-making from the domain of political freedom. This might appear paradoxical, since it would seem to deprive self-governing citizens of the liberty to impose upon themselves the form of government in which they participate. The much-acclaimed liberty of a people to determine the political order under which they live is not, however, either identical to or compatible with the exercise of political freedom. For free political activity to be for its own sake, as justice demands, the end that citizens freely will must be the realization of self-government that comprises the very framework in which they engage in politics. Because self-government, like every other self-determination, is inseparable from the context of interaction in which it proceeds, a citizen cannot exercise political freedom without already being situated within the constitutional institutions by which it operates. What gives them their validity as organs of self-rule is that the only way citizens can act in their context is by governing themselves, exercising an activity that wills that context itself.

By contrast, willing the constitution into being is by its very nature an unconstitutional act, exercised by an agent who wills his constituting action not as an end in itself, but as a means for producing a political order that does not already exist. Both with regard to time and quality, the constitutional activity of any state is completely distinct from the constituting activity responsible for its foundation.

Enacting a constitution is not an activity for its own sake, enjoying the reflexive character of self-determination, but an activity of making by a given determiner who acts in express indifference to his own context in order to will another as the authentic framework of justice. Citizens of the just state can exercise an activity for its own sake, however, because what they engage in is not constitution-making, but participating in existing political institutions of justice.

These institutions of political justice are undermined the moment government gives one, some, or all citizens the power to determine the constitution. If this happens, the political domain becomes hostage to a will that does not act for its own sake, realizing the constitutional order in which political freedom consists, but instead exercises an unrestrained arbitrariness to make government whatever it pleases.

Although the exclusion of constitution-making and amending from the just state may run counter to common views of political self-determination, it directly reflects how the just constitution is an object of reason. Because the just constitution is not merely operative, but unconditionally valid, its provisions must be invariable and universally prescriptive. Conditions may not everywhere be ripe for the best regime, as Aristotle properly recognized. Nevertheless, the just constitution still provides the unchanging standard for judging what kind of regime is the best possible under given circumstances. Sharing the same qualities of universality, objectivity and unconditionality that reason must exhibit to be the vehicle of truth, the just constitution is rationally justifiable and a proper object of political philosophy.

Given this rationality of the just constitution and the apparent irrationality of democratic decision, the need of democracy for constitutionality might seem to present an insoluble contradiction testifying to the impossibility of justifying majority rule. If binding constitutional principles can be prescribed by reason, why allow any room for the arbitrariness of democratic prerogative? The answer lies, as it could only, in the rational character of the just constitution. Its own unconditioned univerality gives good reason for precisely the rationally opaque prerogative that democracy involves.

Since the constitution should prescribe all those activities and institutions that are unconditionally just, constitutional government is charged with one exclusive task: realizing the constitution. Every government, however, faces changing circumstances in society, politics and foreign affairs that concern justice and must therefore be taken account of in implementing the constitution. Consequently, although the just constitution has an *a priori* content prescribed by reason, its realization in practice cannot be determined by concepts alone. It necessarily involves applying the constitution's rationally determinable provisions to a given, changeable reality whose contingent situation can only be known through experience. This predicament calls for the legislation, authorization, and execution of positive laws, not to alter the constitution, but to bring it to bear upon the current state of affairs. Alterable, rescindable positive laws are necessary, for without their continual enactment in reference to the changing factual situation of the nation, the statutes of the constitution cannot be acted upon in any general, yet determinate fashion.

What permits toleration of democratic prerogative are the ensuing conditions of positive legislation. The framing of positive laws is a very different matter from framing the constitution under which they are made. Whereas constitutional law can be an object of reason, positive law can only be an object of judgment. By definition, the just constitution contains all those laws that are invariably valid and rationally prescribable. What positive legislation is left to supply are those variable conditioned laws obedience to which will implement the constitution in the current situation. Although reason must enter in to comprehend the constitution awaiting application, the reality at hand cannot be preordained by reason, but only be perceived after the fact in experience. Formulating positive law to connect the two therefore requires an act of judgment doubly burdened by subjectivity.

To begin with, perception of the given state of affairs is subject to all the limitations of factual knowledge that deprive it of any final objective certainty. The problems are the same that come to the fore in evaluating evidence in a court of law. No matter how detailed and consonant be the testimony of past and present experience, subjective discretion must ultimately be relied upon to decide whether the facts have been accurately and honestly reported, whether they are complete or representative, and whether they have been properly interpreted.

Then, after the facts have been established, not with absolute certainty, but with the subjective limitation of being beyond a reasonable doubt, subjective discretion must again enter in to judge how the laws should be framed to best apply the constitution. Reason alone may be able to specify the just constitution, but it is powerless to dictate the particular measures by which the constitution is realized in every possible situation. Perception, on the other hand, may provide relative knowledge of current facts, but it is blind when it comes to deciding what laws should be made in response to them. Lawmakers must employ reason to understand the constitution and call upon experience to apprehend the reality that is to be constitutionally governed. Yet when it comes to drafting the appropriate laws, there is need for an act of judgment going beyond what reason prescribes and perception observes. This judgment lies as much outside the limits of reason as any interpretation of facts. Reason may reiterate the universal statutes of constitutional law, but without the contribution of subjective discretion, there can be no determination of positive law.

Accordingly, positive legislation is unsusceptible to the rational prescription that would bar democracy from playing any legislative role in the just state. Because knowledge of the factual state of affairs and formulation of the positive laws needed to address it are both opaque to reason and dependent upon subjective judgment, there can be no privileged wisdom dictating absolutely correct laws, nor any privileged experts in legislation. All one needs to be competent to exercise the judgment required for positive legislation is the same unimpaired mind and choosing will permitting the exercise of every other right and duty. If this leaves all mature citizens with equal claim to participate in lawmaking, it also grants legislative authority to majority decision. Because positive laws cannot be framed with any absolute truth, it is as right as unavoidable for positive law to be determined by political opinion instead of by the political wisdom of a philosopher-king or vanguard party. Since reason cannot deduce positive laws from constitutional principles, legislative debate is always an open-ended prospect where no speaker can claim unqualified truth without belying how every legal judgment rests on uncertain observations and subjective discretion. With no rational standards available to certify the truth of competing legislative proposals, and with all mature citizens possessing an equal right to determine legislation, the only factor that can give one opinion more authority than another to ordain the law is the weight of political opinion.

Although this permits laws to be made democratically with the participation of all mature citizens, it does allow for a representative legislature provided its members hold their legislative office through election determined by the same weight of political opinion that they then must rely on among themselves in passing their bills. What it does not permit is any independent claim by some class, group or individual to a privileged role in legislation. Even if one were to follow Marx and grant the proletariat a universal interest determinable by philosophy and in accord with justice, the working class would still be no more reliable than any other legislator. Deciding what legislation promotes its rational interest would still require perceiving the prevailing situation and judging how to apply the rationally knowable proletarian interest to those circumstances. Not only would the legislative programs of workers be as varied and changing as subjective discretion allows, but individuals of other classes might just as well advocate laws realizing proletarian interest more effectively than those of any workers or their self-anointed guides. Just as knowledge of an interest cannot provide an unequivocal determination of the positive laws serving it best, so the political opinion of legislators cannot derive from their place in society, even if their social roles give them a common objective interest that they seek to promote.

Consequently, a corporate legislature with class representation, designed to guarantee the satisfaction of social interests and the integration of society and state, such as Hegel suggests, makes little sense on its own terms. Since the whole purpose of positive legislation is to realize the constitution, rather than a particular social interest, what warrants legislative representation are different political views for governing the whole, not the social interests of different classes. Because the just constitution already commits government to eliminating social disadvantage and preventing social power from turning into political privilege, attending to the universal tasks of politics already mediates society and state in conformity with justice, without any need for direct political representative of social interests.

Within the limited realm of positive legislation, enacting laws to realize the constitution in the current situation, where no policies or goals have *a priori* command other than the constitution itself, and where no groups or individuals have political privileges deriving from non-political factors, majority decision has its place. By contrast, the execution of positive laws does call for expertise corresponding to whatever tasks these laws mandate. Accordingly, executive positions can be filled, not by democratic election, but by objective examinations certifying who is most qualified for the administrative duties already set by law. In this realm, where government policies are not decided, but enforced, a professional bureaucracy, entered by passing civil service exams or the like, and obedient to whatever laws are validly passed, would be perfectly suited to handle the technical duties of executing the law. In the legislative arena itself, however, where given ends, set functions and experts have no relevance, democracy would have its proper terrain.

13.5 Constitutional Self-Government and the Division of Powers

Whereas the conditions of positive legislation allow for democratic lawmaking, the relation of legislation to constitutionality raises the issue of a division of powers, an issue that bears directly upon the legitimate limits of majority rule. This issue arises because the distinction between constitutional and positive law, on which rests all commitment to democracy or any other institution of justice, cannot be sustained solely through the non-amendability of the constitution. Unless constitutional government can be internally regulated to prevent any political agent from wielding unlimited authority, there will be no way of insuring that the constitution be respected. This can be accomplished only through a division of powers separating two political functions from legislation and investing each in a separate branch of government.

One branch of government must be exclusively empowered to authorize the laws proposed and voted upon by the legislative branch. Only when this authorizing power has certified the laws passed by the legislature to be constitutionally valid do they become the actual law of the land, commanding obedience and enforcement. Then a third branch of government must enter in with exclusive authority to execute the authorized laws.

The indispensability of this division can easily be seen by regarding what results from its absence. If, in its place, the legislature could both formulate laws and authorize them, the constitution would be deprived of all reality. By having the power to authorize their own legislation, law-makers could certify the constitutionality of any law they made no matter how much it transgressed the constitution. Constitutionality would be just as much a fiction if a separate authorizing power did exist, but the legislature could execute the authorized laws as it saw fit. Then lawmakers would be free to give their enforcement any form they choose in complete disregard of the constitutional expectations of the authorizing power. In the case of a democratic legislature, either arrangement would enable it to legally eliminate virtually every restriction of constitutional government and make the will of the majority a sovereign power within the state, above all law and unrestrained by any principle of justice. Whether it be celebrated as the sovereign will of the people or the general will that can do no wrong, this is not the working of political freedom, but the mask of tyranny.

Of course, the danger of absolute domination is no less if the authorizing or executive powers are combined with any other branch of government. If the authorizing power were to frame the laws it approves for execution, or execute what it authorizes, it too could rule without any constraints. In the former case, any law whatsoever could be implemented, whereas in the latter case, authorized laws could be executed in complete disregard for the constitution. To prevent these abuses, the authorizing power must be strictly limited to approving or rejecting laws drawn up independently by an entirely separate legislative branch, with no executive powers. This arrangement does make the authorizing power the effective head of state since only its certifying decision allows government actions to be performed in the name of the state. However, because this apex of authority is otherwise powerless, neither it nor any other agent within the state enjoys the internal sovereignty from which absolutism springs. Because the head of state is unable to determine either the content of the laws it rejects or approves, or how authorized laws are executed, it can do nothing more disruptive than stall government by refusing to authorize any proposed legislation.

Under this division of powers, government possesses the organic unity without which neither constitutionality can be maintained nor political freedom exercised. For political as well as non-political rights to be realized, no organ of government should be able to exercise its characteristic power except in conjunction with the complementary constitutional activity of the others. When the legislature cannot make its laws valid without the assent of a separate authorizing power, when the authorizing power has nothing to certify without the preceding legislation of the law-makers, and when the executive cannot govern without authorized laws to administer, no particular will can substitute itself for the universal will of the state, separating ruler and ruled and annulling self-government. With each branch dependent upon the others, the state can only act through the codetermination of all its separate powers, as it must if each citizen is to be both ruler and subject.

Most political philosophers have failed to divide the powers of government in a properly organic fashion. Generally, they either ignore the authorizing power entirely or combine it with the legislature, while supplementing the executive power with a separate judiciary branch whose administration of the law is still wholly executive in function. Hegel is one of the few thinkers to have recognized the need for an organic division of powers where legislative, authorizing and executive functions are divided, yet interdependent. Nevertheless, his theory of the branches of government is marred by two major errors. First, he fails to separate civil society from the state in the radical way necessary to maintain the unconditioned universality of politics that permits the reality of freedom to be thoroughly self-grounded. Borrowing from the institutions of his day, he injects estate relations into government, assigning direct political functions to different classes. This makes the allotment of political powers a matter of social privilege, subjecting politics to the rule of particular interests.[14] Having rooted the branches of government in the divisions of society, Hegel next conflates the proper functions of the different powers of government. Instead of fully dividing them, he disrupts their organic unity by allowing the head of state and the executive to participate in legislation, while rendering the estate assembly a largely advisory body.[15]

If democracy is to enjoy constitutionality, and have any claim to validity, it must be organized without any such deformations of the division of powers. The democracy prescribed by the American Constitution fails in this regard just as does the participatory council democracy advocated in varying forms by council communists and Arendt.

Despite all its famous concern for the balance of powers, the American constitution does not properly separate the authorizing from the legislative and executive branches of government. The power of authorizing laws is divided between the President and the Supreme Court. The president exercises it by signing or vetoing bills of Congress, whereas the Supreme Court does so by judging the constitutionality of laws at issue in cases coming before it. Neither, however, wield powers of authorization as comprehensive, final, and exclusive as those of a head of state should be. Any veto by the President can be overridden by Congress. Although the Supreme Court can later step in and strike down a vetoed law, it does not pass judgment on each and every law before it goes into effect, but only on those currently enforced laws that figure in cases appealed to it. This leaves Congress in a position to authorize its own laws and exercise virtually unlimited power so long as presidential vetoes are overridden and legal challenges have not made their way through the judicial system to the Supreme Court. Until those laws have their constitutionality tested in the highest court, anything can be done, including legal dismemberment of the appeal procedures themselves. To compound matters, the President is also the Chief Executive, conflating the presidential element of the authorizing power with the executive branch of government. Admittedly, these structural problems have not yet led to the usurpations they permit. Nevertheless, American democracy will remain haunted by the danger of legal despotism so long as constitutional change is not undertaken.

The same danger afflicts the proposals for participatory council democracy that have been made in nostalgia for the polis as refracted through the historical experiences of the Paris Commune, the 1905 and 1917 Russian revolutions, the Spanish Civil War and the

Hungarian uprising in 1956. Council democracy has its strongest advocate in Hannah Arendt. She frees its concept of Marxist and syndicalist limitations by purging the oligarchical element of class dictatorship at the hands of which worker councils have suffered in theory and practice. Instead of organizing participatory assemblies on the basis of social boundaries, such as workplace and class, and directing their energies to social concerns of economic self-management, Arendt proposes a pyramid of purely political councils, resting on democratic assemblies open to all who wish to participate, regardless of their place in society. These grass roots councils govern local affairs and elect delegates to the next level of regional assemblies which have their own more encompassing jurisdiction and name members to the succeeding assemblies until finally the whole edifice is crowned by a supreme council governing on a national plane.[16]

Although the resulting state incorporates successive demarcations of authority, these consist in varying degrees of local, regional, and national authority vertically differentiated according to the principle of federalism. What is not provided is a horizontal separation of powers limiting political prerogative at each level of rule, while permitting their respective jurisdictions to be enforced without relying upon a power whose own authority has no limit. With all political functions distributed through a federation of participatory assemblies, the legislative, authorizing, and executive powers of government are conflated at every stage. Since each assembly has exclusive jurisdiction at its own level, there are no institutional means available to prevent assemblies from doing whatever they please in their own domains. The only intervention possible is for the immediately lower assembly to elect new members to the council above it. That, however, does not change what actions have or can be taken, either within the locale of the council or in conflict with assemblies of other regions. Although the different jurisdictions of each successive assembly are presumably defined prior to their respective engagements in governing, the absence of any additional organs of government leaves nowhere to appeal when assemblies violate their own mandate and transgress other levels of political council or non-political relations of justice. Such a council system may grant every citizen the opportunity to govern in person at a local level, provided neither local nor regional assemblies have chosen to abrogate that right. What it can never extend to any citizen are the safeguards of constitutional rule that a proper division of powers makes possible.

13.6 Democracy for its own Sake

If the requirements of constitutionality, positive legislation and the division of powers set ground rules to which democracy must conform to have legitimacy, they do not alone justify democracy as the exclusively valid form of government. Constitutionality and separation of powers may be necessary features of political justice, but they can certainly exist without democracy. By the same token, just government may require positive legislation, whose reliance upon subjective discretion makes room for democracy, but that does not mean that legislative discretion need be exercised democratically. As far as these political factors are concerned, how positive laws are made is a matter of indifference so long as there is a division of powers in accord with constitutionality. Nor does the enforcement of non-political rights require democratic government; witness Jefferson's and Rousseau's failures to justify democracy as the privileged instrument of liberty.

If democracy is to warrant exclusive advocacy as the just regime, it must not only accord with constitutionality, separation of powers, and the non-political relations of justice, which all should be constitutionally guaranteed, but also be the unique form of constitutional government that has unconditioned validity. This can only be if democratic rule is an end in itself. In that case, democracy would be indispensible, for what justifies it would be its own existence and not the achievement of some independent goal that might be fulfilled by other means. The legitimation of democracy therefore ultimately rests upon a demonstration that none of its traditional defenders have undertaken. This is the demonstration that democracy, fit for positive legislation, but qualified by constitutionality, separation of powers and respect for the non-political relations of justice, is nonetheless for its own sake.

It is a long line of argument that leads to the threshold at which the justice of democracy can be established. Every last vestige of any antinomy of willing and reason must be uprooted to clear the way. This has already been achieved by showing how normative validity consists in self-determination, and how justice consists in the reality of freedom. The last step in the demonstration is now virtually complete. Because political justice must consist in the institutions of political freedom, through whose autonomous rule all other institutions of right are united into a self-grounded, self-determining whole, the exercise of political self-determination is an end in itself. Accordingly, the just state requires a body politic where citizens codetermine an order of self-government that is the very framework by which they exercise their agency as free citizens. All relations of justice, however, depend on the political realization of constitutionality. This can be an activity of political self-determination only when all citizens participate in codetermining the legislation, authorization and execution of the law that governs themselves. Accordingly, democracy must enter in for no other sake than permitting the very exercise of political freedom of which it forms a constitutive element.

Admittedly, because constitutionality entails separating the legislative, authorizing, and executive functions, political democracy cannot consist in direct participation by every citizen in all three branches of government. That would conflate all powers into one and place the will of the majority above all law and justice. Instead, the legislature, head of state, and perhaps some element of the executive should be democratically determined such that legislative, authorizing, and executive wills are institutionally distinct from one another, yet still codetermined by the will of every citizen. In this form, democratic government is an end in itself, for it comprises the vehicle of political self-determination that is the ultimate *raison d'etre* of the just state.

Admittedly, these bare outlines of political justice leave much of the actual structure of self-government yet to be determined. Whether the legislative power should involve participatory and/or representative assemblies, single or multiple chambers, proportional or majority representation, or any federal arrangement; whether the head of state should be an individual or a collective leadership, directly or indirectly elected; and which, if any, executive officials should be elected, are all questions given no immediate answer by the identity of justice and freedom, and the need for constitutionality and division of powers. Nevertheless, if these matters of government can be rationally decided, it will only be by thinking through the reality of political self-determination, which gives democracy legitimacy while freeing justice from foundations.

Chapter 14

The Historical Genesis of Justice

Although the concept of justice can be derived no more from history than from any other foundation, the theory of justice is not complete without a consideration of how the institutions of justice can come to be in history. This topic can only arise as the conclusion of the theory of justice, for only after the theory has established what all the institutions of freedom are can their genesis be systematically discussed. The philosophy of right can then treat the historical coming to be of justice to the extent that it signifies not a factual matter, but the purely normative topic of what must occur for the reality of freedom to emerge. What course history has actually taken and whether or not the institutions of freedom have factually arisen or passed away has no bearing whatsoever on the question of what must occur for justice to come into being. If events have given birth to institutions of freedom, the prescriptive theory of the genesis of justice may have descriptive applicability to the course of historical development. However, no description of what is or has been, nor any prophecy of what will be can prescribe the institutional developments necessary for the reality of freedom to arise.

Consequently, the possibility of a prescriptive rational theory of the genesis of justice in no way depends upon the possibility of a descriptive philosophy of factual history. It it did, conceiving the genesis of justice would be a very doubtful enterprise.

14.1 The Grounds for Rejecting any Philosophy of Factual History

Contrary to all philosophers of progress or decline, any *a priori* theory of factual history is precluded by both the character of historical reality and the way it which it can be known.

History can only arise from the course of nature by being made by individuals endowed with choosing wills allowing for novel developments undetermined by the cycles of natural necessity. Thus, the aggregate result of what the individual makers of history do over time involves an arbitrariness as devoid of universal order as it is opaque to conceptual comprehension. Because history issues from the combined actions of individuals who enact and tear down institutions according to how they choose to act towards one another, historical process involves entirely conventional activities pursued by individuals in their plurality. For this reason, factual history is not defined by any natural functions, whose unwilled alterations, such as aging and evolution, may have a universal order, but not historical character.

Because of the wholly conventional character of historical development, no individual action in history can be preordained or baptized with necessity after the fact. Further, no historical "meaning" can be deduced from any action, since whatever historical significance it acquires will depend not upon itself, but upon how all other individuals decide to act in conjunction with it. Since their concomitant actions proceed on the same terms, as contributing elements to a process whose course cannot be unilaterally determined, historical reality presents an all-inclusive continuum governed by an endemically all-sided arbitrariness.

This leaves action seeking historical change in an insoluble ethical predicament. Because each individual can precipitate historical change by taking action influencing what others do, no one can escape an ethical responsibility for history. Nevertheless, since the historical effect of each deed is ultimately determined by the actions others independently take, the assignment of responsibility always remains problematic. If this leaves the makers of history at once guilty and innocent no matter what their intentions may be, it also reflects how any pattern to the course of events is simply a matter of circumstance that can only be perceived after the fact. It makes no difference what conditions prevail. The very conventionality of historical action bars any guarantee that individuals will not overthrow the existing order, enact novel institutions, reestablish previous formations, or perpetuate the status quo.

Indeed, not only is every historical pattern subject to chance, but so is the very continuation of history. Since history can only be made by a plurality of willing individuals and the natural preconditions of their agency can be eliminated, either through their own chosen actions or by natural events, the continuity of history is itself contingent. That the sun will burn out, that galaxies may collide, and that we have brought ourselves to the brink of nuclear and ecological holocaust all testify how history not only has no necessary past, but no necessary future.

If the arbitrariness infesting historical reality disallows any certain conformity between the course of history and *a priori* schemes of historical development, how factual history is given to our knowing precludes any philosophical knowledge of it as well. Since the facts of history appear only through observable ruins, received documents, and the testimony of the dead and the living, acquiring knowledge of what has happened raises all the difficulties besetting interpretation, where the knower has no criteria for judging the true story of events except what his own discretion warrants. Just as in a court of law, where the facts of the case can only be known beyond a reasonable doubt, so in the court of history, there is nothing for historical knowledge to rest upon than faith in the honesty and accuracy of available testimony, faith in the prudence of interpretations of given records, and faith in the representative character of the chosen data that historical understanding addresses. Because recorded history is first rendered an object of investigation through these acts of subjective judgment, theories of historical fact cannot provide universal truths, but only prudent opinions resting on subjective assumptions that determine what is putatively given.

These considerations rule out any philosophy of historical fact that purports to conceive the course of events by reason alone. It would be a mistake, however, to reject all philosophy of history in their name. Even if a descriptive philosophy of history is suspect, this does not preclude a prescriptive philosophy of history that conceives not what has or will occur, but what should occur for justice to come into existence. Precisely because the historical existence of institutions only testifies to their being and not to their legitimacy, knowledge of historical fact is not needed to conceive either what justice is, nor what must happen for it to arise.

14.2 Freedom and the Genesis of Justice

If the conventionality of history and the limits of historical knowledge pose no ultimate barriers to conceiving the genesis of justice, what makes that endeavor an appropriate conclusion to the philosophy of right is the identity of freedom and justice. Because freedom is itself a structure of right, consisting in a self-determined system of interactions, no natural law or propensity of the self can bring its justice into being. Instead of arising by nature or in virtue of the self, freedom can only emerge when individuals choose to inter-relate in the different modes of right. As a consequence, the realm of justice does not exist in any state of nature, but only in history as a product of convention. Although this does not make historical occur-rence a criterion of justice, it does mean that history can alone realize what ought to be. Therefore, history cannot be ignored by the theory of justice. If its own conceptions of right are not to be utopian ideals incapable of coming into being, it must certify how the institutions of freedom can emerge in history.

This certification has nothing to do with the hopeless task of con-ceiving *a priori* what has happened or will happen in history. Rather than entailing a descriptive philosophy of history, it involves conceiv-ing what historical change must occur for justice to arise. Since justice is the reality of freedom, what lies at issue is conceiving how the institutions of freedom can emerge within history. For this reason, the prescriptive theory of history that concludes the theory of justice addresses nothing but the history of freedom.[1]

It must not be forgotten that conceiving this history is a strictly normative enterprise entirely independent of past and future events. Furthermore, the genesis of justice is not something limited to the par-ticular destiny of homo sapiens, but a universal development of what ought to be that bears upon any setting where there are individuals with wills. Just as rights cannot be tied to the natural particularities of species being without violating their universal non-natural character, so the history of freedom cannot be restricted to humanity without confusing what is naturally given with what is self-deter-mined. The genesis of justice does not concern how men have erected or can erect the institutions of freedom, but how any thinking and willing individuals can do so.

Although these warnings serve to focus the universal character of the history in question as it is determined by the philosophical inves-tigation of justice, what remains unclear is whether anything else can be conceived about this history. If the conventional character of history leaves the course of events willfully contingent and neither nature nor historical fact can guide the genesis of justice, how can the historical emergence of freedom have any necessary and universal form susceptible to philosophical treatment? A prescriptive philosophy of history seems just as questionable as a descriptive philosophy of historical fact.

Two factors weigh against such scepticism. First, no past, present, or future events can independently dictate what must occur for justice to arise. Their contingent givenness prevents them from playing any role as necessary preconditions of subsequent consequences, whereas the foundation-free character of justice precludes any role for them as antecedent grounds for the validity of institutions. Establishing how freedom can emerge in history therefore involves no immersion in historical facticity, which lies outside conceptual determination and the scope of philosophical inquiry.

Second, both the starting point and end point of the genesis of justice are conceptually available, granted the efforts of a systematic philosophy of nature and mind, as well as those of the theory of justice. Since the material out of which history develops is nothing more than the plurality of individuals inhabiting a common world, the conceptions of nature and individual selves provide the philosophically transparent starting point from which the coming into being of freedom must be conceived. As for the end point of the history of freedom, it is already given by the conception of justice itself. The structures of freedom conceived within the philosophy of right are precisely the terminus whose development from the given reality of nature and individuals comprises the entire genesis of justice. The task of the prescriptive philosophy of history therefore consists in conceiving how these relations of right can arise from those preconditions of history. Naturally, this question can only be addressed at the end of the theory of justice after all the institutions of freedom have been worked out.

Far from lacking a rationally determinable beginning and end, the history of freedom does not even arise as a problem until its commencement and conclusion are already conceptually established in the systematic determinations of nature and self on the one hand, and of right on the other. Once, however, the theory of justice provides the final destination of freedom's genesis, what remains to be determined is how convention can produce its structures of right from the given reality of nature and selves.

Admittedly, little direction is offered by the conceptual starting point of the history of freedom. By itself, the reality of nature and the plurality of selves provides nothing to guide the genesis of justice other than the ever present possibility that individuals will happen to choose to interact in harmony with all the relations of right, albeit in a natural setting where geographical, temporal and other natural differences will add their own particular cast to that conformity. If the only resource for determining the genesis of justice lay in these preconditions of historical development, then the prescriptive philosophy of history would be reduced to repeating the truism that freedom can arise whenever individuals choose to act in accord with justice.

However, there is another term available to provide the realization of right with more definite a genesis. This is the structure of its end point, the reality of justice. If the composition of the institutions of freedom mandate how they themselves can come into being, then the prescriptive philosophy of history is not condemned to virtual silence.

14.3 The Political Character of the Genesis of Justice

What can alone concretize the history of freedom is the concrete character of justice. Because the reality of right consists in a self-determined system of different structures of interaction, the genesis of freedom comprises the very determinate process of generating all these institutions in their unity as a self-grounded whole.

Due to the systematic character of justice, this genesis cannot be understood by focusing on each institution in isolation from the others. Because the different structures of freedom incorporate and act upon one another, their relationship is of central importance in determining how they may arise. As we have seen, the institutions of justice stand in a dual relationship, common to the elements of any self-determined whole.

In one respect, the different structures of right join in an order of increasing complexity where the less determinate relations form the structural prerequisites incorporated by the more determinate ones. This ordering, which proceeds from property relations to morality, the family, society, and the state, is followed by the conceptual development of justice because none of its institutions can be systematically conceived if their presupposed components have not been accounted for already.

Property relations come first in this succession insofar as they comprise the most elementary structure of right, incorporating no others, but presupposed by all the rest. The self-determination of ownership involves nothing more than a plurality of choosing individuals who lay their wills in different entities that they reciprocally recognize as their respectively entitled domains. Moral, family, social, and political relations may add their own dimensions to affairs of property, but they do not themselves constitute property relations. They cannot possibly do so because their own structures of right rest upon the existence of property. As we have seen, if individuals do not already have ownership of at least their own bodies, without which they are no better then slaves, there is no way they can recognizably express their free wills to others and exercise any further rights.

Whereas this leaves morality subsequent to ownership, to the extent that one cannot be held responsible for one's actions if they do not belong to one, moral relations come second since acting on conscience not only depends on no further institutions, but requires disregarding what family, social, or political relations may ordain, unless personal duty sanctions their command.

Family relations come next because their adult participants are already morally accountable property owners, who do not, however, interact within the family through social or political institutions. Civil law may regulate marriage, divorce, and the responsibilities of parents to children, extending legal protection to household right, but this enforcement does not comprise the reality of domestic freedom.

Civil society follows upon the family because its social domain incorporates households into the economic, legal, and public welfare activities of social justice. Civil society precedes the state, however, because neither the market, economic interest groups, civil courts, or welfare agencies engage in the self-government of politics, whose constitutive sovereignty requires that it come last as the institution of justice presupposing all others by virtue of ruling over them.

Although this sequence of successive incorporation is a conceptual succession, expressing how the coexistent elements of justice are prerequisites of one another, it has direct bearing upon the history of freedom. This is because its line of presupposition reveals how each structure of right can exist independently of those that incorporate it, but only if those that it encompasses exist as well. Because property relations incorporate no other institutions of justice, they can arise in history without accompaniment of moral accountability, households organized in terms of domestic freedom, a civil society, or a self-governing republic. By contrast, a more concrete institution like civil society cannot come into existence until its component structures have emerged as well, allowing individuals to exercise their rights as owners, moral subjects, and family members.

These structural connections between institutions of justice and their components allow for a differentiation of possible stages in the genesis of freedom. Following the parallel orders of conceptual constitution and internal presupposition, this sequence consists in distinct periods, however local or widespread, where the spheres of justice that have so far been enacted are: (1) property relations alone; (2) property and morality; (3) property, morality, and the free family; (4) property, morality, the free family, and civil society, and finally; (5) the free state that brings to realization all the other relations of right as components of its just reign. This sequence does not present the only institutions that might prevail during a certain period. In those periods where certain relations of justice are lacking, there may well be alternative institutions coexisting with what structures of right are at hand. Since these could not be interactions of self-determination without canceling the distinctions between periods, they would have to be determined by factors other than freedom. Accordingly, they could conceivably take any of the countless forms that illegitimate convention could assume.

In this fashion, the conception of justice provides an *a priori* morphology of the possible way stations in the historical emergence of freedom. However, due to the supreme role that politics plays within the reality of freedom, the concept of justice further entails that the genesis of right is preeminently a political history. Because what alone brings into being the totality of freedom is the just state, the genesis of justice has nothing to do with the Marxist vision of a socially determined history terminating in a just society. Instead, the history of freedom has a political order as its goal and political develoment as an overriding feature.

As the theory of justice has shown, the self-governing state brings all justice into being not only because it incorporates every other structure of right within its dominion, but because its autonomous rule makes their realization a product not of historical accident, but of an activity of freedom falling within justice itself. By enforcing the property, moral, household, and civil rights of its citizens in conformity with their political autonomy, the free state enables justice to ground itself by providing a political order whose freedom posits all the other structures of freedom in reproducing its own. Although it arises in history, once it comes into being, the free state breaks its dependence upon antecedent conditions by securing both the existence and authority of its own constitutive institutions as part and parcel of its own constitutional actuality.

Due to this totalizing character of the just state, the genesis of justice involves more than the sequence by which the different institutions of freedom can arise in their increasing complexity. Because the history of freedom has a free political order as its ultimate result, it must also encompass the possible stages of political development allowing all the necessary structures of self-government to emerge. Accordingly, the genesis of justice entails a differentiation of possible historical periods in terms of an *a priori* political morphology of possible forms of government distinguished according to how fully they realize the political institutions of freedom.

The resulting typology of political regimes has a very different status from that usually afforded forms of government in the metaphysics of justice or liberal theory. In general, these traditional theories tend to treat forms of government as a proper theme of political justice rather than as a matter of history. This is particularly true of the liberal theorists, who, with the inconsistent exception of Rousseau, give equal sanction to monarchy, oligarchy, and democracy insofar as the non-political ends of natural right can be achieved by any of these regimes. Aristotle gives the different forms less blanket approval, but still grants them affirmative value when distinguishing the types of legitimate regimes. Only Plato approaches a proper handling of the matter by accounting for the different forms of government in terms of the history that results from the dissolution of the ideal polis.[2] In so doing, he duly recognizes that because the just state must be unconditionally universal, it can comprise but one invariable form of government. This signifies that the normative theory of politics addresses the just state per se and not the different forms of government. The separate powers of self-government might exhibit monarchical, oligarchical and democratic features, as Hegel suggests,[3] but as a whole, the just state has only one form, that of the regime of political freedom. By contrast, the normative genesis of justice does require treating forms of government, recasting the classic differentiation of tyranny, oligarchy, democracy, and monarchy into an array of possible stages in the development of political freedom.[4]

Although such forms of government can be ordered with respect to their varying realization of the institutions of political freedom, this does not mandate that they must come to be in a fixed sequence,[5] nor that the just state requires any of them as a direct historical precondition of its emergence. All these forms provide are the range of political orders that may precede the rise or succeed the fall of the just state. Giving their catalogue still leaves undetermined the political act by which the just state can be founded. Since it is this act of foundation that brings the genesis of justice to a close, the history of freedom remains stalled until it is comprehended.

What does illuminate the foundation of the just state is the totalizing character of its politics. It involves a second ordering of the institutions of justice that proceeds conversely to the first order, whose sequence of increasing complexity led from property relations to self-government. Whereas that ordering arrived at the state as a result of the pre-political institutions that comprise its prerequisite components, this second ordering relates the different institutions of justice in terms of the actuality of the state. The move from one sequence to the other is not the result of a change of perspective, but rather a reflection of what occurs when the just state comes into being. At that moment, the emergent state does not stand merely as the result of the less concrete structures of freedom, which can arise before it and which its own rule presupposes. In virtue of its own sovereign activity, the resultant state exists as their one and only ground, giving them all a secured realization that none can supply for themselves.

We have already seen how property relations, morality, and the household all lack the resources to adjudicate disputes, prevent violations of right, punish wrongdoers, and retribute victims. Without the aid of a higher public authority, property owners cannot resolve cases of non-malicious wrong, fraud, and crime anymore than family members can enforce household rights and duties. For its part, morality can never be objectively realized, for all conscience has to determine the good is its own subjective discretion.

Left to its own devices, the just society is caught in similar straits. Although its civil law and welfare administraiton do secure the property, household, and economic rights of individuals, the just society lacks both the legislative power to make the laws enforced within it and the source of constitutionality that can give its public institutions proper authority.

As has been shown, only a self-governing state can supply these lacking features through freedom, instead of letting them be provided by some resource lying outside justice. In furnishing this service, the self-govering state frees itself from the presuppositions of the non-political institutions of justice by positing them as elements whose regulated form and guaranteed existence emanate from its own sovereign rule. At the same time, the just state secures its own positive independence by governing constitutionally. In so doing, the state achieves normative self-sufficiency, setting the measure of its own politics within it in its constitution. By this continuous deed, the just state grounds not only all other institutions of justice, but its self-government as well. Through this dual achievement, logically foreshadowed in the totality of categories concluding the theory of determinacy, the constitutional state brings freedom to a self-grounded whole, as justice requires.

Although this foundation-free character of the valid body politic establishes that nothing in the genesis of justice can be a basis of legitimacy, it adds a final specification to the history of freedom that bears directly upon the foundation of the just state. Because the genesis of justice ultimately involves founding the free state and because the free state is constitutional, the history of freedom must conclude with the enactment of the just constitution.

14.4 The Foundation of the Just State and the Riddle of Constitution-Making

The supreme importance of constitution-making in the genesis of justice directly reflects its total unimportance in legitimating the institutions of right. Since the coming to be of the just state is something different from its actuality, conceiving its genesis is, as Aristotle pointed out in Book I of the *Politics*, quite a separate task from determining the state's legitimate reality. The dilemmas of foundationalism and the validity of self-determination serve to underline just how total is the separation between the founding and the legitimate actuality of the just state.

As we have seen, the state cannot derive its legitimacy from factors independent of right without making justice relative to what is unjust. Nor can the state have legitimacy by solely serving non-political institutions of justice. Although their ends may be valid, their lack of self-sufficiency leaves their own justice dependent upon injustice unless the institution securing their existence is itself just. The state can have this character, however, only if it is itself an institution of freedom, grounding itself while uniting the other structures of right into an independent whole. The body politic achieves this normative self-sufficiency when it exists for its own sake as the self-determined totality of freedom that has its own standard of legitimation within itself in its own constitution.

What makes the state just therefore cannot be how it came into being, but the structure it actually has. Because that actuality must be an end in itself to enjoy the foundation-free character of justice, any attempt to base the state's legitimacy in the process of its creation auto-matically destroys its normative validity by grounding the political order in something other than the state's own constitutional politics. For this reason, no procedural theories of justice, be they social con-tract conceptions or not, are capable of determining the just state.

The radical demarcation of the state's legitimacy from its genesis signifies that the founding of the state is not itself a relation of right, but a matter of history, subject to all the contingencies of convention. Although founding constitutional conventions may facilitate general acceptance of a new regime, they do not enjoy any independent legitimacy of their own, nor can there be any guarantee that they pro-vide the privileged means for achieving the minimal respect required for a political order to have reality.

Furthermore, as we have seen, constitution-making has no place within the domain of political freedom. Whereas self-government is an activity for its own sake, proceeding through institutions that must already exist for political freedom to be exercised, the founding of the just state is an instrumental activity, producing a new order within which justice can first be realized. To maintain that order of right, citizens must have the power not to alter the constitution, but to realize it in face of changing circumstances through legislation, authorization and execution of positive laws. Consequently, although the foundation of the just state brings the history of freedom to its perennial end, the just state has a history of its own consisting not in the enactment or alteration of its constitution, but in the positive legislation and governing that proceed on its basis. By contrast, the power legislating constitutions necessarily falls outside the just state into the prior history of freedom that introduces the history of the just state's own rule.[6]

Although the very concept of constitutional government entails this conclusion, the relegation of constitution-making to history appears to cast in doubt the constitutive autonomy of the just state, and with it, the history of freedom by which it arises. That political freedom does not include the right to determine the constitution seems to contradict the self-determined character the state must have to be just. If political action cannot determine the constitution of the state, but must receive it from history, then the political order appears to be preordained by the prior historical enactment of the constitution and anything but self-ordering. How then can the state remain legitimate if, instead of being self-determined, its own form is given independently of political freedom? Does this not condemn the whole enterprise of justice to the dilemmas of foundationalism?

Here, at its final moment, on the very verge of accounting for the realization of right, the entire quest for justice seems to collapse in an insurmountable antimony. If justice is to come into existence and the philosophy of right is to be more than speculative fiction, then the history of freedom must run its course and culminate in the enactment of the just constitution. Yet if constitutional self-government can only issue from a preceding constitution-making, it seemingly can never have the self-determined character needed for normative validity. Paradoxically, the only way the just state can be founded seems to make it impossible for the state to be just.

The solution to this dilemma is already contained in the concept of political freedom. It removes the antimony of constitution-making and political autonomy by rendering each not just compatible but indispensable for one another. What it reveals is that the state can be both self-determined and the product of a historical constitution-making provided it comprises a constitutional self-governing regime whose citizens freely will the realization of the same institutions through which they exercise their rights of political self-determination. Although the political participation of every citizen is constitutionally restricted to enacting, authorizing and executing positive laws, it still realizes the constitution as a political order existing for no other sake than its own self-government. Thus, it is precisely by coinciding with and conforming to a constitution it can never bring into being, but must always already possess, that political freedom gets realized as an end in itself, as the continual product of its very own activity.

Because of this unity between antecedently-given constitutionality and political freedom, the historically-enacted just constitution is but a meaningless piece of paper unless citizens actually practice constitutional self-government. Only then does politics become a self-activity of political freedom, just as only then does the enacted constitution underlying political freedom become what it is meant to be. Far from excluding one another, the foundation of the just state and the normative actuality of politics are inseparable correlates. The just constitution has not really come into being as a product of enactment unless it stands actualized in a political order of freedom, whereas the state canot have the constitutionality it needs to be autonomously self-grounded, unless history has provided it with its constitution. In virtue of their respective characters, it is simply impossible for the just constitution to be enacted without the actuality of political freedom, and vice versa. Consequently, the just state is not at odds with the conditions of its foundation. On the contrary, the just state cannot help but be both self-determined and dependent upon history for the enactment of its constitution.

14.5 Formal versus Real Constitution-Making

If this solution to the ostensible antimony of constitution-making redeems the history of freedom, it also introduces a feature of constitutionality that is, at least at first glance, full of paradox. Because the just constitution enters into being only insofar as citizens actually interact in terms of the political and non-political relations of right, it would appear that the just constitution cannot be made through a purely political act, let alone through any act at all.[7] Yet to deny that the just constitution can be made seems to be a contradiction in terms, since, by definition, a constitution is not a natural given, but a product of convention that must be enacted to come into being.

Nevertheless, thinking of the constitution as the product of a making becomes difficult once it is realized how it cannot come into existence simply in virtue of the willing of a single agency. Although it cannot be denied that a Napoleon or a Stalin may unilaterally impose their constitutions for republics and people's democracies, there are decisive reasons why no such imposition can make a constitution the internal standard of a just state on the sole force of its command.

First, a constitution cannot have any reality as the internal measure of the just state if the non-political structures of right are not in place themselves. Without valid property relations, moral accountability, free households, and civil society all at hand, the constitution may exist on paper, but the constitutional enforcement of non-political freedoms is as lacking as the preconditions of political freedom. These structures of freedom cannot be brought into being in the self-same act of constitution-making because the process of their formation is something quite separate from ordaining a constitution. Constitutional government may require an enacted constitution for its own existence, but each non-political institution can very well arise independently of the emergence of political institutions of freedom. Conversely, political activity cannot create non-political relations of justice for the simple reason that they consist in self-determinations that do not concern self-government. Laws can be made, authorized, and executed, but it is another matter having citizens exercise sufficient rectitude to establish non-political institutions.

This problem of enforcement applies equally to the political domain. No unilaterally willed constitution can have a just reality if the prospective citizens refuse to engage in constitutional self-government and instead regard the constitution as a piece of paper signifying either the decree of illegitimate domination or the unobserved fiction of a powerless regime. Because every right is a structure of interaction, only the multilateral actions of citizens can give life to the institutions of justice and guarantee that the just constitution is actually the internal measure of a self-ordered state.

For these reasons, it can well be said that the founding of a just constitution is not the result of any unilateral deed, but the product of the development of the entire life of the people it orders, involving the eventual multilateral enactment of every sphere of justice. What must be remembered is that the subject of this development is not an ethnically-defined people, as Hegel tends to suggest,[8] but a citizenry, whose unity rests not on nature or tradition, but on political relations of freedom. The genesis of justice cannot be subordinated to ethnic givens when the institutions of right it engenders must define themselves through freedom.

Although the emergence of the just state encompasses this full breadth of institutional development, at some point a constitution will have to be made to bring the emerging whole to its finished, self-legitimating form. Nevertheless, this act will found the just state only in conjunction with the recognizant political participation of the citizenry and their establishment of free property, moral, household, and civil relations among themselves. Then the enactment of the constitution will usher in the final hour of the history of freedom, for it will have followed upon the liberation of all spheres of right from the hold of privileged givens and authorized their reconstitution as spheres of self-determination.

By combining these two sides of liberation and constitution, which together provide freedom from foundations and self-grounding legitimacy, the founding of the state comprises the genuine revolution. This is not the upheaval that rises out of social necessity to impose a new class rule in preparation for the withering away of the state. It is instead the revolution that strips away all conditioned institutions and then constitutes the positive reality of freedom in its political totality. The prescriptive history of freedom has this as its end, for the genesis of justice aims at nothing else.

14.6 Factual History and the Genesis of Justice

The *a priori* history of freedom with which the theory of justice concludes is a normative conception bearing no direct relation to the course of human events. Nevertheless, it can serve as a framework for interpreting and evaluating, as well as altering that course. By consisting in the reality of justice, the destination of the history of freedom provides the only valid standard for judging to what degree human history has given rise to the institutions of right. Similarly, its theory of the genesis of justice offers the only conceptual aid for answering the abiding question of what still must be done to bring these institutions to a universal and complete realization.

Because of the arbitrariness of convention, there is no necessity that the history of mankind will ever bring justice into being. Yet, if modernity happens to have realized central features of property relations, morality, the free family, civil society, and constitutional self-government, then the *a priori* concepts of the history of freedom can have a descriptive power in the interpretation of past events. By the same token, if modernity happens to have fostered developments violating the relations of right, then the concepts of justice can serve as standards to critique the wrongs of modern times, while the conception of the genesis of justice can suggest what historical change must occur for these wrongs to be remedied.[9] Either way, any conclusions that are drawn result not from an employment of systematic philosophy, but only from an exercise of interpretaion, bound to all the limits of any hermeneutic study. Whether simply describing the course of events or evaluating their contribution to justice, one is faced with the task of applying rational categories to a perceived reality. As in making positive law to realize the constitution in the given situation, one must rely on subjective judgment to apply universal concepts to particular events. Since this limits all conclusions to educated opinion, the resulting discussion does not properly fall within the philosophy of right and its systematic theory of how justice can come into being. Instead of entering into conflict with philosophical conception, it rather stands outside philosophy entirely, as an interpretative application of philosophical concepts to facts that must be experienced and recorded to be known.

For just this reason, one can argue endlessly over interpretations and evaluations of the past and present without ever reaching certain truth. Where subjective discretion must be employed to reach conclusions, the unconditioned validity of philosophical thought can never be attained. Yet, the interpretation of events should not be ignored in total deference to systematic argument. So far as we are rational agents, it is our duty to orient ourselves to the facts of modern times and judge to what extent our history has been a history of freedom and to what extent justice remains to be done. As thinkers, it is our task to conceive the institutions of right with the autonomy of reason that allows philosophical discourse to ground itself. As citizens, it is our responsibility to erect and safeguard a self-grounded state of freedom in which the autonomy of action is fully realized. Although the rational will is the free will, only the contributions of reason can aspire to any finality. Because the reality of justice can always be overturned if enough individuals endeavor to do so, the history of freedom is always open in practice. Its course may be theoretically conceivable once and for all, but its practical completion is an ever present political toil.

Like philosophy's strivings to bring truth to light, the genesis of justice falls within time. Nevertheless, the temporality of its appearance no more taints its validity than do the historical expressions of the concepts of philosophical thought. No matter where we stand in the order of events, we have the opportunity to redeem the transience of our theory and practice by thinking without foundations and by enacting the timeless conventions of justice. Only then will we have freed reason of history and made history in which there is reason.

Notes

Introduction

1. Plato makes this point in the *Meno*, where he takes account of the difference between knowing and willing that he tends to ignore when he develops his notion of the philosopher-king in the *Republic*.

2. For a further discussion of their positions, see Richard Dien Winfield, "The Reason For Democracy," *History of Political Thought*, Vol. VI, No. 1.

3. Hannah Arendt, *The Human Condition*, (Chicago: University of Chicago Press, 1958).

4. Leo Strauss, *Natural Right and History*, (Chicago: University of Chicago Press, 1953).

5. Alasdair MacIntyre, *After Virtue*, (South Bend, Ind.: University of Notre Dame Press, 1981).

6. Robert Nozick, *Anarchy, State, and Utopia*, (New York: Basic Books, 1974).

7. John Rawls, *A Theory of Justice*, (Cambridge: Harvard University Press, 1971).

8. Karl-Otto Apel, "Das A priori der Kommunikationsgemeinschaft und die Grundlagen der Ethik," in *Transformation der Philosophie*, (Frankfurt am Main: Suhrkamp, 1973).

9. See, for example, Habermas' essay, "Moral und Sittlichkeit," in *Merkur*, Heft 12, December 1985, pp. 1041–1052.

10. MacIntyre, op. cit., pp. 183 ff.

11. Habermas, op. cit., p. 1041.

12. Ibid., p. 1052.

13. See Hans-Georg Gadamer, *Truth and Method*, (New York: Seabury Press, 1975), and Alasdair MacIntyre, op. cit.

14. See Gadamer, op. cit., and Richard Rorty, *Philosophy and The Mirror of Nature*, (Princeton: Princeton University Press, 1979).

15. See Leo Strauss, op. cit.

Chapter 1 Given Determinacy and Justification

1. See Willard Van Orman Quine, "Two Dogmas of Empiricism," in *From a Logical Point of View*, (New York: Harper and Row, 1973).

2. See T. S. Kuhn, *Structure of Scientific Revolutions*, (Chicago: University of Chicago Press, 1970).

3. Aristotle, *Metaphysics*, 982b.

4. Leo Strauss develops this point in *Natural Right and History*, (Chicago: University of Chicago Press, 1953) without recognizing the insoluble dilemmas that arise, nor the alternative that self-determination provides.

5. Immanuel Kant, *Werke VI*, (Wiesbaden: Insel Verlag, 1958), p. 511.

6. See A. J. Ayer, *Logic, Truth and Language*, (Middlesex, England: Penguin Books, 1982).

7. See Quine, "Two Dogmas of Empiricism."

8. Plato, *The Republic*, Book VII, 533c–d.

9. Aristotle, *Nichomachean Ethics*, Book I, Chapter ii.

10. I am indebted to Robert Berman for pointing this out.

11. Bertrand Russell, *A Critical Exposition of the Philosophy of Leibniz*, (London: George Allen & Unwin, 1971), p. 22.

12. Aristotle, *Metaphysics*, Book Gamma, Chapter 7.

13. Ibid., Book Gamma, Chapter 4.

Chapter 2 The Metaphysics of Justice

1. M. B. Foster emphasizes this point in his neglected work, *The Political Philosophies of Plato and Hegel*, (Oxford: Oxford University Press, 1968).

2. Aristotle, *Politics*, 1252b30.

3. Ibid., 1275a33.

4. Because Aristotle supports aristocracy as the best constitution, he later admits that the absolutely good man is not merely the citizen of the best state, but rather its ruler. See Ibid., 1278b3.

5. Ibid., 1279a–1279b.

6. Ibid., 1282b3, 1287a32, 1292a33.

7. Ibid., 1269a14, *Nicomachean Ethics*, 1134b18–1135a.

8. Aristotle, *Nicomachean Ethics*, 1137a31–1138a.

9. Aristotle, *Politics*, 1259b5, 1287a15–25.

10. Ibid., 1301b30.

11. Ibid., 1259b5.

12. Ibid., 1294a5.

13. Ibid., 1281b.

14. Ibid., 1295b.

15. Ibid., 1328b–1330b.

16. Ibid., 1297b–1298a.

17. Ibid., Book V.

18. Ibid., 1284a.

19. Ibid.

20. Ibid., 1277a.

Chapter 3   The Futile Temptation of Transcendental Argument

1. Immanuel Kant, *The Critique of Pure Reason*, translated by Norman Kemp Smith (New York: St. Martin's Press, 1965), Axxi, A14/B28.

2. The varieties of transcendental philosophy that have dominated twentieth century thought have shown through their own example that these assumptions apply not merely to the Kantian formulation of noumenal subjectivity but equally to any transcendental condition, no matter what content it may have. In this regard, the problems of Husserl's egological transcendental theory are no different from those of the ordinary language theory of the late Wittgenstein, the hermeneutic transcendentalism of Gadamer, or the ideal language theory of the early Wittgenstein, Habermas and Apel, and French structuralism.

3. In the Introduction to the *Phenomenology of Spirit*, Hegel makes these arguments, without taking up the other alternative notion of knowing as a structure of referring whose act generates its own referent.

4. Although Fichte, the young Schelling and Husserl all sought to eliminate the last vestiges of metaphysics by conceiving the transcendental structure as self-constituting, none of them realized that once the constituting act of the ego becomes its own constituted object, the intentionality of the ego collapses.

5. Hegel has described this very donouement in his discussion of Absolute Knowing in the *Phenomenology of Spirit*.

Chapter 4 *The Justice of Liberty*

1. Michael B. Foster has discussed this in detail in reference to Plato's *Republic* in *The Political Philosophies of Plato and Hegel*.

2. See Richard Dien Winfield, "The Injustice of Human Rights," *Philosophy and Social Criticism*, Volume 9, Number 1, Spring 1982.

3. A recent example of the latter form of foundationalism is provided by Rawls' theory of justice and its "original position" version of social contract theory.

4. A recent example of work in this vein is Robert Nozick's *Anarchy, State, and Utopia* (New York: Basic Books, 1974).

5. Hegel has taken this insight to its radical extreme, and the following discussion closely draws upon his analysis of the universal, particular, and individual aspects of the will, an analysis compactly stated in paragraphs 5 through 7 of his *Philosophy of Right*.

6. The importance of the two aspects of mutual covenant and consent has been discussed at length by Hannah Arendt in *On Revolution* (New York: The Viking Press, 1976), p. 169f.

7. See Chapter X of Locke's *The Second Treatise of Government*.

8. See Chapter XIX, paragraphs 240–241 of John Locke's *Second Treatise On Civil Government*.

Chapter 5 *The Promise and Illusion of Practical Reason*

1. The importance of the distinction between practical reason and practical understanding has been largely ignored by John Rawls, among others, who tends to reduce practical reason to practical understanding in his *A Theory of Justice*. As a result he never leaves entirely behind the empirically conditioned framework of Utilitarianism, which makes practical understanding the principle of justice. This is evident in Rawls' conception of the so-called original position, with which he replaces the state of nature of traditional social contract theory. There the given alternatives of choice are merely rendered indeterminate through a postulated veil of ignorance, instead of being replaced by a positive principle of self-determination that can grant the will a content deriving from itself. As a result, appeal must be made to a variety of given factors in order for the original position to lead to any determinate principles of justice. See section 4 following for a further analysis of Rawls' theory.

2. Immanuel Kant, *Critique of Pure Reason*, translated by Norman Kemp Smith (New York: St. Martin's Press, 1965), A69/B94, A299/B356.

3. Ibid., A56/80, A69/B94.

4. Ibid., A300–301/B356–357.

5. Ibid., A301/B357.

6. Ibid., A322/B379.

7. Ibid., A316/B372.

8. Immanuel Kant, *Critique of Practical Reason*, A35.

9. Ibid., A52.

10. G. W. F. Hegel, *Philosophy of Right*, translated by T. M. Knox (New York: Oxford University Press, 1967), remark to paragraph 135; and G. W. F. Hegel, *Lectures On The History of Philosophy*, translated by E. S. Haldane and F. H. Simson (New York: Humanities Press, 1968), Volume III, pp. 460–461.

11. Immanuel Kant, *Metaphysical Elements of Justice*, translated by J. Ladd (New York: Bobbs-Merrill, 1965), AB 45, 48.

12. Ibid., AB 33.

13. Ibid., AB 33.

14. Ibid., AB 74.

15. Ibid., AB 75.

16. Ibid., AB 184.

17. Ibid., A165–166/B195–196.

18. Ibid., A229–230.

19. Ibid., A217.

20. Ibid., A235.

21. Rawls, *A Theory of Justice*, (Cambridge: Harvard University Press, 1973), p. 86.

22. Ibid., pp. 60, 302–303.

23. Ibid., pp. 120, 129–130.

24. Ibid., pp. 131–135.

25. Ibid., pp. 130.

26. Ronald Dworkin, *Taking Rights Seriously*, (Cambridge: Harvard University Press, 1978), Chapter 6: "Justice and Rights," pp. 169 ff.

27. Rawls, op. cit., p. 137.

28. Ibid., p. 143.

29. Ibid., pp. 92–93.

30. Ibid., p. 86.

31. Ibid., p. 179.

32. Alasdair MacIntyre, *After Virtue*, (Notre Dame: University of Notre Dame Press, 1981), pp. 227–237.

33. Robert Nozick, *Anarchy, State, and Utopia* (New York: Basic Books, 1974), pp. 207–208.

34. Rawls, op. cit., pp. 20–21, 48–51.

35. Dworkin, op. cit., p. 155.

Chapter 6   Self-Determination and Systematic Philosophy

1. Hans-Georg Gadamer, *Truth and Method*, (New York: Seabury Press, 1975).

2. Alasdair MacIntyre, *After Virtue*, (Notre Dame: Notre Dame Press, 1981).

3. Richard Rorty, *Philosophy and The Mirror of Nature*, (Princeton: Princeton University Press, 1980).

4. Hilary Putnam, *Reason, Truth and History*, (New York: Cambridge University Press, 1981).

5. This is the topic with which Hegel begins his *Phenomenology of Spirit*, namely, sense certainty, and not the indeterminacy of being with which his *Science of Logic* begins.

6. This is the fundamental point which Hegel argues in the chapter, "With What Must Science Begin?", in his *Science of Logic*.

7. See Kenley R. Dove, "Hegel's Deduction of The Concept of Science," *Boston Studies In The Philosophy of Science*, Vol. XXIII; William Maker, "Hegel's *Phenomenology* As Introduction to Science," *Clio*, No. 10, 1981; Richard Dien Winfield, "The Route To Foundation-Free Systematic Philosophy," *The Philosophical Forum*, Vol. XV, No. 3, Spring 1984, and "Conceiving Reality Without Foundations: Hegel's Neglected Strategy For *Realphilosophie*," *The Owl of Minerva*, Vol. 15, No. 2, Spring 1984.

Chapter 7   The Theory of Determinacy and the Quests for Truth and Justice

1. G.W.F. Hegel, *Science of Logic*, p. 68.

2. G.W.F. Hegel, Ibid., p. 838.

3. G.W.F. Hegel, *Logic*, translated by W. Wallace, (Oxford: Oxford University Press, 1978), paragraph 159.

4. G.W.F. Hegel, *Philosophy of Mind*, translated by W. Wallace and A.V. Miller, (Oxford: Oxford University Press, 1978), paragraph 440.

5. Ibid., paragraph 535.

6. See William Maker, "Does Hegel Have A Dialectical Method?", *The Southern Journal of Philosophy*, Vol. XX, No. 1, for a parallel critique of realism and idealism.

7. Hegel, *Science of Logic*, p. 50.

8. Ibid., p. 843.

9. Ibid., p. 843; G.W.F. Hegel, *Philosophy of Nature*, translated by A.V. Miller (Oxford: Clarendon Press, 1971), paragraphs 574–577.

10. Hegel, *Philosophy of Nature*, op. cit., paragraph 247.

Chapter 8   *The Elementary Structures of Freedom*

1. For an alternative discussion of the logical structure of the interaction of freedom, see Kenley R. Dove, "Logik und Recht bei Hegel," *Neue Hefte Fur Philosophie*, 17.

2. Hegel, *Philosophy of Right*, remark to paragraph 57, paragraph 71.

3. Hegel attempts to conceive it as such in his "Logic of The Concept." See Hegel, *Science of Logic*, p. 575 ff.

4. Alexandre Kojeve, *Introduction a la lecture de Hegel*, (Paris: Editions Gallimard, 1947).

5. Hannah Arendt, *The Human Condition*, (Chicago: University of Chicago Press, 1973), p. 175 ff.

6. Jürgen Habermas, "Vorbereitende Bemerkungen zu einer Theorie der kommunikativen Kompetenz," in Habermas and Niklas Luhmann, *Theorie der Gesellschaft oder Sozialtechnologie*, (Frankfurt am Main: Suhrkamp, 1972).

7. Karl-Otto Apel, "Das Apriori der Kommunikationsgemeinschaft und die Grundlagen der Ethik" in Apel, *Transformation der Philosophie*, (Frankfurt am Main: Suhrkamp, 1976).

8. Hegel, *Philosophy of Right*, paragraph 33.

9. Joachim Ritter points this out in the essay, "Person and Property," in his book, *Hegel and The French Revolution: Essays on The Philosophy of Right*,

translated and introduced by Richard Dien Winfield (Cambridge: MIT Press, 1982).

10. Hegel discusses these options in paragraphs 54 through 58 of his *Philosophy of Right*.

11. Hegel has made this point in paragraphs 43, 47, and 48 in the *Philosophy of Right*.

12. Hegel points out the significance this has for making possible the selling of labor power in paragraph 57 of the *Philosophy of Right*.

13. For a further critique of Marx's theory of alienation, see Richard Dien Winfield, "The Dilemma of Labor," *Telos*, No. 24, Summer 1975.

14. Hegel fails to develop this point in his discussion of property, even though it is a prerequisite for conceiving the common property of the household and corporate ownership in civil society.

15. Hegel, *Philosophy of Right*, paragraph 86.

16. Ibid., paragraph 102.

17. Hegel, *Philosophy of Right*, paragraphs 136–140.

Chapter 9   *The Family as an Institution of Freedom*

1. Hegel, *Philosophy of Right*, paragraphs 158–180.

2. Ibid., paragraph 164.

3. Ibid., paragraphs 165–166.

4. "Polygamy" here signifies any family arrangement with more than two spouses, including polygamy and polyandry in their traditional senses, as well as households whose multiple spouses are not heterosexual.

5. Ibid., paragraph 167.

6. Ibid., paragraph 168.

Chapter 10   *Economic Freedom and the Just Society*

1. This is particularly evident with regard to the most elementary property relation: ownership of one's own body.

2. See Adam Smith, *The Wealth of Nations*, (New York: Random House, 1937), pp. 13, 259.

3. David P. Levine, *Contributions to the Critique of Economic Theory*, (London: Routledge and Kegan Paul, 1977), pp. 198, 236.

4. Karl Marx, *Capital: Volume I*, (New York: International Publishers, 1970), pp. 46, 167.

5. Hannah Arendt, *The Human Condition*, (Chicago: University of Chicago Press, 1958), p. 96 ff.

6. Martin Heidegger, *The Question Concerning Technology and Other Essays*, trans. W. Lovitt (New York: Garland Publishing, Inc., 1977), pp. 3–35.

7. Jürgen Habermas, *Theory and Practice*, (Boston: Beacon Press, 1973), "Labor and Interaction," p. 142 ff.

8. Aristotle, *Politics*, 1254a1–8, 1258b.

9. Adam Smith, op. cit., p. 14.

10. Adam Smith, op. cit., p. 5.

11. Ibid., p. 13.

12. Ibid., p. 11.

13. Ibid., p. 30.

14. Ibid., p. 259.

15. See Richard Dien Winfield, "The Social Determination of The Labor Process From Hegel To Marx," *The Philosophical Forum*, Vol. XI, No. 3, Spring 1980, *The Social Determination of Production*, (dissertation, Yale University, 1977), Part III, and *The Just Economy*, (New York and London: Routledge, 1988), pp. 61–75.

16. For a detailed attempt to conceive the institutions of economic freedom by recasting some of Marx's arguments, see Richard Dien Winfield, *The Social Determination of Production*, Part III, and *The Just Economy*, Part II.

17. Karl Marx, *Capital: Volume III*, (New York: International Publishers, 1967), pp. 819–820.

18. See Arendt's analysis of Engels's remark in *On Revolution*, (New York: Viking Press, 1976), p. 276.

19. Marx and Engels, *Basic Writings On Politics and Philosophy*, edited by Lewis S. Feuer (New York: Doubleday, 1959), p. 254.

20. Hegel, *Philosophy of Right*, paragraph 37.

21. Hegel makes this point in his discussion of the right of distress (*Notrecht*), in paragraph 127 of the *Philosophy of Right*.

Chapter 11   Capital and the Legitimacy of Commodity Relations

1. Hegel makes this point in paragraphs 190–191 in the *Philosophy of Right*.

2. See Smith, *The Wealth of Nations*, p. 13, Marx, *Capital: Volume I*, p. 36.

3. See G.W.F. Hegel, *Vorlesungen Über Rechtsphilosophie–Vierter Band*, Edition Ilting, (Stuttgart-Bad Cannstattt: Frommannn-Holzboog, 1974), p. 475.

4. Ibid., p. 605; Hegel, *Philosophy of Right*, paragraph 195.

5. Although Hegel does not use the term "exchange value," he foreshadows its concept in paragraph 77 of the *Philosophy of Right* and treats it thematically in paragraph 192.

6. Eugen V. Bohm-Bawerk's "Zum Abschluss des Marxschen Systems," in *Aspekte der Marxschen Theorie 1: Zur methodischen Bedeutung des 3. Bandes des "Kapital*," ed. F. Eberle (Frankfurt am Main: Suhrkamp, 1973), identifies this problem in Marx's theory.

7. Marx, *Capital: Volume I*, p. 71 ff.

8. Ibid., p. 38 ff.

9. In Part III of the *Social Determination of Production*, I have attempted to reconstruct Marx's theory of the forms of commodity exchange by excluding all the illicit references to production.

10. Marx, *Capital: Volume I*, p. 166 ff.

11. Ibid., Chapters VI and VII.

12. Marx, *Capital: Volume I*, Part VIII, "The So-Called Primitive Accumulation."

13. For a critique of Hegel's class theory, see Richard Dien Winfield, "Hegel's Challenge To The Modern Economy," in *History and System*, ed. R. L. Perkins (New York: State University of New York Press, 1984), and *The Just Economy*, pp. 149–156.

Chapter 12   The Realization of Social Justice

1. See Hegel, *Philosophy of Right*, paragraphs 200, 230, 236, and 237.

2. For an analysis of why Hegel erroneously restricts economic interest groups to members of just one class, see Richard Dien Winfield, "Hegel's Challenge To The Modern Economy," p. 242, and *The Just Economy*, pp. 149–156, 172.

3. See Hegel, *Philosophy of Right*, paragraph 245.

4. Ibid., paragraph 245.

5. Hegel makes this point in the *Philosophy of Right*, remark to paragraph 299.

Chapter 13   Democracy and the Just State

1. For a critical discussion of Hegel's politicization of classes, see Winfield, "Hegel's Challenge To The Modern Economy," pp. 242–243, and *The Just Economy*, pp. 149–156.

2. For a parallel discussion of democracy, see Richard Dien Winfield, "The Reason For Democracy," in *History of Political Thought*, Vol. VI, No. 1, Spring 1985.

3. Cited in *Social and Political Philosophy*, edited by J. Somerville and R. E. Santini, (New York: Doubleday, 1963), pp. 266–270.

4. Ibid., pp. 261–266.

5. Ibid., pp. 251, 269.

6. See John Locke, *Second Treatise On Civil Government*, Chapter XIX, paragraphs 240–241.

7. See Jean-Jacques Rousseau, *The Social Contract*, Book I, Chapter VII, and Book II, Chapter IV.

8. Ibid., Book II, Chapter III, and Book IV, Chapter I.

9. Ibid., Book II, Chapter VII, and Book IV, Chapter VIII.

10. V. I. Lenin, *State and Revolution*, (Moscow: Progress Publishers, 1965), pp. 14–15.

11. Ibid., p. 80.

12. Ibid., pp. 18–19, 75, 90.

13. Ibid., pp. 81, 93.

14. G.W.F. Hegel, *Philosophy of Right*, paragraphs 291, 303–308, and 312–313.

15. Ibid., paragraph 300.

16. Hannah Arendt, *On Revolution*, (New York: Viking Press, 1965), pp. 282–284.

Chapter 14   The Historical Genesis of Justice

1. For a discussion of to what extent Hegel's philosophy of history undertakes this investigation, see Richard Dien Winfield, "The Theory and Practice of The History of Freedom: On the Right of History in Hegel's Philosophy of Right," in *History and System: Hegel's Philosophy of History*.

2. See Book VIII of Plato's *Republic*.

3. See the *Philosophy of Right*, note to paragraph 273.

4. G.W.F. Hegel, *The Philosophy of Mind*, translated by W. Wallace (Oxford: Oxford, 1971), note to paragraph 544.

5. In Book V (1316a) of the *Politics*, Aristotle properly criticizes Plato for offering his history of regimes as a necessary sequence, when in fact, the forms of government he describes can just as well precede as follow one another.

6. See G.W.F. Hegel, *Vorlesungen Über Rechtsphilosophie–Vierter Band*, edited by K.-H. Ilting (Stuttgart-Bad Cannstattt: Frommann-Holzboog, 1974), p. 696.

7. Hegel stresses this point in the note to paragraph 273 and the note and addition to paragraph 274 of the *Philosophy of Right*.

8. See the note to paragraph 273 and paragraph 274 of the *Philosophy of Right*.

9. For an attempt to judge contemporary regimes in light of the concept of justice, see Richard Dien Winfield, "Capital, Civil Society and The Deformation of Politics," in *History of Political Thought*, Vol. IV, No. 1.

Index